Palgrave Studies in Economic History

Series Editor
Kent Deng, London School of Economics, London, UK

Palgrave Studies in Economic History is designed to illuminate and enrich our understanding of economies and economic phenomena of the past. The series covers a vast range of topics including financial history, labour history, development economics, commercialisation, urbanisation, industrialisation, modernisation, globalisation, and changes in world economic orders.

More information about this series at
http://www.palgrave.com/gp/series/14632

Zoi Pittaki

Exploring the Roots of Systematic Tax Avoidance in Greece

Business, the Tax System and Tax Conscience, 1955–2008

palgrave
macmillan

Zoi Pittaki
Brunel Business School
Brunel University London
London, UK

ISSN 2662-6497 ISSN 2662-6500 (electronic)
Palgrave Studies in Economic History
ISBN 978-3-030-71978-4 ISBN 978-3-030-71979-1 (eBook)
https://doi.org/10.1007/978-3-030-71979-1

Cover illustration: ZU_09/GettyImages

This Palgrave Macmillan imprint is published by the registered company Springer Nature Switzerland AG
The registered company address is: Gewerbestrasse 11, 6330 Cham, Switzerland

Contents

Abbreviations

ASDY	Public Service Commission
CET	Common External Tariff
EEC	European Economic Community
EMU	European Monetary Union
FGI	Federation of Greek Industrialists
GDP	Gross Domestic Product
IMF	International Monetary Fund
OECD	Organisation for Economic Co-operation and Development
OEEC	Organisation for European Economic Co-operation
PASOK	Panhellenic Socialistic Movement

List of Charts

List of Tables

CHAPTER 1

Introduction

In a letter leaked to the *Financial Times* in early March 2015, the ex-Finance Minister of Greece Yanis Varoufakis suggested that the Greek state could use undercover tax agents in order to curb tax evasion. The idea was for the government to have 'students, housekeepers and even tourists to serve as undercover tax inspectors', by wiring them 'with audio and video equipment to track down lawbreakers'.[1] Such a measure would act as a deterrent to potential tax evaders and would also '[engender] a new tax compliance culture' in Greece.[2]

No matter how absurd this idea sounds, the mere fact that it was proposed by a then member of the Greek government indicates how serious the problem of tax evasion has been for Greece and how difficult it has been for state mechanisms to cope with it.[3] More recently,

[1] The letter was addressed to the president of the Eurogroup and Dutch minister of Finance Jeroen Dijsselbloem and it contained a number of suggested measures for the reform of the Greek economy (see Peter Spiegel, 'Greece Proposes Tourists as Tax Inspectors', *The Financial Times*, 6.3.2015. http://www.ft.com/cms/s/0/b65fa81c-c411-11e4-a02e-00144feab7de.html#axzz3pOaWCPUW [accessed 2.11.2015]).

[2] Spiegel, and Ian Traynor and Helena Smith, 'Wired-Up Tax Snoopers Could Be Unleashed in Greece', *The Guardian*, 6.3.2015. http://www.theguardian.com/world/2015/mar/06/wired-up-tax-snoopers-could-be-unleashed-in-greece [accessed 2.11.2015].

[3] For the purposes of this research, tax evasion is defined as every illegal act or omission aiming to the reduction of the tax liability or the payment of no tax at all. Tax avoidance,

Z. Pittaki, *Exploring the roots of systematic tax avoidance in Greece*, Palgrave Studies in Economic History,
https://doi.org/10.1007/978-3-030-71979-1_1

reports suggested that the country has the second-highest level of VAT tax evasion in Europe.[4] It is characteristic that, according to Varoufakis, 'the prospects of successfully countering tax dodging are dismal because of the demoralised and understaffed state of the tax inspection service'.[5]

This last point indicates that tax evasion, a 'burning issue' all around the EU,[6] is, for the Greek case, also an outcome of administrative problems that have been burdening the country's system of taxation for decades. These problems mainly stem from the characteristics of the tax system such as its complexity, constant change and tax officers' inadequate training. This reality has made it particularly challenging for Greek taxpayers to understand and comply with the tax legislation, and equally difficult for the members of the tax services to manage the tax administration mechanism.

In fact, the problems of tax administration have been a topical issue in a number of European states. This is indicated through the European Commission's 2014 Competitiveness Report, which contained the results of a survey exploring the dimensions of public administration that most impede firms' operations across a number of European countries.[7] The survey utilised business perceptions methodologies and drew primary data from the World Bank's Enterprise Surveys. It examined 15 different dimensions of public administration, among which were corruption, ineffective justice systems, customs and trade, labour regulation, tax administration and tax rates. The finding of the survey was that the most severe obstacles to firm growth are tax administration (not tax rates),

a term also used here, has the same results, but is achieved through technically legal acts, which do not entail the breach of the rule of law (for a more extensive analysis see Nikos Tatsos, *Shadow Economy and Tax Evasion in Greece* [Athens: Papazisi, 2001], pp. 16–26, in Greek).

[4] Spyros Dimitrelis, 'Greece Loses the Revenue from Three ENFIA Taxes Due to VAT Evasion', *Capital.gr*, 05.09.2019, https://www.capital.gr/oikonomia/3380524/treis-enfia-xanei-i-ellada-apo-ti-forodiafugi-fpa [accessed 10.07.2020].

[5] Traynor and Smith, 'Wired-Up'.

[6] Vanessa Houlder, 'Europe's Shadow Economy Costs €454bn in 'Lost' Taxes', *The Financial Times*, 24.9.2015. http://www.ft.com/cms/s/0/9c30cc14-5e1c-11e5-a28b-50226830d644.html?siteedition=uk#axzz3mpp1uGbt [accessed 5.12.2015].

[7] The study covered 11 European Union Member States, four candidate countries, one applicant country and one country that is neither a candidate nor an applicant.

corruption and ineffective justice systems.[8] Therefore, the study indicates that tax administration is perceived as a common problem in many European states. Due to this reason, the implications of the examination done here can prove useful not only for Greece but for these countries too.

This book examines the problems in the Greek system of taxation, explaining also how they affected business, from the mid-1950s up to the late 2000s. The mid-1950s were chosen as a starting point because they witnessed efforts to reform the tax system as well as promote industry and the development of the economy as a whole, in the aftermath of the Second World War. The late 2000s were another critical point for the Greek economy, since they marked the period before the devastating economic crisis that erupted in the country.

It should be noted that, in economic terms, the period examined here experienced high rates of growth for the most part. Still, and this is telling of how much taxation has contributed also to the economic crisis currently affecting the country, even during these years of growth, the problematic aspects of the tax system were perceived to have negatively affected the economy. The analysis here shows this by focusing on entrepreneurship; there is an emphasis on manufacturing industry, the largest industry of the secondary sector, which, as explained later, was the most dynamic sector of the Greek economy for the majority of the years covered here.

The view of Xenophon Zolotas, the eminent economist who served as the Head of the Bank of Greece for more than 20 years,[9] confirms

[8] European Commission, *Helping Firms Grow, European Competitiveness Report 2014*, Commission Staff Working Document SWD(2014)277 final. http://ec.europa.eu/growth/industry/competitiveness/reports/eu-competitiveness-report/index_en.htm [accessed 12.3.2016], pp. 136–137.

[9] Zolotas served as a co-Governor of the Bank of Greece in 1944–1945 and as a Governor in 1955–1967 and 1974–1981. See Kostas Mavragannis, '110 Years from the Birth of Xenophon Zolotas: His Life Through Unpublished Photographs', *The Huffington Post*. http://www.huffingtonpost.gr/2014/12/13/110-xronia-xenophon-zolotas_n_6317764.html?utm_hp_ref=greece [accessed 15.12.2014], in Greek. Zolotas was also the non-party Prime Minister of Greece in 1989–1990, see 'Xenophon Zolotas'. http://www.intercomprehension.eu/modules/intercom_new/template.php?module=3&activity=1&sc=9&langID=en&w_langID=gr [accessed 15.12.2014], in Greek. Also, Zolotas, along with Randolph Burgess of the United States, Sir Paul Gore-Booth of Great Britain and Bernard Clappier of France, was part of the group of the 'four wise men' which, in early 1960, being appointed to work upon the United States' proposal for a reorganisation of the OEEC, prepared a report that led to the creation of the OECD

that the sort of problematic aspects of the tax system examined here created difficulties for business. According to the journalist Nikos Nikolaou, Zolotas always had a standard response when asked about how to promote business investment in the country: 'What the entrepreneur needs is not the introduction of incentives but the removal of disincentives. That is, he needs to stop being chased by the tax officers, the ministries' bureaucrats, the immoral members of the local authorities, etc'.[10] In broad terms, Zolotas' view was similar to that of Johannes Witteveen, the director of the International Monetary Fund from 1973 to 1978. Witteveen considered that a stable tax regime is one of the most important conditions for the promotion of private investment.[11]

The coming chapters show that the Greek tax system was burdened by the complexity and continuous changes of the tax laws as well as the insufficient organisation and bureaucratic rigidities[12] of the tax services. Entrepreneurs' relations with tax officers were also problematic, with tax officers often accused to be lacking in training,[13] arbitrary in their decisions[14] and sometimes corrupt. It seems that such problems created difficulties for business in the post-Second World War setting. Due to the complexity and the frequent change of tax legislation, entrepreneurs knew that they were constantly at risk of being accused of breaking the tax law. It becomes clear from the evidence that will be presented here that this was a source of constant upset for them. At the same time, because of the arbitrariness of the system, taxes were the object of a constant negotiation between business and the tax authorities. Entrepreneurs could never be certain about where they stood with regard to their tax liabilities. This increased their vexation even more.

in December of the same year. See 'OECD agreement', *CQ Almanac*. http://library.cqpress.com/cqalmanac/document.php?id=cqal61-1373318 [accessed 15.12.2014].

[10] Nikos Nikolaou, 'We Need to Get Rid of Disincentives', To Vima, 14.11.2004. http://www.tovima.gr/finance/article/?aid=162410 [accessed 15.12.2014], in Greek.

[11] See Chapter 5, p. 20.

[12] The term bureaucratic rigidities denotes the various cumbersome, time-consuming and inflexible practices that were followed in the tax offices.

[13] That is, tax officers were the object of criticism with regards to their knowledge of accounting and tax legislation.

[14] That is, that their decisions were contingent solely upon their discretion, without been controlled by law or any relevant regulations.

With this evidence in mind, the research also throws light on some of the main causes of the current economic crisis affecting Greece, as the difficulties facing entrepreneurship seem to have contributed to the general weakness of the economy and to the gradual emergence of the crisis. Of course, what also contributed to the crisis was the great increase in public deficit from the 1980s onwards, from 8.7 between 1980 and 1985 to 11.7 between 1990 and 1995.[15] One of the causes of the continuously growing public deficit was tax evasion, which also started growing significantly from the late 1970s.[16]

It will be argued in Chapter 2 that tax evasion occurred mainly as a result of the perceptions that the tax system was money-driven and unfair. Indeed, tax evasion has been to a large extent an outcome of Greeks' low tax conscience, where tax conscience can be defined as the moral sense of right and wrong guiding tax-paying behaviour.[17] Through this perspective, tax evasion in Greece has often taken the form of a justified reaction towards an unfair, untrustworthy and therefore illegitimate tax system. The term tax conscience is considered of value here, precisely because it denotes that Greeks were aware that avoiding paying taxes was an unlawful act, they did commit it though because their conscience allowed it: as noted above, it seems that they considered tax evasion to be a justifiable practice.

For example, a 1953 article noted that the fact that there were people having their salaries 'decimated by the state each month' whereas others managed to 'slip through the fingers' of tax authorities, was a sign of an undeveloped tax conscience. The state never managed to cultivate citizens' tax conscience, it was noted, mainly because it lacked the necessary 'inspiring ethos'. According to the author, this was one of the reasons why tax evasion had become 'exonerated', taking the form of taxpayers' 'just

[15] Barry Bosworth and Trifon Kollintzas, *Economic Growth in Greece: Past Performance and Future Prospects, in Greece's Economic Performance and Prospects*, eds Ralph C. Bryan, Nikolaos C. Garganas and Georgios S. Tavlas (Athens: The Bank of Greece and The Brookings Institution, 2002), p. 177.

[16] K. Kalyvianakis et al., *Tax Regime, Shadow Economy and Tax Evasion in Greece* (Athens: Papazisis, 1993), pp. 275–279.

[17] In *Oxford Dictionaries* conscience is defined as '[a] person's moral sense of right and wrong, viewed as acting as a guide to one's behaviour' (see 'Conscience', *Oxford Dictionaries*. http://www.oxforddictionaries.com/definition/english/conscience [accessed 2.12.2015]).

defence'. In order to have conscientious taxpayers, it was stressed, the state should 'impose taxes with dispassionate and honest conscience'.[18]

The illegitimacy of the tax system was an outcome of other factors too. When the independent Greek state was established right after the end of the Second World War, the system's primary scope was to collect revenues, without having any significant redistributive and social dimensions.[19] Due to this reason, people saw the tax system mostly as a mechanism that 'drained' money away from their pockets and this naturally made them eager to avoid paying taxes. To this also contributed the fact that the distribution of the tax burden was considered unfair, because, among others, the burden for the lower income brackets was significantly higher than that of the higher ones.[20] There were also a series of features of the tax system that affected all tax-paying citizens, irrespective of income class. One such feature, which again harmed severely the system's legitimacy, was taxes in favour of third parties. As explained in more detail in the next chapter, these taxes were imposed on transactions in order to fund groups with great negotiating power, such as lobbies, trade unions, professional bodies, etc.

A further cause of tax evasion has been the very high level of corruption in the country,[21] which damaged people's confidence towards the state and again increased incentives to avoid paying taxes. The first study examining Greeks' perceptions about corruption, that is, their perceptions about 'the abuse of public office for private gain',[22] took place in 1996

[18] Vovolini Archive, 'Notes—Tax Evasion', *Viomichaniki Epitheorissis*, Vol. 20, September 1953, p. 302.

[19] As Giouras and Psalidopoulos' work indicates, this was also the character of tax policies followed by the German occupation forces during the war: Thanasis Giouras and Michalis Psalidopoulos, *Occupation, Nazism and Greek Economy—Official Reports and Memoirs* (Athens: Metamesonikties Ekdoseis, 2015), pp. 19–20; 34; 224–246, in Greek.

[20] Tatsos, *Shadow Economy*, p. 287.

[21] International Monetary Fund, *Greece, Selected Issues*, Country Report No.13/155, June 2013. https://www.imf.org/external/pubs/ft/scr/2013/cr13155.pdf [accessed 1.11.2015], p. 26.

[22] International Monetary Fund, *Corruption: Costs and Mitigating Strategies*, IMF Staff Discussion Note, May 2016. http://www.imf.org/external/pubs/ft/sdn/2016/sdn1605.pdf [accessed 8.10.2016], p. 3. One of the means through which corruption is facilitated is bribing, that is, the offering, to those holding public office, of 'something, usually money, to gain an illicit advantage' (see 'What Is Bribery and Corruption?', *Tackling Bribery and Corruption*. http://www.anticorruption.ie/en/acjs/pages/fq08000018 [accessed 8.10.2016]).

and was based on an opinion poll conducted on a national level. The survey indicated that 67% of the respondents agreed with the statement that 'the State is corrupt', with the tax services characterised as the most corrupt sector of public administration.[23]

This latter point shows that tax evasion has been an indication of the taxpayers' doubt about the legitimacy of taxes and, by an extension, the legitimacy of the state that imposed such taxes. Ultimately, it was an expression of doubt about the authority of the Greek state itself. Apart from being a factor of uncertainty that affected business, taxation was also an issue, about which the lack of trust between the state and civil society in Greece was expressed in its most direct manner.

By analysing the administrative weaknesses of the Greek system of taxation, this work suggests some of the reforms that the system needs today, especially in view of the current economic situation of the country.[24] However, the argument presented here has wider theoretical implications too, as it shows that the socio-political and economic environment is of crucial importance for the development of entrepreneurship. This was suggested through the work of William Baumol, who indicated that tax rules influence the allocation of entrepreneurship into either productive or unproductive and even destructive activities.[25] Not only that, but, as the work of the Austrian sociologist Rudolf Goldscheid has shown, taxation influences and shapes state policies.[26]

The present research follows a perspective which differs from the usual economic one, by focusing mainly on the problems eroding the administrative structures of the tax system and not on the level of taxes or on tax rates. Of course, as will be shown in the next pages, there have been theoretical contributions indicating that tax rates and the amount of money that people pay in taxes do indeed affect entrepreneurship. And

[23] Tatsos, *Shadow Economy*, pp. 247–249.

[24] Philip Stephens, 'An Offer That Greece Should Not Refuse', *The Financial Times*, 4.6.2015. http://www.ft.com/intl/cms/s/0/f6127244-09e1-11e5-b6bd-00144feabdc0.html#axzz3dJwTCDQG [accessed 12.9.2015].

[25] See pp. 10–12 for an analysis of Baumol's perspective.

[26] See Joseph A. Schumpeter, 'The Crisis of the Tax State', in *Joseph A. Schumpeter: The Economics and Sociology of Capitalism*, ed R. Swedberg (Princeton, NJ: Princeton University Press, [1918], 1991), p. 100 and also Rudolf Goldscheid, 'A Sociological Approach to Problems of Public Finance' in *Classics in the Theory of Public Finance*, eds R. A. Musgrave and A. T. Peacock (London: Macmillan & Co. Ltd., [1925], 1958), p. 202; 210.

it is well-noted that Greek entrepreneurs complained about the level of tax rates too, especially after the mid-1970s, when the tax burden for the whole of the economy started to increase significantly. However, it is interesting to note that, as will be shown in detail in the next chapter, after the mid-1970s, it was not entrepreneurs who bore the majority of the tax burden in Greece. Additionally, their share of this burden was continuously decreasing for the majority of the years explored here. More generally, Greece's share of taxes on income, profits and capital gains (but also that of total tax revenue) over GDP was for most of the period examined significantly lower than the OECD average.[27] Therefore, it seems that the obstacles that the tax system created for entrepreneurship came from the way it functioned, and not from the level of taxes.

The Tax System as an Institution

The theoretical basis behind the topic of the present research is that the system of taxation is an institution of great significance for every economy. The work of Douglas North is famous for indicating the importance of institutions. He defined them as 'the humanly devised constraints that structure political, economic and social interaction'.[28] North noted that humans use their perceptions about the world in order to structure their environment and reduce uncertainty when interacting with each other. In such a process, the way that perceptions transform the 'human environment' has to do with the institutional structure. North viewed such a structure as 'a combination of formal rules, informal constraints, and their enforcement characteristics'.[29] It must be noted here that the system of taxation is viewed not from the perspective of Douglas North, but that of historical institutionalism, more details about which will be offered in the next pages.

A set of rules that plays a fundamental role in every function of the modern state is the system of taxation. This was demonstrated through

[27] See Chapter 2.

[28] Douglass C. North, 'Institutions', *Journal of Economic Perspectives*, 5, 1 (1991), p. 97. See also Geoffrey M. Hodgson, 'What Are Institutions?', *Journal of Economic Issues*, XL, 1 (2006), p. 2, who defined institutions as 'systems of established and prevalent social rules that structure social interactions'.

[29] Douglass C. North, *Understanding the Process of Economic Change* (Princeton: Princeton University Press, 2005), p. 6.

the work of Rudolf Goldscheid. Specifically, in *The Crisis of the Tax State,* Schumpeter quoted the following famous phrase by Goldscheid: 'The budget is the skeleton of the state stripped of all misleading ideologies'.[30] This phrase denotes that, a state's needs for funding, usually covered through taxes, is the decisive factor for the various policies undertaken and, eventually, for the general economic profile the state will adopt. According to this perspective, the emergence of specific types of economic activities, the economic prevalence of specific social classes as well as the establishment of specific types of industry, are all an outcome of the way the system of taxation of a state has been structured.

The importance of taxation is underlined also in a subsequent work of Goldscheid, where he embarked on an analysis that demonstrated the way that society affects and largely shapes financial and political conditions within a state. According to his view, social needs determine to a great extent the interconnection between public revenue and public expenditure. In such a framework, taxation seems to be a factor of crucial importance, as '[t]ax struggles were the oldest form of class struggle', 'fiscal matters were an important contributory cause even in the mightiest spiritual movements of mankind' and even 'the great religious revolutions can be proved to have been strongly rooted in intolerable tax pressure'.[31]

Goldscheid also maintained that there is a direct link between the state and households, as the latter are merely a reflection of the former. The 'soundness' of the state, he noted, defines public economy and morality and thus also the economic and moral position of individuals. Therefore, he asked: '[w]hat is the point of eternal complaints about low tax ethics, if the financial practices of the State and other public authorities cannot stand the test even of economic standards, let alone moral ones?'[32]

The arbitrary character of the tax system and the regressive distribution of the tax burden in Greece[33] was, for me, an example of state practices that did not seem to follow specific economic or moral standards of fairness. In this way, they contributed to the very high levels of tax

[30] Schumpeter, p. 100. This phrase is found in this work: Rudolf Goldscheid and Robert Lazarsfeld, 'Staatsozialismus oder Staatskapitalismus - Ein finanzsoziologischer Beitrag zur Lösung des Staatsschulden-Problems, Archiv für Rechts- und Wirtschaftsphilosophie, 11, 2 (1917/1918), pp. 255–259.

[31] Rudolf Goldscheid, 'A Sociological Approach', p. 202.

[32] Ibid., p. 210.

[33] See Chapter 2, for more detail.

evasion plaguing the economy.[34] However, in the Greek case, it was also political practices which did not often seem to stand the test of moral standards. Seraphim Seferiades, a political scientist, notes that for the period 1946–1981 'no two consecutive elections were carried out under exactly the same electoral law'.[35] This strategy seems to have been followed for purely electioneering purposes. For example, according to Keith Legg, the National Radical Union, the leading political party in 1956, changed the electoral system to its advantage, a movement that resulted 'in a massive failure of the opposition parties'.[36] In 1958, the system was revised again in such a way in order to prevent the Left from becoming the second largest political force in Parliament. This tactic was repeated in the elections of 1961, 1963 and 1964.[37] These manipulations left a mark on the political scene of Greece of the time. They undoubtedly undermined the legitimacy of the governments (which had been formed from the parties adopting such strategies) and therefore also the legitimacy of the tax policies such governments implemented. Of course, any such legitimacy was severely damaged also because the governments of the time were not successful in remedying the various administrative weaknesses of the tax system.

Goldscheid's work belongs to the genre of fiscal sociology[38]; also, given the period that he wrote, it is considered a contribution to old institutionalism. The perspective followed here is, as already mentioned, that of historical institutionalism, a sub-category of new institutionalism that emerged in the 1960s and 1970s.

[34] The following chapter will explore this in more detail.

[35] Seraphim Seferiades, 'Polarization and Nonproportionality: The Greek Party System in the Postwar Era', *Comparative Politics*, 19, 1 (1986), p. 71.

[36] Keith R. Legg, *Politics in Modern Greece* (California: Stanford University Press, 1969), p. 139.

[37] Ibid., p. 144.

[38] Isaac William Martin, Ajay K. Mehrotta and Monica Prasad, 'The Thunder of History: The Origins and Development of the New Fiscal Sociology' in *The New Fiscal Sociology, Taxation in Comparative and Historical Perspective* eds Isaac William Martin, Ajay K. Mehrotta and Monica Prasad (Cambridge: Cambridge University Press, 2009), p. 5.

In more detail, there are three kinds of new institutionalism: rational choice institutionalism, historical institutionalism and sociological institutionalism.[39] Rational choice institutionalism is an approach that has been followed by rational choice theorists[40] and has to a large extent been based on North's perspective.[41] North wrote of 'well-specified'[42] rules that define 'the way the game is played',[43] tools that humans devise 'to make the environment more predictable', an 'ongoing response to the various levels of uncertainty that humans have confronted and continue to confront in the evolving physical and human landscape'.[44] However, by focusing on the Greek system of taxation, this research examines an institution/rule that was by no means well-specified. This poorly functioning institution decreased the predictability of the economic environment.

More broadly, for rational choice institutionalism, people have 'a fixed set of preferences or tastes...behave entirely instrumentally so as to maximize the attainment of these preferences and do so in a highly strategic manner that presumes extensive calculation.'[45] In contrast, historical institutionalists 'posit a world that is more complex than the world of tastes and institutions often postulated by rational choice institutionalists'.[46]

Moreover, rational institutionalism is interested in examining how rules structure choices,[47] and therefore, actions. Historical institutionalists are also interested in specifying the relation between institutions and action,[48]

[39] Kathleen Thelen, 'Historical Institutionalism in Comparative Politics', *Annual Review of Political Science*, 2 (1999), pp. 369–370. See also Peter A. Hall and Rosemary C. R. Taylor, 'Political Science and the Three New Institutionalisms', *Political Studies*, XLIV (1996), pp. 936–942.

[40] Thelen, p. 377.

[41] Hall and Taylor, p. 943.

[42] North, *Understanding the Process*, p. 15.

[43] Ibid., p. 48.

[44] Ibid., pp. 14–15.

[45] Hall and Taylor, p. 945.

[46] Ibid., p. 942.

[47] Ibid., pp. 942–943.

[48] Ibid., p. 940.

however they are 'especially attentive to the relationship between institutions and ideas or beliefs'.[49] They focus on the 'meanings that historical actors attribute to their own actions'.[50]

Last, rational choice institutionalism views institutions in terms of their 'coordinating functions' whereas historical institutionalism sees them as 'the legacy of concrete historical processes'.[51] Indeed, for historical institutionalism, institutions are the outcome of historical processes 'that is, the outcomes of past events and interpretations of those events'.[52] As Suddaby et al. write, '[a]dopting a rational-deductive perspective limits our understanding of institutions as outcomes of historical processes. It forces us to treat institutions as things, rather than as processes and encourages the reduction of complex causality into simple variables'.[53]

Through a historical institutionalism lens, notes Sven Steinmo, people's expectations are 'moulded by the past'[54] and '[h]ow one behaves, depends on the individual, on the context and on the rule'.[55] Historical processes but also the social, political, economic and cultural environments shape such a context.[56]

Following a historical institutionalist approach, this monograph examines the Greek tax system in terms of the interactions between various agents relating to it (predominantly, between tax officers and entrepreneurs/taxpayers), but also in terms of the collective interpretations of those interactions.[57] That is, the sources used here also reflect how Greek society viewed the interactions between tax officers and

[49] Ibid., p. 941.

[50] Ibid., p. 954.

[51] Thelen, p. 382.

[52] Roy Suddaby, William M. Foster and Albert J. Mills, 'Historical Institutionalism', in *Organizations in Time: History, Theory, Methods*, eds Marcelo Bucheli and R. Daniel Wadhwani (Oxford: Oxford University Press, 2013), p. 111.

[53] Ibid., p. 109.

[54] Sven Steinmo, 'Historical Institutionalism', in *Approaches and Methodologies in the Social Sciences, a Pluralist Perspective*, eds Donatella Della Porta and Michael Keating (Cambridge: Cambridge University Press, 2008), p. 128.

[55] Ibid., p. 126.

[56] Ibid., pp. 127–128.

[57] Suddaby et al., pp. 111; 118.

entrepreneurs. The analysis also takes into consideration the 'contextualised worldviews'[58] of the agents under study. In other words, it examines entrepreneurs' perceptions about the way that the tax system affected them, primarily through its complexity and arbitrariness. Equally, it examines the tax officers' own perspectives with regard to the difficulties they had to overcome in order to adequately perform their duties.[59] One of the perceptions about the functioning of the tax system had to do with clientelism. As explained in the next chapter, here clientelism is defined as the exchange of favours and payoffs between either members of the public and those holding public office, or among the people holding public office themselves. For example, taxpayers knew that bribery was one of the ways to reduce their tax liability. Such dynamics, of course, undermine the effectiveness of any institution, and the Greek tax system could be no exception. The general public's view about the way that the tax system functioned was that it was burdened by clientelism. This perception had been moulded by the past, that is, as historical institutionalism suggests, it was the result of people's past experiences with the system and their interpretations of such experiences.

Additionally, in this work the system of taxation is seen as a quite static structure.[60] In other words, the type of historical institutionalist approach followed here views institutions as 'relative persistent features of the historical landscape'.[61] Or, as W. Richard Scott wrote, as 'multifaceted, durable social structures…[that] are relatively resistant to change…[and]

[58] R. Daniel Wadhwani and Marcelo Bucheli, 'The Future of the Past in Management and Organization Studies', in *Organizations in Time: History, Theory, Methods*, eds Marcelo Bucheli and R. Daniel Wadhwani (Oxford: Oxford University Press, 2013), p. 10.

[59] Ibid. For an analysis of the importance of historical actors' experiences and perceptions see also Jeff Fear, 'Mining the Past: Historicizing Organizational Learning and Change', in *Organizations in Time: History, Theory, Methods*, eds Marcelo Bucheli and R. Daniel Wadhwani (Oxford: Oxford University Press, 2013), pp. 179–180.

[60] It must be stressed here that what is characterised as static is the broader structure of the system of taxation. That is, there were indeed many changes in the tax legislation (this was actually one of the main complaints of entrepreneurs/tax payers) but not any substantial improvement or meaningful reform in the way that the tax administration mechanisms functioned. For example, the complexity of legislation was an ongoing problem, throughout the examined period.

[61] Hall and Taylor, p. 941.

tend to be transmitted across generations, to be maintained and reproduced'.[62] This perspective relates to some extent to Arthur Stinchcombe's idea of 'imprinting'. The concept of imprinting regards organisations which 'survive far into the future with their founding structures largely intact because the latter continue to be efficient, because of inertial forces such as tradition, vested interests or ideology, or because of lack of competition'.[63] A quite similar perspective is followed by John Meyer and Bryan Rowan, who view institutional rules as 'myths…with enhanced survival prospects'.[64] This theoretical perspective explains, to a certain extent, why there was so little progress in the Greek system of taxation throughout the period examined here.

Taxation and Entrepreneurship

Not only the system of taxation, but also entrepreneurship can be viewed through the perspective of historical institutionalism. In general, as Geoffrey Jones and Daniel Wadhwani note, entrepreneurial processes are embedded in certain institutional and historical settings,[65] and therefore '[t]ime and geography often act as fundamental boundary constraints that need to be taken into account in developing more useful generalizations about entrepreneurship'.[66] This is the reason why, as they stress, 'many of the most interesting and intriguing research questions about entrepreneurship beg for institutionalist methodologies…. The perennially engaging question of how and why the character of entrepreneurship

[62] W. Richard Scott, *Institutions and Organizations—Ideas and Interests* (California: Sage Publications, 2008), pp. 48–49.

[63] Arthur Stinchcombe, in Victoria Johnson, 'What Is Organizational Imprinting? Cultural Entrepreneurship in the Founding of the Paris Opera', *American Journal of Sociology*, 13, 1 (2007), p. 98.

[64] John W. Meyer and Bryan Rowan, 'Institutionalized Organizations: Formal Structure as Myth and Ceremony', *American Journal of Sociology*, 83, 2 (1977), p. 340. See also Elisabeth Clemens and James Cook, who refer, among others, to institutional 'durability' (Elisabeth S. Clemens and James M. Cook, 'Politics and Institutionalism: Explaining Durability and Change', *Annual Review of Sociology*, 25 [1999], p. 447).

[65] Geoffrey Jones and Rohit Daniel Wadhwani, 'Schumpeter's Plea: Rediscovering History and Relevance in the Study of Entrepreneurship', *Harvard Business School Working Paper*, No. 06-036 (2006). http://www.hbs.edu/faculty/Publication%20Files/06-036.pdf [accessed 10.10.2013], p. 13.

[66] Ibid., p. 22.

has differed in various cultures begs for good historical institutionalist methodology if it is to ever transcend vague cultural notions and stereotypes'.[67]

As used by this monograph, historical institutionalism views the past not only as a source of information but also as a theoretical tool that is ideal for the examination of socio-economic events.[68] Specifically, according to Wadhwani, historical research examining entrepreneurship is divided into two broad categories. The first one regards history as 'the cumulative sequence of events that took place in the past', providing thus 'a vast store of evidence and information against which to test and modify theory'.[69] The second category adopts a more meaningful approach, regarding history as a source of reasoning. Through such a perspective, history does not merely provide a pool of data regarding the past; it is, rather more importantly, the means through which to examine social phenomena (such as entrepreneurship) in the framework in which they developed. In this way, historical reasoning is used 'to expand understanding of the origins or development of a phenomenon or its relationship to other phenomena that are not perceptible through current experience alone and hence often lie outside contemporary theory'.[70]

As Jones and Wadhwani note, William Baumol's work 'provides an excellent illustration of how a critical understanding of historical context and variation can help create useful and robust generalizations that are nevertheless bounded by time'.[71] He focused on the importance of institutions, and, among others, examined the relationship between taxation and entrepreneurship.[72]

Baumol is considered to have pioneered the importance of institutions for entrepreneurship, maintaining that a reallocation of entrepreneurial efforts towards productive activities can be achieved through a change

[67] Ibid., p. 27.

[68] R. Daniel Wadhwani, 'Historical Reasoning and the Development of Entrepreneurship Theory', in *Historical Foundations of Entrepreneurship Research*, eds Hans Landström and Franz Lohrke (UK: Edward Elgar, 2010), p. 352.

[69] Ibid. Wadhwani notes that Foreman-Peck's (2005) and Nicholas' (2008) works are examples of such kind of research.

[70] Ibid., p. 353.

[71] Jones and Wadhwani, 'Schumpeter's Plea: Rediscovering History', p. 22.

[72] William J. Baumol, 'Entrepreneurship: Productive, Unproductive, and Destructive', *Journal of Political Economy*, Vol. 98, 5, 1 (Oct., 1990), p. 917.

in the tax rules, which indeed constitute a big part of what is called 'the rules of the game' in a society.[73] Specifically, in his famous article on productive, unproductive and destructive entrepreneurship, he argued that the rules of the game in an economy (for example tax rules) create incentives that influence entrepreneurship in different ways and allocate it between either productive activities (e.g. innovation), or unproductive activities, such as rent seeking and organised crime. As he wrote, '[h]ow the entrepreneur acts at a given time and place depends heavily on the rules of the game -the reward structure in the economy- that happen to prevail'.[74]

Using examples from history, Baumol showed that such a reward structure or, in other words, the relative payoffs that society attributes to each kind of activity, is what determines the allocation of entrepreneurship into various activities.[75] In more detail, he maintained that Schumpeter's list regarding what could be considered as innovation in an economy (that is, technological improvement, a new good, a new method of production, an opening of a new market, a new source of supply of raw materials or the emergence of 'the new organization of any industry')[76] should be extended so as to include 'items such as innovation in rent seeking procedures'.[77] In such a case, entrepreneurship can be unproductive, or even destructive.

The decisive factor determining whether entrepreneurship will focus on productive or unproductive activities is the set of rules of the game in each society, influencing the relative payoffs attributed to different entrepreneurial activities. As Baumol writes, 'when the supply of productive entrepreneurs declines this is likely to be attributable not to an autonomous contraction in the total number of innovating entrepreneurs, but to a change in the structure of rewards that has led the entrepreneurs to transfer their innovative talents from production to rent seeking or worse'.[78]

[73] Ibid.

[74] Ibid., p. 894.

[75] Ibid., p. 895.

[76] Joseph Schumpeter, in Baumol, 'Entrepreneurship', pp. 896–897.

[77] Ibid., p. 897.

[78] William J. Baumol, 'Formal Entrepreneurship Theory in Economics: Existence and Bounds', *Journal of Business Venturing*, 8 (1993), p. 203.

Therefore, according to Baumol, the term 'unproductive entrepreneurship' encompasses a large spectrum of activities: rent seeking through takeovers, litigation, tax avoidance and even tax evasion schemes are all unproductive activities, having an entrepreneurial character though, given the possible rewards yielded and the effort exerted by business executives to pursue them.[79] Assar Lindbeck demonstrated the way that in high-tax environments, entrepreneurs channel their efforts to unproductive entrepreneurship such as financial speculation or even illegal activities.[80] Baumol also noted that 'taxes can serve to redirect entrepreneurial effort'.[81]

It should be noted at this point that, when writing about 'taxes' or 'tax rules' Baumol referred to the level of taxation.[82] However, the narrative he developed seems capable to accommodate also other aspects of taxation, even if this is never clearly stated in his works. In general, a large part of the literature examining how taxes affect entrepreneurship does not make any clear distinction between various aspects of taxation. For example, Robin Douhan and Magnus Henrekson note that when the cost of abiding by tax regulations increases, tax evasion increases too, but also that when the level of taxes increases, entrepreneurs are channelling their efforts towards unproductive forms of entrepreneurship, such as tax avoidance.[83] Similarly, Henrekson notes that the effects of taxes on entrepreneurial behaviour are complex because of the 'complexity of the tax code'.[84] However, his main interest is in examining the effects of tax rates on business activity and entrepreneurial behaviour, arguing that 'high taxes may spur self-employment but reduce productive entrepreneurship'.[85]

[79] Baumol, 'Entrepreneurship', p. 915.

[80] Assar Lindbeck, 'Consequences of the Advanced Welfare State', *The World Economy*, 11, 1 (1988), p. 27.

[81] Baumol, 'Entrepreneurship', p. 915.

[82] That is, he refers to rules that concern the level of the various tax rates (ibid., p. 917).

[83] Robin Douhan and Magnus Henrekson, 'The Political Economy of Entrepreneurship', *IFN Working Paper* No 716, Research Institute of Industrial Economics (2007), p. 20.

[84] Magnus Henrekson, 'Entrepreneurship and Institutions', *IFN Working Paper* No 707, Research Institute of Industrial Economics (2007), p. 17.

[85] Ibid., p. 19. There have been of course, works focusing solely on tax rates and the level of taxes, such as, for example, Evsey Domar and Richard Musgrave and Hans-Werner

Equally, there is little distinction in the literature between the level of taxation and the methods of tax collection and enforcement. Saul Estrin, Klaus Meyer and Maria Bytchkova mention two early 2000s studies following such a distinction, based on survey data from transitional EU economies. The first one, by Ruta Aidis and Tomasz Mickiewicz, suggests that '[t]he measure of taxation is correlated with two omitted variables, "frequent changes to tax policy" and "ambiguity of taxes", suggesting that all aspects of the system of corporate taxation, rather than the level alone, may inhibit entrepreneurial growth'. Also, Meyer et al's 2005 study indicates that unstable rules and regulations, 'rather than the actual state of these variables', are considered by foreign investors as a 'major obstacle'.[86]

This monograph focuses on the administrative aspects of the Greek system of taxation (although there will be some references to the level of taxes and tax rates as well), because it seems that it is not the level of taxes that matters the most, but the complexity and arbitrariness of the tax system. Baumol's model incorporates this flexibility and is suitable to analyse the effects of such aspects of the system of taxation. His wider perspective is appropriate because it shows the importance of examining entrepreneurship within specific historical and institutional contexts.[87]

It should also be noted that, as will be shown later, Baumol approaches entrepreneurship mostly in Schumpeterian terms. The great importance Schumpeter ascribed to history[88] makes him particularly relevant to the present research. However, Greek entrepreneurship could also be seen

Sinn, which concluded that under the assumption of risk aversion higher taxes encourage risk taking and therefore also entrepreneurship (Douhan and Henrekson, p. 21). There have also been a number of empirical literature contributions on the effects of taxation on small business creation. For example, the studies of Julie Berry Cullen and Robert Gordon and Donald Bruce and Mohammed Mohsin, which show a 'weak negative relation' between tax levels and self-employment (ibid.).

[86] Saul Estrin, Klaus E. Meyer and Maria Bytchkova, 'Entrepreneurship in Transition Economies', in *The Oxford Handbook of Entrepreneurship*, eds Mark Casson, Bernard Yeung, Anuradha Basu and Nigel Wadeson (Oxford: Oxford University Press, 2006), p. 705.

[87] Wadhwani, 'Historical Reasoning', p. 354.

[88] Hans Landström and Matts Benner, 'Entrepreneurship Research: A History of Scholarly Migration', in *Historical Foundations of Entrepreneurship Research*, eds Hans Landström and Franz Lohrke (UK: Edward Elgar, 2010), p. 22.

in terms of Israel Kirzner's concept of alertness towards profit opportunities.[89] In fact, in transition economies, there are usually plenty of opportunities for the development of low-level Kirznerian entrepreneurship.[90] For large parts of the period examined here, Greece was indeed an economy in transition. For example, in the early 1950s the country had to absorb the impact of its participation in the Second World War and the civil war that followed. Also, in the period from the late 1960s to the early 1970s it witnessed three different polity regimes: from being a constitutional monarchy, it entered a phase of dictatorship in 1967 and finally became a parliamentary democracy in 1974. Equally, from a previously associate member of the EEC, it became a full member in the early 1980s.

In fact, Kirzner's perspective does not seem to be focused on a specific kind of entrepreneurial behaviour. That is, the concept of alertness to opportunities seems capable to accommodate not only profit-seeking through price differentials, but also entrepreneurship from a Schumpeterian standpoint, involving the introduction of a totally new product or method of production. This line of thought, viewing opportunity also in Schumpeterian terms, has been exploited by a large part of the current literature on entrepreneurial opportunity. According to Scott Shane, an important part of this literature focuses on the opportunity nexus and examines issues such as 'the characteristics of opportunities; the individuals who discover and exploit them; the processes of resource acquisition and organizing; and the strategies used to exploit and protect the profits from those efforts'.[91] Through such a perspective, entrepreneurial opportunity is defined in both Schumpeterian and Kirznerian terms, as opportunities arise through either 'changes in technology, political forces, regulation, macro-economic factors and social trends', or through differential access to information, which leads to 'errors when [people] make decisions, which in turn create shortages and surpluses'.[92] In a way, the

[89] Israel M. Kirzner, *Competition and Entrepreneurship* (Chicago: University of Chicago Press, 1973), p. 48.

[90] Estrin et al., p. 694.

[91] Scott Shane, *A General Theory of Entrepreneurship* (UK: Edward Elgar, 2003), p. 4.

[92] Ibid., p. 20. It should be noted at this point that, apart from the Kirznerian and Schumpeterian perspectives, there have also been other major contributions in the theory of entrepreneurship, focusing on the meaning of entrepreneurship or the role of entrepreneurs or both, like for example the works of Frank Knight, Edith Penrose and

perspective followed here is similar to that of Mark Casson, who proposes an overall definition of entrepreneurship. He does so by arguing that there is no difference between the manager of a firm and an entrepreneur, and that the main characteristic of the entrepreneur is judgement in decision-making.[93] Casson sums up this idea in the following phrase: 'Good judgment leads to timely innovation and profitable arbitrage'.[94]

Therefore, in entrepreneurship theory, judgement in decision-making and alertness towards profit opportunities are crucial in terms of understanding investment behaviour. This also holds for the Greek case. Even so, little attention has been paid to institutions and even less to the institution of the tax system. One of the few works utilising an institutional approach is that of Sapelli, who identifies the cause of the problems of Greek industry and economy in deeply entrenched institutional weaknesses of the society. His view is that Greek businessmen 'operated under structural conditions which did not encourage the profitability of industrial investment'.[95] Specifically, according to Sapelli, businessmen avoided productive investment mainly because they were part of a society that

Harvey Leibenstein. Specifically, Knight examined in detail the role of the entrepreneur, distinguishing between the concepts of risk and uncertainty and developing a theory of profit that associated uncertainty with economic change and differences in entrepreneurial ability (Robert Hébert and Albert N. Link, *The Entrepreneur: Mainstream Views and Radical Critiques* (New York: Praeger, 1988), p. 95). As for Leibenstein, he argued that in contrast to what the standard model of competition proclaims, entrepreneurship plays a vital role in the process of development and that the basic role of entrepreneurs is to intervene and make up for market inefficiencies (Harvey Leibenstein, 'Entrepreneurship and Development', *The American Economic Review*, 58, 2 (1968), pp. 72–75. Last, in her work, which is regarded to be the first ever theory of the growth of the firm (Mark Casson and Peter J. Buckley 'Entrepreneurship and the Growth of the Firm: An Extension of Penrose's theory' in *Entrepreneurship—Theory, Networks, History* [UK: Edward Elgar, 2010], p. 88), Penrose indicated that entrepreneurship is the major force behind firms' growth (see also Edith Penrose, 'Limits to the Growth and Size of Firms', *The American Economic Review*, 45, 2 [1955], p. 531). For an overview of the plethora of literature that built on those and other major contributions on entrepreneurship theory see also *The Oxford Handbook of Entrepreneurship* and Hans Landström and Olle Persson, 'Entrepreneurship Research: Research Communities and Knowledge Platforms', in *Historical Foundations of Entrepreneurship Research*, eds Hans Landström and Franz Lohrke (UK: Edward Elgar, 2010), pp. 46–76.

[93] Mark Casson, *Entrepreneurship: Theory, Networks, History* (UK: Edward Elgar, 2010), pp. 3; 8–9.

[94] Ibid., p. 3.

[95] Giulio Sapelli, *Southern Europe Since 1945, Tradition and Modernity in Portugal, Spain, Italy, Greece and Turkey* (London and New York: Longman, 1995), p. 66.

traditionally had a strong preference for wealth accumulated without production.[96]

The present monograph does not find such an approach convincing, because it does not provide any evidence about whether there was such a preference for wealth without production, or, assuming that there was indeed one, any explanations about how it emerged. Here Greek entrepreneurship is examined by focusing on manufacturing industry, a productive sector which, in spite of what Sapelli argued, was the 'engine of growth' for Greece until the mid-1970s, being the largest industry of the secondary sector. This was the most dynamic sector of the Greek economy during this period,[97] as its participation over total GDP kept increasing in contrast to the two other sectors of the economy, the primary (agriculture) and the tertiary (services) one.[98]

In spite of its dynamism, the Greek industrial sector did not prove capable of fulfilling its potential, and this becomes clear when compared with similar countries throughout the broader post-war period. It is a fact, for example, that the share of Greek manufacturing industry in total GDP has 'always been the lowest between Portugal, Greece and Italy'.[99] This book will explore whether and to what extent the system of taxation created difficulties for Greek industry.

This examination will to some extent confirm the perspective of Ingrid Verheul et al., who, apart from noting that high taxes 'reduce the returns on entrepreneurship and can impede the … expansion of established firms',[100] also stressed that the language of tax legislation is usually ambiguous and difficult to comprehend. This fact, they continued, along with the 'frequent changes, expiration clauses and different layers of taxation', often confuses entrepreneurs and thus inhibits firms' growth.[101]

[96] Ibid., p. 67.

[97] Konstantinos Drakatos, *The Big Cycle of the Greek Economy (1945–1995)* (Athens: Papazisis, 1997), pp. 62–63.

[98] See Bank of Greece, *Long-term Statistical Series of the Greek Economy* (Athens: Bank of Greece, 1992), pp. 10–12, in Greek.

[99] Sapelli, p. 95.

[100] Ingrid Verheul, Sander Wennekers, David Audretsch and Roy Thurik, 'An Eclectic Theory of Entrepreneurship: Policies, Institutions and Culture', in *Entrepreneurship: Determinants and Policy in a European-US Comparison*, eds David Audretsch, Roy Thurik, Ingrid Verheul and Sander Wennekers (USA: Kluwer Academic Publishers, 2002), p. 43.

[101] Ibid., p. 47.

The view that Verheul et al. offer is particularly informative, because it shows that taxation affects entrepreneurship in many different ways. It is not only high taxes that might have a negative impact on the propensity to invest, but also the complexity and frequency of change of tax regulations. This latter point is directly pertinent to the Greek system of taxation, which was significantly complex, confusing and sometimes also corrupt. Compliance with the Greek tax legislation was a difficult task and created a burden that was more important than tax levels.

That taxation imposes compliance burdens on taxpayers is something that has been recognised in works as major as that of Adam Smith's *Inquiry into the Nature and Causes of the Wealth of Nations*. The *Wealth of Nations* is considered to offer '[t]he first systematic study of the functions and objectives of taxation'.[102] In it, Adam Smith refers to four 'maxims' that should characterise taxation systems. Apart from the first maxim, which refers to the equality of tax contributions,[103] and the fourth one, according to which every tax should 'take out and…keep out of the pockets of the people as little as possible, over and above what it brings into the public treasury of the state',[104] the remaining two relate to the minimisation of the compliance burden taxation systems entail. Specifically, he stresses that taxes 'ought to be certain, and non-arbitrary. The type of payment, the manner of payment, the quantity to be paid, ought all to be clear and plain to the contributor…'. Otherwise, taxpayers are 'put more or less in the power of the tax-gatherer, who can either aggravate the tax…, or extort, by the terror of such aggravation, some present or perquisite to himself'. Also, '[e]very tax ought to be levied at the time, or in the manner, in which it is most likely to be convenient for the contributor to pay it'.[105] This study of the Greek taxation system will confirm Adam Smith's insights.

Early nineteenth-century economists largely ignored Adam Smith's points about the compliance burden of taxation. An exception to this

[102] Cedric Sandford, Michael Godwin and Peter Hardwick, *Administrative and Compliance Costs of Taxation* (Great Britain: Fiscal Publications, 1989), p. 24.

[103] 'The subjects of every state ought to contribute towards the support of the government, as nearly as possible, in proportion to their respective abilities' (Adam Smith, *An Inquiry into the Nature and Causes of the Wealth of Nations*, Volume II [London: Methuen & Co, 1904], p. 310).

[104] Ibid., pp. 310–311.

[105] Ibid.

tendency has been McCulloch, who argued that 'no tax…can be a good tax unless it correspond[s] pretty closely with the last three maxims of Smith'.[106] The subject remained neglected also in the twentieth century, up until 1935, when Haig constructed a questionnaire addressed to more than 1500 large US corporations in order to investigate their costs of compliance with the tax laws.[107] Among Haig's conclusions were that the compliance cost for corporations in 1934 amounted to 2.3% of the total taxes they had paid, that there was 'a wide variation in the weight of the burden of compliance as one passes from one type of tax to another' and that the administration's expenses were lower for those taxes which caused the greater compliance costs for the taxpayers and vice versa.[108] In spite of the fact that Haig's conclusions are considered suspect 'because of a low response rate and a bias towards large corporations',[109] his contribution is important, as it signified the renewal of interest on the subject of the compliance burden of taxation.[110]

Following Haig, it took almost four decades for the next influential work on the compliance burden of taxation to appear. This was Cedric Sandford's research that started in the early 1970s and is now considered to be the most authoritative source in the field.[111] Sandford, a Professor of Political Economy and head of the Centre for Fiscal Studies at Bath University[112] had a major role in turning the field of tax compliance costs into an established academic discipline, by 'developing a systematic and clearly articulated methodology' for the subject.[113] Sandford believed

[106] Sandford, Godwin and Hardwick, p. 26.

[107] Robert Murray Haig, 'The Cost to Business Concerns of Compliance with Tax Laws', *Management Review*, 24, 11 (1935), p. 325. An analysis of Haig's work is given in Chris Evans, 'Studying the Studies: An Overview of Recent Research into Taxation Operating Costs', *eJournal of Tax Research*, 1,1 (2003), p. 67.

[108] Haig, p. 327.

[109] Sandford, Godwin and Hardwick, p. 27.

[110] Ibid.

[111] Binh Tran-Nam and Chris Evans, 'The Impact of Cedric Sandford on the Discipline of Tax Compliance Costs', *Australian Tax Forum*, 17 (2002), p. 395 and Chris Evans, 'The Operating Costs of Taxation: A Review of the Research', *Economic Affairs*, 21, 2 (2001), p. 5.

[112] Chris Evans, 'Cedric Sandford', *The Guardian*, 16.4.2004. http://www.theguardian.com/money/2004/apr/16/publicfinances.guardianobituaries [accessed 3.9.2015].

[113] Tran-Nam and Evans, pp. 394–396.

that the growth of the discipline in the 1970s should be attributed to a number of reasons, among which were the technological advancements of the time, which facilitated computer-based surveys, the introduction of VAT in many countries, which entailed 'high and visible compliance costs', as well as 'the increasing complexity of the tax systems and of the affairs of taxpayers'.[114]

Sandford's study involved the collection of survey data in order to examine 'personal compliance costs of direct taxes' for the UK.[115] However, his analysis offers insights on business compliance costs too. Sandford characterised compliance costs of taxation as 'hidden' or 'disguised' costs, which are 'incurred...over and above actual tax payments'.[116] Compliance costs take the form of time costs, psychological costs, but also money costs, such as 'fees to accountants or bankers for continuing assistance and advice'.[117] Specifically for firms, he noted that compliance costs relate to the taxes imposed on profits, such as 'corporation tax, or income tax and surtax for the individually owned business or partnership', which might 'necessitate the keeping of much more elaborate accounts than would otherwise be considered necessary'.[118] Therefore, compliance costs affect entrepreneurship and this study argues that they are primary for understanding Greek entrepreneurship too.

In a later work with Godwin and Hardwick, Sandford added to the business compliance costs 'the cost of collecting, remitting and accounting for tax on...the wages and salaries of its employees together with the costs of acquiring the knowledge to enable this work to be done including knowledge of their legal obligations and penalties', but also the costs 'incurred by representative bodies (paid for by their members) in making presentations and lobbying for tax changes'.[119] A more general

[114] Ibid., pp. 394–395.

[115] Cedric Sandford, *Hidden Costs of Taxation* (London: Institute for Fiscal Studies, 1973), p. 144.

[116] Ibid., p. 8.

[117] Ibid., pp. 8–9.

[118] Ibid., p. 10.

[119] Sandford, Godwin and Hardwick, pp. 11–12.

but very crucial factor that generates compliance costs is also the 'ignorance and incomprehension' resulting from the complexity of the tax laws.[120]

Since Sandford's work, tax compliance burden literature has flourished and followed many different paths. Such proliferation of works is apparently related to 'the growing burden of costs that have fallen on the business community'[121] but also to the fact that complexity of the tax laws and thus the burden associated with it increased too.[122] Before the mid-1990s, tax compliance cost literature was mostly based on surveys that generated quantitative data on the compliance costs related to specific taxes or characteristics of the tax system.[123] From the mid-1990s onwards, a need for the examination of 'more incremental and varied issues' led to qualitative approaches.[124] However, on the whole, it should be noted that a general outcome of the quantitative literature is that the costs of tax compliance, 'however measured – whether in absolute money terms or relative to tax yield, GDP or administrative costs',[125] are 'both highly significant and highly regressive'.[126] Confirming also Adam Smith's points, the research suggests that among the main causes of tax compliance costs are the '[c]omplexity of legislative provisions together with the frequency of legislative change'.[127] The literature also suggests that generally the burden of tax compliance is a very significant issue, a source of continuous concern for most business taxpayers and a problem that does not seem to diminish over time, 'despite attempts by governments (ostensibly) designed to reduce the burden faced by taxpayers'.[128]

[120] Sandford, p. 122.

[121] Evans, 'The Operating Costs', p. 5.

[122] Evans, 'Studying the Studies', p. 68.

[123] Evans, 'The Operating Costs', p. 7.

[124] Ibid.

[125] Evans, 'Studying the studies', p. 71.

[126] Evans, 'The Operating Costs', p. 7. By regressive here is meant that small taxpayers are burdened with higher compliance costs (Lillian F. Mills, 'Corporate Tax Compliance and Financial Reporting', *National Tax Journal*, XLIX, 3 [1996], p. 429).

[127] Evans, 'Studying the Studies', p. 72.

[128] Ibid.

With regard to the Greek case, there are tax studies indicating that the issue of continuous alterations of the tax system made economic planning for Greek companies a very difficult task.[129] Nikos Tatsos has also noted that, as the indications suggest, compliance cost of taxation in Greece was and is higher than in other European countries, something which negatively impacts upon the indigenous firms' competitiveness.[130]

In his study, Tatsos characterises tax compliance costs as difficult to measure and stemming from a multitude of factors. For example, the costs form a long list: the costs of paying tax experts, accountants and lawyers for the provision of tax advice, the costs of the time lost in performing tasks such as completing tax returns and keeping the accounting books and records, the psychological costs because of the taxpayers' uncertainty for the precise level of their tax burden as well as their 'anxiety about whether they have closely followed the tax law provisions or not', but also 'third parties' costs', for example, the costs relating to the operation of courts dealing with tax disputes.[131]

The issues leading to some of the kinds of costs described above will be analysed in detail in this study, which examines how the various administrative problems burdening the system of taxation from the mid-1950s to the late 2000s, for example, the complex and frequently changing tax legislation, created obstacles to business.

Sources

The data used in this book were collected in Athens and are predominantly archival. However, there were also a number of interviews conducted; data were also retrieved from two documentary series aired by Greece's state broadcaster.

The main aim here was to show how the problems in the way that the tax system functioned affected business. However, an important part of the material concerns the broader dysfunctionality of the tax system. Also, the views about this dysfunctionality came not only from entrepreneurs,

[129] See for example G. I. Agapitos, *Income Taxation in Greece* (Athens: Centre of Planning and Economic Research, 1986), p. 35, in Greek.

[130] Tatsos, *Shadow Economy*, p. 408.

[131] Ibid., pp. 406–407.

but from other parts of society too, such as tax professionals, ordinary citizens, politicians, etc. Moreover, an important part of the material regards entrepreneurial criticism expressed through articles in business magazines, newspapers and publications from business organisations. This variety of sources reflects, on the one hand, the scarcity of business archival material indicating how taxes and the tax regime affected business behaviour. In other words, it was quite difficult to find out how entrepreneurs felt about the system of taxation and what they believed about the way it affected their investment activities by merely focusing on business archives. This is mainly because many of the aspects of the tax system that this book explores, for example, arbitrariness of the tax authorities, tax evasion and corruption, are issues that would not be recorded in business archival material.

At the same time however, the variety of sources that is used here shows that entrepreneurial complaints and concerns about the way that the tax system functioned were not isolated. That is, one could have thought that entrepreneurs complained about the tax system simply because they did not like to pay taxes. However, the fact that criticism came from many different directions, and the consistency of this criticism, shows that the functioning of the tax system was indeed a systemic problem for the Greek state. It affected the general public, not only entrepreneurial classes.

A significant part of directly expressed opinions about the tax system came from the Board meeting minutes of the Union of Corporations and Limited Liability Companies,[132] publications from business organisations as well as articles found in newspapers and business magazines. With regard to publications from business bodies, the *Bulletin of the Chamber of Commerce and Industry of Athens*, kept in the Library of the Chamber of Commerce and Industry of Athens, was a particularly rich source of information. Useful information were also found in the *Bulletin of the FGI*. Also, a wealth of material came from articles and various publications in the following daily and economic newspapers: *Dimokratia, Eleftheria, Empros, Imerisia, I Avgi, I Kathimerini, I Naftemporiki, O*

[132] The Union of Corporations and Limited Liability Companies is the representative body for corporations and limited liability companies in Greece. It was established in Athens in 1922, by the largest corporations of the time (see 'The Course of the Union of Corporations and Limited Liability Companies', *Union of Corporations and Limited Liability Companies*. http://sae-epe.gr/istoriko [accessed 8.11.2015], in Greek).

Economicos Tahydromos, Makedonia, Rizospastis, Ta Nea, To Vima and *To Vima tis Kyriakis.*[133] An important amount of information was also found in the *Viomichaniki Epitheorissis*, a monthly business magazine that has been continuously published since 1934.[134] The volumes of the magazine, hosted in the Vovolini Archive, contained also the proceedings of the various congresses of the Chambers of Commerce and Industry of Greece.

Information about the tax policies enforced by the state were found in such publications but also in Ministers of Finances' or Prime Ministers' archives held in the Konstantinos G. Karamanlis Foundation, specifically the Konstantinos Papakonstantinou, Ioannis Mpoutos and Konstantinos Karamanlis collections. Similar information came from the Index of Parliamentary Discussions 1946–1967, held in the Library of the Parliament of Greece and from the *Accountant* magazine, held in the Athens Bar Association. Data were also retrieved from the Eftaxias Family archive, which is part of the Vovolini Archive and held in the Gennadius Library of the American School of Classical Studies in Athens, the Economic Development Financing Organisation Archive hosted in the Historical Archives of the Piraeus Bank Group Cultural Foundation as well as the Hellenic Literary and Historical Archive (ELIA).

A limited amount of material also came from the archives of two manufacturing companies, CHROTEX and IZOLA. Archival material regarding CHROTEX, a paint industrial company that was established in 1945 and is active in the sector to date,[135] is kept in the company. The material utilised for the present study came from Board meeting minutes and newspaper cuts. As far as IZOLA is concerned, it was a manufacturing company focusing on construction materials and household equipment, established in 1930 and closed down in 1991.[136] The material used from

[133] A number of contemporary articles were also used in the study, from newspapers such as I Kathimerini, to VIma, Dimokratia, Capital and Imerisia.

[134] The name of the magazine has currently changed into Economiki Epitheorisi.

[135] 'CHROTEX', The Company. http://www.chrotex.gr/article_detail.asp?e_lang_id=0&e_cat_serial=001001&e_cat_id=2&e_article_id=417 [accessed 12.9.2015], in Greek. For more information about the history of the company see Margarita Dritsas, *The Colour of Success: The Greek Paint industry, 1830–1990* (Athens: Trohalia, 1995), in Greek.

[136] See Takis Katsimardos, 'IZOLA: A Greek Fairytale Without Happy Ending', *Imerisia*, 24.5.2008. http://www.imerisia.gr/article.asp?catid=26510&subid=2&pubid=1953170 [accessed 30.9.2015], in Greek and Toula Dimoudi, 'The (legendary) IZOLA Comes Back After 24 Years Through Poland', *Dimokratia*, 15.3.2015, http://www.dimokratianews.gr/content/36481/i-thryliki-izola-epistrefei-24-hronia-meta-meso-polonias [accessed 30.9.2015], in Greek.

IZOLA's archive was the annual Board of Governors reports, kept in the Hellenic Literary and Historical Archive (ELIA). As noted before, it was difficult to find information about the aspects of the Greek tax system that this research focuses on in business archives. The two companies just mentioned were selected precisely because their archives provided useful material.

A number of interviews complemented the information found in the archives. Specifically, five owners of industrial companies were interviewed, some of whom held executive positions in various business bodies, as well as a former president of the National Union of Tax Officers, a former executive of the Ministry of Finance and a retired tax officer. Interviewees were found through snowball sampling and then selected depending on their position and their ability to comment on Greek tax policy. Also, two documentary series were used for the period of dictatorship (1967–1974), during which information appearing in newspapers and magazines was censored by the state and therefore of questionable validity.

Apart from the interviews conducted, views and opinions regarding the administrative problems of the tax system coming from the tax officers themselves were found in newspaper articles as well as articles published in two relevant magazines, the *Tax Review*, the issues of which are kept in the Library of the National Federation of Tax Officers [P.O.E-D.O.Y]) and the Library of the Athens Bar Association, as well as the *Bulletin of Tax Legislation*, also kept in the Library of the Athens Bar Association.

For triangulation purposes,[137] all of the primary data mentioned above were analysed in relation to information from a variety of studies and publications such as the *Statistical Yearbook of Greece* published annually by the Hellenic Statistical Authority, the *Proposals of the Disincentives Committee*, the *Bank of Greece Governor's Annual Reports* and the *Long-term Statistical Series of the Greek Economy* by the Bank of Greece as well as the *National Accounts of Greece* and the *Annual Reports for the Execution of the Budget* from the Ministries of Coordination and Finance respectively.

[137] Kenneth Lipartito, 'Historical Sources and Data', in *Organizations in Time: History, Theory, Methods*, eds Marcelo Bucheli and R. Daniel Wadhwani (Oxford: Oxford University Press, 2013), p. 290.

Structure of the Book

The rest of this book comprises six main chapters and a concluding one. The second chapter provides basic information about the Greek tax system, the Greek state, political system and parties, but also the civil service as well as the role of the trade unions, with a special focus on that of the tax officers.

The next five chapters explore how disadvantages of the tax system such as the complexity of legislation, the insufficient organisation[138] of the tax services, excessive bureaucracy and also problematic relations between tax officers and entrepreneurs created difficulties for business initiative. Such disadvantages undermined the effectiveness of developmental tools that had been introduced for the promotion of investment, such as the one of tax incentives. This examination starts from 1955, because this year saw the initiation of tax reforms that were part of a broader effort of revamping the Greek economy and promoting industrialisation, and ends in the late 2000s, shortly before the eruption of the government-debt crisis the country faced.

In more detail, Chapter 3 focuses on 1955–1967, a period which saw an important growth in the Greek economy but within a context of a 'feeble' democratic regime, for the 'peculiar mixture of authoritarianism and democracy, exclusion and prosperity, ideological backwardness and cultural vigour' it witnessed.[139] These years saw the enactment of laws that introduced a series of reforms in the tax system which, however, did not bring about any long-lasting improvement in the organisation of the tax bureaus. The various weaknesses burdening the tax administration structures seemed to cause difficulties to business and, as the evidence indicates, appeared to be a factor of uncertainty that discouraged industrial investment, even within a wider framework of rapid economic growth.

The situation in the system of taxation deteriorated in the period from 1967 to 1974, one in which the democratic regime was abolished and a military coup was imposed. The fourth chapter examines those years, during which the considerable increase in the rate of growth gave

[138] The term insufficient organisation is used here to denote primarily that the procedures followed in the tax offices were complex and not adequately standardised.

[139] Ilias Nikolakopoulos, *The Cachectic Democracy-Political Parties and Elections: 1946–1967* (Athens: Patakis, 2001), p. 9, in Greek.

way, towards the end of the period, to the gradual overheating of the economy. The system of taxation continued to create difficulties for business, as, in spite of its declarations, the junta regime did not implement any measures for the modernisation of the system. Even worse, the policies that the regime introduced essentially dismantled the Central Service of the Ministry of Economics, which was responsible for managing the functioning of the tax services.

The actual dimensions of the problems in the system of taxation would become clearer during the period 1974–1981, which is examined in the fifth chapter. In those years, in the aftermath of the dictatorship and in the midst of an international economic recession, the Greek economy was faced with a deterioration in all of its basic macroeconomic indicators. The country had also entered a stage of industrial stagnation, marked by the reduction of the share of investment in manufacturing over GDP. In this period, the system of taxation was pointed out more regularly as a component of the economic environment that created difficulties to business conduct. Various complaints and critique indicate that the tax legislation's complexity and frequency of change increased during this period, but also that the arbitrariness of the tax authorities did not diminish, in spite of the fact that the government implemented relevant measures. Arbitrariness created opportunities for tax officials to extort taxpayers and ask for bribes. Indeed, there was an increasing number of incidences of tax officers being accused of corruption and blackmailing, phenomena that were not unheard of in previous periods, but, within a climate of generalised economic instability, poisoned even more the already dysfunctional relations between tax authorities and the taxpayers.

The sixth chapter shows how these problems were exacerbated in the 1980s. During this time the structural weaknesses of the Greek economy had become more than manifest, in the form of stagflation, increasing deficits and deteriorating competitiveness. However, what distinguishes those years is that the problems burdening the functioning of the tax system became of a more direct impact than ever before, and a matter of open conflict, not only between entrepreneurs/taxpayers and the members of tax administration, but also, and interestingly enough, between the latter and the Ministry of Economics. The issue of the complexity of the tax legislation, recognised also by tax officers themselves, actually grew larger, the arbitrariness of tax officers did not seem to abate, cases of bribe-taking continued to appear in the press, tax evasion increased, and there were not any reforms that would reduce the bureaucracy and great complexity burdening the tax system.

The seventh chapter covers the period 1989–2008 and shows how, in the context of mixed results as far as the economy's performance was concerned, the structural weaknesses of the Greek tax system remained as present and corrosive as ever before. It is shown how the rigidities and dysfunctionalities of the tax administration kept on creating difficulties for the development of business and the promotion of entrepreneurship, in a fashion strikingly similar to previous decades.

On the basis of the analysis done in the six main chapters of this book, the concluding one suggests a series of possible steps that could be taken in order to improve the current situation in the Greek system of taxation. The chapter also analyses the ways in which this study contributes to Greek historiography, to institutional analyses about taxation, but also to the literature concerning the interaction between institutions and entrepreneurship, and more precisely, the interaction between entrepreneurship and taxation. It is stressed that the 'extended' version of Baumol's model suggested here could be utilised by further research, because, as it seems, Greece is not the only European country where the tax administration creates difficulties for business.

Bibliography

Primary Sources

Vovolini Archive, 'Notes – Tax Evasion', *Viomichaniki Epitheorissis*, Vol. 20, September 1953.

Official Publications

Bank of Greece, *Long-term Statistical Series of the Greek Economy* (Athens: Bank of Greece, 1992), pp. 10–12, in Greek.

European Commission, *Helping Firms Grow, European Competitiveness Report 2014*, Commission Staff Working Document SWD(2014)277 final. http://ec.europa.eu/growth/industry/competitiveness/reports/eu-competitiveness-report/index_en.htm.

International Monetary Fund, *Greece, Selected Issues*, Country Report No.13/155, June 2013. https://www.imf.org/external/pubs/ft/scr/2013/cr13155.pdf [accessed 1.11.2015].

International Monetary Fund, *Corruption: Costs and Mitigating Strategies*, IMF Staff Discussion Note, May 2016. http://www.imf.org/external/pubs/ft/sdn/2016/sdn1605.pdf [accessed 8.10.2016].

Web Resources

'CHROTEX', The Company. http://www.chrotex.gr/article_detail.asp?e_lang_id=0&e_cat_serial=001001&e_cat_id=2&e_article_id=417, in Greek.

Dimitrelis, S., 'Greece Loses the Revenue from Three ENFIA Taxes Due to VAT Evasion', Capital.gr, 05.09.2019. https://www.capital.gr/oikonomia/3380524/treis-enfia-xanei-i-ellada-apo-ti-forodiafugi-fpa.

'OECD Agreement', *CQ Almanac*. http://library.cqpress.com/cqalmanac/document.php?id=cqal61-1373318.

Oxford Dictionaries. http://www.oxforddictionaries.com/definition/english/conscience.

Spiegel, P., 'Greece Proposes Tourists as Tax Inspectors', *The Financial Times*, 6.3.2015. http://www.ft.com/cms/s/0/b65fa81c-c411-11e4-a02e-00144feab7de.html#axzz3pOaWCPUW.

Spiegel, P., I. Traynor and H. Smith, 'Wired-Up Tax Snoopers Could Be Unleashed in Greece', *The Guardian*, 6.3.2015. http://www.theguardian.com/world/2015/mar/06/wired-up-tax-snoopers-could-be-unleashed-in-greece.

Stephens, P., 'An Offer That Greece Should Not Refuse', *The Financial Times*, 4.6.2015. http://www.ft.com/intl/cms/s/0/f6127244-09e1-11e5-b6bd-00144feabdc0.html#axzz3dJwTCDQG.

'The Course of the Union of Corporations and Limited Liability Companies', *Union of Corporations and Limited Liability Companies*. http://sae-epe.gr/istoriko, in Greek.

'What Is Bribery and Corruption?', *Tackling Bribery and Corruption*. http://www.anticorruption.ie/en/acjs/pages/fq08000018.

'Xenophon Zolotas'. http://www.intercomprehension.eu/modules/intercom_new/template.php?module=3&activity=1&sc=9&langID=en&w_langID=gr.

Secondary Literature

Agapitos, G. I., *Income Taxation in Greece* (Athens: Centre of Planning and Economic Research, 1986), in Greek.

Baumol, W. J., 'Formal Entrepreneurship Theory in Economics: Existence and Bounds', *Journal of Business Venturing*, 8 (1993).

Ibid., 'Entrepreneurship: Productive, Unproductive, and Destructive', *Journal of Political Economy*, Vol. 98, 5, 1 (Oct., 1990).

Bosworth, B., and T. Trifon Kollintzas, *Economic Growth in Greece: Past Performance and Future Prospects, in Greece's Economic Performance and Prospects*, eds Ralph C. Bryan, Nikolaos C. Garganas and Georgios S. Tavlas (Athens: The Bank of Greece and The Brookings Institution, 2002).

Casson, M., *Entrepreneurship: Theory, Networks, History* (UK: Edward Elgar, 2010).

Casson, M. and P. J. Buckley, 'Entrepreneurship and the Growth of the Firm: An Extension of Penrose's Theory', in *Entrepreneurship—Theory, Networks, History* (UK: Edward Elgar, 2010).

Clemens, E. S., and J. M. Cook, 'Politics and Institutionalism: Explaining Durability and Change', *Annual Review of Sociology*, 25 (1999).

Douhan, R., and M. Henrekson, 'The Political Economy of Entrepreneurship', *IFN Working Paper* No. 716, Research Institute of Industrial Economics (2007).

Drakatos, K., *The Big Cycle of the Greek Economy (1945–1995)* (Athens: Papazisis, 1997).

Dritsas, M., *The Colour of Success: The Greek Paint industry, 1830–1990* (Athens: Trohalia, 1995), in Greek.

Estrin, S., K. E. Meyer and M. Bytchkova, 'Entrepreneurship in Transition Economies', in *The Oxford Handbook of Entrepreneurship*, eds Mark Casson, Bernard Yeung, Anuradha Basu and Nigel Wadeson (Oxford: Oxford University Press, 2006).

Evans, C., 'Studying the Studies: An Overview of Recent Research into Taxation Operating Costs', *eJournal of Tax Research*, 1, 1 (2003).

Evans, C., 'The Operating Costs of Taxation: A Review of the Research', *Economic Affairs* 21, 2 (2001).

Evans, C., 'Cedric Sandford', *The Guardian*, 16.4.2004. http://www.theguardian.com/money/2004/apr/16/publicfinances.guardianobituaries.

Fear, F., 'Mining the Past: Historicizing Organizational Learning and Change', in *Organizations in Time: History, Theory, Methods*, eds Marcelo Bucheli and R. Daniel Wadhwani (Oxford: Oxford University Press, 2013).

Giouras, T. and M. Psalidopoulos, *Occupation, Nazism and Greek Economy—Official Reports and Memoirs* (Athens: Metamesonikties Ekdoseis, 2015), in Greek.

Goldscheid, R., 'A Sociological Approach to Problems of Public Finance', in *Classics in the Theory of Public Finance*, eds R. A. Musgrave and A. T. Peacock (London: Macmillan & Co. Ltd., [1925], 1958).

Goldscheid, R. and R. Lazarsfeld, 'Staatsozialismus oder Staatskapitalismus - Ein finanzsoziologischer Beitrag zur Lösung des Staatsschulden-Problems, Archiv für Rechts- und Wirtschaftsphilosophie', 11, 2 (1917/1918).

Haig, R. M., 'The Cost to Business Concerns of Compliance with Tax Laws', *Management Review*, 24, 11 (1935).

Hall, P. A. and R. C. R. Taylor, 'Political Science and the Three New Institutionalisms', *Political Studies*, XLIV (1996).
Hébert, R. and A. N. Link, *The Entrepreneur: Mainstream Views and Radical Critiques* (New York: Praeger, 1988).
Henrekson, M., 'Entrepreneurship and Institutions', *IFN Working Paper* No 707, Research Institute of Industrial Economics (2007).
Hodgson, G. M., 'What Are Institutions?', *Journal of Economic Issues*, XL, 1 (2006).
Houlder, V., 'Europe's Shadow Economy Costs €454bn in 'Lost' Taxes', *The Financial Times*, 24.9.2015, http://www.ft.com/cms/s/0/9c30cc14-5e1c-11e5-a28b-50226830d644.html?siteedition=uk#axzz3mpp1uGbt.
Johnson, V., 'What Is Organizational Imprinting? Cultural Entrepreneurship in the Founding of the Paris Opera', *American Journal of Sociology*, 13, 1 (2007).
Jones, G. and R. D. Wadhwani, 'Schumpeter's Plea: Rediscovering History and Relevance in the Study of Entrepreneurship', *Harvard Business School Working Paper*, No. 06-036 (2006). http://www.hbs.edu/faculty/Publication%20Files/06-036.pdf.
Kalyvianakis, K. et al., *Tax Regime, Shadow Economy and Tax Evasion in Greece* (Athens: Papazisis, 1993).
Kirzner, I. M., *Competition and Entrepreneurship* (Chicago: University of Chicago Press, 1973).
Landström, H. and M. Benner, 'Entrepreneurship Research: A History of Scholarly Migration', in *Historical Foundations of Entrepreneurship Research*, eds Hans Landström and Franz Lohrke (UK: Edward Elgar, 2010).
Landström, H. and O. Persson, 'Entrepreneurship Research: Research Communities and Knowledge Platforms', in *Historical Foundations of Entrepreneurship Research*, eds Hans Landström and Franz Lohrke (UK: Edward Elgar, 2010).
Legg, K. R., *Politics in Modern Greece* (California: Stanford University Press, 1969).
Leibenstein, H., 'Entrepreneurship and Development', *The American Economic Review*, 58, 2 (1968).
Lindbeck, A., 'Consequences of the Advanced Welfare State', *The World Economy*, 11, 1 (1988).
Lipartito, K., 'Historical Sources and Data', in *Organizations in Time: History, Theory, Methods*, eds Marcelo Bucheli and R. Daniel Wadhwani (Oxford: Oxford University Press, 2013).
Martin, I. W., A. K. Mehrotta and M. Prasad, 'The Thunder of History: The Origins and Development of the New Fiscal Sociology', in *The New Fiscal Sociology, Taxation in Comparative and Historical Perspective*, eds Isaac William Martin, Ajay K. Mehrotta and Monica Prasad (Cambridge: Cambridge University Press, 2009).

Mavragannis, K., '110 Years from the Birth of Xenophon Zolotas: His Life Through Unpublished Photographs', *The Huffington Post*. http://www.huffingtonpost.gr/2014/12/13/110-xronia-xenophon-zolotas_n_6317764.html?utm_hp_ref=greece.

Meyer, J. W. and B. Rowan, 'Institutionalized Organizations: Formal Structure as Myth and Ceremony', *American Journal of Sociology*, 83, 2 (1977).

Mills, L. F., 'Corporate Tax Compliance and Financial Reporting', *National Tax Journal*, XLIX, 3 (1996).

Nikolakopoulos, I., *The Cachectic Democracy- Political Parties and Elections: 1946–1967* (Athens: Patakis, 2001).

North, D. C., 'Institutions', *Journal of Economic Perspectives*, 5, 1 (1991).

North, D. C., *Understanding the Process of Economic Change* (Princeton: Princeton University Press, 2005).

Penrose, E., 'Limits to the Growth and Size of Firms', *The American Economic Review*, 45, 2 (1955).

Sandford, C., M. Godwin and P. Hardwick, *Administrative and Compliance Costs of Taxation* (Great Britain: Fiscal Publications, 1989).

Sandford, C., *Hidden Costs of Taxation* (London: Institute for Fiscal Studies, 1973).

Sapelli, G., *Southern Europe Since 1945, Tradition and Modernity in Portugal, Spain, Italy, Greece and Turkey* (London and New York: Longman, 1995).

Schumpeter, J. A., 'The Crisis of the Tax State', in *Joseph A. Schumpeter: The Economics and Sociology of Capitalism*, ed. R. Swedberg (Princeton, NJ: Princeton University Press, [1918], 1991).

Scott, W. R., *Institutions and Organizations—Ideas and Interests* (California: Sage Publications, 2008).

Seferiades, S., 'Polarization and Nonproportionality: The Greek Party System in the Postwar Era', *Comparative Politics*, 19, 1 (1986).

Shane, S., *A General Theory of Entrepreneurship* (UK: Edward Elgar, 2003).

Smith, A., *An Inquiry into the Nature and Causes of the Wealth of Nations*, Volume II (London: Methuen & Co, 1904).

Steinmo, S., 'Historical Institutionalism', in *Approaches and Methodologies in the Social Sciences, a Pluralist Perspective*, eds Donatella Della Porta and Michael Keating (Cambridge: Cambridge University Press, 2008).

Suddaby, R., W. M. Foster and A. J. Mills, 'Historical Institutionalism', in *Organizations in Time: History, Theory, Methods*, eds Marcelo Bucheli and R. Daniel Wadhwani (Oxford: Oxford University Press, 2013).

Tatsos, N., *Shadow Economy and Tax Evasion in Greece* (Athens: Papazisi, 2001).

Thelen, K., 'Historical Institutionalism in Comparative Politics', *Annual Review of Political Science*, 2 (1999).

Tran-Nam, B. and C. Evans, 'The Impact of Cedric Sandford on the Discipline of Tax Compliance Costs', *Australian Tax Forum*, 17 (2002).

Verheul, I., S. Wennekers, D. Audretsch and R. Thurik, 'An Eclectic Theory of Entrepreneurship: Policies, Institutions and Culture', in *Entrepreneurship: Determinants and Policy in a European-US Comparison*, eds David Audretsch, Roy Thurik, Ingrid Verheul and Sander Wennekers (USA: Kluwer Academic Publishers, 2002).

Wadhwani, R. D., 'Historical Reasoning and the Development of Entrepreneurship Theory', in *Historical Foundations of Entrepreneurship Research*, eds Hans Landström and Franz Lohrke (UK: Edward Elgar, 2010).

Wadhwani, R. D. and M. Bucheli, 'The Future of the Past in Management and Organization Studies', in *Organizations in Time: History, Theory, Methods*, eds Marcelo Bucheli and R. Daniel Wadhwani (Oxford: Oxford University Press, 2013).

Articles in National Newspapers

Dimoudi, T., 'The (Legendary) IZOLA Comes Back After 24 Years Through Poland', *Dimokratia*, 15.3.2015. http://www.dimokratianews.gr/content/36481/i-thryliki-izola-epistrefei-24-hronia-meta-meso-polonias, in Greek.

Katsimardos, T., 'IZOLA: A Greek Fairytale Without Happy Ending', *Imerisia*, 24.5.2008. http://www.imerisia.gr/article.asp?catid=26510&subid=2&pubid=1953170.

Nikolaou, N., 'We Need to Get Rid of Disincentives', *To Vima*, 14.11.2004. http://www.tovima.gr/finance/article/?aid=162410.

CHAPTER 2

Unstable Politics, Unfair Taxation and a Public Administration Afflicted by Clientelism: Key Information About the Greek State

Introduction

This chapter offers key information about the Greek state throughout the period analysed here. It is shown that Greece was a country with a highly unstable political structure in which patronage was often more important than ideology. It also had a regressive and unfair system of taxation in which certain parts of society were favoured at the expense of others, and a system of public administration that was burdened by clientelism. The depiction of clientelism here follows the perspective of Susan Rose-Ackerman and Bonnie Palifka, who note that '…clientelistic systems develop where favours and payoffs are exchanged that undermine the transparency and effectiveness of public and private institutions'.[1] In the case of the Greek public administration, a frequently commented upon example of clientelism was the fact that citizens obtained favours from politicians in exchange for their votes.

The chapter is divided into four parts, the first of which presents the starting point of the Greek state immediately after the end of the Second World War and up to the point when, following successful reconstruction efforts, it managed to become again part of the international economy in the decade of the 1950s.

[1] Susan Rose-Ackerman and Bonnie J. Palifka, *Corruption and Government—Causes, Consequences, and Reform* (New York: Cambridge University Press, 2016), p. 251.

Z. Pittaki, *Exploring the roots of systematic tax avoidance in Greece*, Palgrave Studies in Economic History,
https://doi.org/10.1007/978-3-030-71979-1_2

The second and third parts raise certain points that are necessary for an understanding of Greece's constitutional arrangements, political system, as well as the system of public administration and civil service. Apart from practical information, the analysis stresses that spoils and clientelistic practices characterised relations to a large extent. They not only dominated transactions between the members of the public services, but also among the citizens and the members of political parties, which were, in many cases, also members of these same public services.

The last part of the chapter offers key information about the Greek tax system. It is shown that the system was replete with features that made it highly unfair, for example, taxes in favour of third parties, the revenue of which was given to professional classes and organisations with great negotiating power. By harming the legitimacy and fairness of the tax system, such and other similar features contributed to the ongoing problem of tax evasion, which is arguably Greece's most serious fiscal problem nowadays.

Historical Background—Greece in the Aftermath of the Second World War

Greece entered the Second World War in 1940. Upon its ending, a civil war erupted, one that lasted up to 1949. Ten years of continuous devastation left the country ravaged in all possible respects: during the 3.5 years of occupation following the German invasion, 7–8% of the population was lost[2]; on the whole, from 1941 to 1949, human losses exceeded half a million lives.[3] By 1944, almost 30% of the national wealth was lost,[4] 9000 villages and 23% of all dwellings had been destroyed.[5] The railway and a large part of the road network suffered extensive damage,

[2] Jean Meynaud, *Political Forces in Greece, vol. I*, trans. by P. Merlopoulos (Athens: Savvalas, 2002), p. 62. The source used here is a Greek translation, the original work's title was *Les forces politiques en Grèce*.

[3] A. J. Sbarounis, in Theodore C. Kariotis, 'The Economy: Growth Without Equity', in *Greece in the Twentieth Century*, eds Theodore A. Couloumbis, Theodore Kariotis and Fotini Bellou (Athens: Hellenic Foundation for European and Black Sea Studies, 2004), p. 240.

[4] Meynaud, p. 62.

[5] C. A. Coombs, in Nikos Mouzelis, *Modern Greece, Facets of Underdevelopment* (London: The Macmillan Press Ltd., 1978), p. 118.

as 100% of railway bridges and 90% of road bridges were obliterated. 93.5% of railway infrastructure and 65.7% of all vehicles were also ruined; this severely disrupted communication between the various areas of the country, destroying any existing internal markets. Seventy-two per cent of the capital that was invested in the shipping industry pre-war was also unrecoverable, with 429 commercial vessels and 1,372,353 registered tonnages being destroyed between 1939 and 1944.[6]

Before the 1940s Greece was mainly an agricultural country.[7] However, the impact of war was severe: all productive sectors of the economy were gravely affected, with agriculture and livestock being reduced to 25–40% of their pre-war levels.[8] One of the biggest problems the Greek economy was faced with during the immediate post-war years was the emptying of bank deposits and the loss of confidence towards paper money, which, along with serious shortages in consumer goods, increased inflation significantly.[9]

Greece was a country that 'from…its independence from the 19th century until the eve of the Second World War was wrestling with poverty'.[10] In such a setting, during the first post-war period, the country needed foreign aid in order to, first of all, feed its population, and then resume any kind of productive activity it had developed in the past.[11] The organisation that contributed to the first cause was the United Nations Relief and Rehabilitation Administration (UNRRA) that up until June 1947 provided support that reached $415 million.[12] Regarding the rehabilitation of the infrastructure and the economic support of Greece, this was to an important degree a result of the implementation of the US aid plan (Marshall Plan) in the country. In monetary terms and for the two decades between 1947 and 1966, total US aid in Greece reached $3.75

[6] Panos Kazakos, *Between State and Market* (Athens: Patakis, 2001), pp. 59–60, in Greek.

[7] Only exception was the shipping sector, the magnitude of which was amongst the largest of the world, and, in the category of tramp freighters, the second largest one (ibid., p. 59).

[8] Sbarounis, pp. 240–241.

[9] E. A Eliades, 'Stabilization of the Greek Economy and the 1953 Devaluation of the Drachma' Staff Papers, *International Monetary Fund*, 4, 1 (Sep., 1954), p. 23.

[10] Meynaud, p. 42.

[11] Kazakos, p. 64.

[12] Ibid., p. 65.

billion, about half of which was economic aid and the remaining military assistance.[13]

There exist many views regarding the purpose of American aid to Greece and the obstacles to its implementation. Indicatively, Kostas Kostis, in addressing the reasons why the United States economically supported Greece's recovery, notes that the industrialisation of the country was one of the main proclaimed aims of the American aid. He argued that it 'was a…solution which…had been put forward as a way to confront the communist danger on the basis of the American-type rationale that a consumer society is the only solution to such kind of problems…such a rationale related later to the country's internationalisation through its connection with the European Economic Community'.[14]

American officials functioned as counsellors and supervisors of the Greek economy during the late 1940s to early 1950s period. As for the obstacles faced by the implementers of the aid programme, Michalis Psalidopoulos' work is very helpful in providing some examples of the perceptions of these American officials. He demonstrates that the difficulties they had to overcome were mainly in respect to the interminable procedures of the Greek bureaucracy and the procrastinating mentality of the officials in the various Ministries.[15]

Nevertheless, it is widely accepted that American aid, combined with a 50% devaluation of the national currency in 1953, greatly assisted the country to recover.[16] In such a framework, production and national

[13] N. V. Giannaris, *Greece and Yugoslavia, an Economic Comparison* (New York, Praeger, 1984), pp. 29–30.

[14] Kostas Kostis, *State and Enterprises in Greece, the History of 'Aluminium of Greece'* (Athens: Polis, 2013), pp. 52–53, in Greek. See also the following works: A. Sutcliffe, *An Economic and Social History of Western Europe Since 1945* (London and New York, Longman, 1996) p. 82; A. Vetsopoulos, 'Efforts for the Development and Stabilization of the Economy During the Period of the Marshall Plan', *Journal of Modern Greek Studies*, 27, 2 (October 2009), p. 280; D. H. Close, *Greece Since 1945* (Great Britain: Pearson Education Limited, 2002), p. 32 and Kazakos, pp. 86–87.

[15] Michalis Psalidopoulos, *Desperate Supervisors, American Consultants in Greece, 1947–53—From Paul A. Porter to Edward A. Tenenbaum* (Athens: Metamesonikties Ekdoseis, 2013), pp. 256–262, in Greek. Psalidopoulos is a Professor of Economics at the University of Athens. He also currently serves as Greece's representative at the IMF. For further information on the implementation of American aid to Greece see Vetsopoulos, pp. 220–221; 247 and Kazakos, p. 95.

[16] See for example Vetsopoulos, p. 296; N.A. Michas, 'Economic Development, Social Mobilization and the Growth of Public Expenditures in Greece', *American Journal of*

income reached their pre-war levels by 1950–1951.[17] This shows that stabilisation efforts quickly proved successful, especially taking into consideration that war in Greece was not over in 1944 but continued, in the form of civil conflict, for 5 or, depending on the perspective, even 8 years more.[18] However, in spite of the economic stabilisation, Greece was also a country in which, as the next pages will show, clientelism and instability burdened the political and public administration structures and taxation was unfair.

Polity, Political Parties and Clientelism

From its independence from the nineteenth century and up to 1967, Greece was a constitutional monarchy. A seven-year dictatorial regime was imposed in April 1967; democracy was restored in July 1974 and the referendum that took place in December of the same year brought about the abolition of the monarchy. From this point onwards, the Greek state became a parliamentary republic.[19]

In terms of party representation, there was a range of opinion across the political spectrum.[20] Throughout the period of examination (1955–2008) thirty-six governments were brought to power, the majority of which were right wing.[21] With the exception of various transitional and coalition governments, Konstantinos Karamanlis' right-wing party was in power from late 1955 to late 1963, and Georgios Papandreou's centre party ruled from late 1963 to July 1965. A number of short-lived governments followed the fall of Papandreou's government from July 1965 to April 1967. From that point and for seven consecutive years, the country entered a phase of military dictatorship. The restoration of democracy

Economics and Sociology, 39, 1 (January 1980), p. 39 and A. F. Freris, *The Greek Economy in the Twentieth Century* (London and Sydney, Croom Helm, 1986), p. 143.

[17] Eliades, p. 25.

[18] The civil war officially over in 1949, with the battle between the government forces and the guerrilla groups in the mount Grammos in Northern Greece. However, guerrilla groups continued to act in the provinces until 1952 (Kazakos, pp. 64–77).

[19] 'Hellenic Parliament', *Constitutional History*. http://www.hellenicparliament.gr/Vouli-ton-Ellinon/To-Politevma/Syntagmatiki-Istoria/ [accessed 20.11.2015], in Greek.

[20] Meynaud, p. 74.

[21] 'The General Secretariat of the Government', *Governments from 1909 to Date*. http://www.ggk.gov.gr/?page_id=776&sort=time [accessed 20.08.2020], in Greek.

in July 1974 saw the return of Karamanlis to power in the head of New Democracy, the new right-wing political party he established. In May 1980, Karamanlis was succeeded by Georgios Rallis, one of the members of his party. Rallis' government remained in power from May 1980 to October 1981. From that point and up to July 1989 the country was ruled by the Panhellenic Socialist Movement, the left-wing party of Andreas Papandreou, Georgios Papandreou's son. For the majority of the 1990s and up to 2004 the country was still ruled by the same party. From 2004 and up to 2008 the right-wing party New Democracy governed the country, this time under the leadership of Karamanlis' nephew. [22]

A general characteristic of the Greek political parties, not only in the post-Second World War period, but actually since the late nineteenth century, is that they were unstable and weak. This was primarily as their formation and development was dependent on personal relations rather than a core of common ideological beliefs.[23] This characteristic, which undoubtedly undermined the legitimacy of such parties and also of the broader political system they represented, becomes clearer when looking at the past, specifically the 1880s. This period, shortly after the establishment of a Parliamentary system in the country,[24] witnessed the emergence of two distinctive political formations, one representing the middle classes and another one having a conservative character and being connected to old political families. Both political formations were not bodies with a bureaucratically organised structure, but 'merely groups of parliamentarians linking up around a leader'.[25] The executive members of such groups were local elites who 'struggled to create a network of relations and solidarity around them'.[26] A factor which also undermined the legitimacy of such political formations was that, 'in a still underdeveloped society', as the political scientist Jean Meynaud noted, the networks sustaining them 'were necessarily established on the basis of clientelistic relations

[22] Karamanlis was assigned the government by the Crown in October 1955, after the death of Prime Minister Alexandros Papagos (Meynaud, pp. 124–125). For more information about the governments of the period see 'Governments from 1909 to date'.

[23] Meynaud, pp. 47–48.

[24] The Parliamentary system was introduced in 1875 (ibid.).

[25] Ibid, p. 47.

[26] Ibid., pp. 47–48.

and spoils'.[27] In other words, the main duty of parliamentarians was 'to be vigilant over protecting their constituencies' interests', in return for those constituencies' votes.[28]

Writing in 1965 and in an effort to throw light on the role of clientelism and spoils in Greek political life, Meynaud focused mainly, but not exclusively, on the spoils requested by people living in the mountainous (and thus also poorer) areas of the country. He noted the following:

> An observer from a developed country could condemn such a phenomenon as being equal to fraud and consider it as an indication of amorality for those getting involved in it. But this would be a view of a person whose everyday life is not about covering basic needs. However, the populations we are talking about live in conditions of such impoverishment that 'spoil-protection' could be considered necessary for the continuation of their very existence. Given that the vote[29] is one of the few goods the society provides to those outcasts, it is only natural that they are trying to make the most of this vote...In a country still as poor as the agrarian Greece, any kind of services a member of the Parliament could offer are important.[30]

In other words, and through such a perspective, spoils and the system of clientelism built around them could be seen as a balance against poverty and the deficiencies of the Greek economic system in general.

According to Dimitris Sotiropoulos, the way clientelism functioned changed from the moment the socialist party PASOK came to power, in 1981. It was then that 'personal clientelism was replaced by party-bureaucratic clientelism'.[31] This was, as he notes, a major transition from citizens contacting politicians or, more broadly, people who had access

[27] Ibid., p. 48.

[28] Ibid.

[29] According to the Constitution of 1844, all men above 25 years old and in possession of land had the right to vote. In 1877, the right was extended to all men regardless of land possession. Women gained full voting rights in 1952 (see 'The right of voting in Greece', *Kyros-Education*, 18.2.2002. https://kyros.wordpress.com/2012/02/18/δικαίωμα-ψήφου-στην-ελλάδα/ [accessed 26.2.2016], in Greek and Margarita Papantoniou, 'Greece Marks 61 Years After Suffrage', *Greek Reporter*, 28.5.2013. http://greece.greekreporter.com/2013/05/28/greece-marks-61-years-after-suffrage/ [accessed 26.2.2016]).

[30] Meynaud, pp. 66–67.

[31] Dimitris A. Sotiropoulos, *The Tip of the Clientelist State—Organisation, Staffing and Politicisation of the Higher Echelons of the Central Administration in Greece, 1974–2000* (Athens: Potamos, 2001), p. 149, in Greek.

to the government to gain rewards. The new form of clientelism was organised by the bureaucratic mechanisms of the ruling party.

In such a state, voters who sought spoils no longer turned to specific politicians, but, instead 'to the local political mechanism of the party they supported, or directly to the party's headquarters'.[32] This could arguably have created institutionalisation and, therefore, a solidification of clientelistic practices. Yet, for the purpose of this study, it is not considered to have fundamentally changed either the meaning or implications of clientelism. The important point to note is that clientelistic relations appeared more or less concurrently with the establishment of the modern Greek state and quickly spread through the public service mechanism.

Public Administration, Civil Service and the Trade Union of Tax Officers

The Greek public administration was created after the establishment of the Greek state in 1830[33] and had, according to Sotiropoulos, all the Weberian characteristics of a hierarchically structured bureaucracy. However, because of the level of development of Greece at the time, such an establishment meant that certain 'liberal institutions...were transplanted into a pre-modern, agricultural society'.[34] As a result, alongside the official structure of public administration, a network of unofficial relations appeared between state institutions and citizens. Indeed, it constituted a similar kind of clientelism to those governing relations between politicians and their constituencies and quickly started to grow: 'As was also the case in other countries with premature parliamentarism and late industrialisation, political participation but also the organisation of the state were governed by relations of patronage'.[35]

In this context, it is no surprise that finding a job in the public sector was often the result of such clientelistic relations and spoils, not only in the years following the establishment of the Greek state, but also in the twentieth century, as the relevant literature indicates. The sociologist Konstantinos Tsoukalas has argued that up to a certain degree, even in

[32] Ibid., pp. 149–150.

[33] Ibid., p. 14.

[34] Ibid.

[35] Ibid., pp. 14–15.

the first decade after the end of the Second World War, politicians used appointments in the civil service as a means of controlling the masses.[36]

Of course, this system of spoils existed side-by-side with a formal one of admissions through competitions organised by the state. Specifically, 1951 saw the introduction of the Civil Service Code,[37] which was drafted 'with help from the US'[38] and initially functioned under the supervision of a Public Service Commission (ASDY). The duty of this Commission was, among others, 'the organization and conduct of competitive examinations for public service posts, with the twin goals of stemming ingrained clientelist practices and of mainstreaming merit in public service recruitment'.[39] However, the Commission was abolished by the junta regime in 1967 and did not function again.[40] Even before the junta though, that is, even when the Commission functioned normally, as Antonis Makrydimitris noted, there were 'countless exceptions' in public sector recruitment. In addition to this, in this same period, a large number of people who were considered to be political dissidents were excluded from public service posts.[41]

In later periods such exclusion was avoided, but the criteria with which civil servants were appointed remained less than satisfactory. For example, as late as the 1980s, a system of 'social criteria' for recruitment of public servants was established, which was however considered unfair.[42] Specifically, a formal 'points' system was introduced which gave much more weight to the candidates' 'social background and antecedents (family, place of birth etc.)' and downplayed the importance of '[e]ducational accomplishments, professional experience and demonstrated skills'.[43] Demetrios Argyriades noted that the logic behind the

[36] Konstantinos Tsoukalas, *State, Society, Labour in post-war Greece* (Athens: Themelio, 2005), p. 93, in Greek.

[37] Antonis Makrydimitris, *The Administration in Crisis, Texts on Administration and Society* (Athens: Nea Sinora-Livanis, 1996), p. 170, in Greek.

[38] Demetrios Argyriades, 'Greek Exit from the Crisis—A Pressing and Much-Needed Public Service Reform', *Social Sciences*, 2 (2013), p. 82.

[39] Ibid.

[40] Ibid.

[41] Makrydimitris, p. 170.

[42] Ibid.

[43] Argyriades, p. 85.

new system was to increase the 'representation of disadvantaged groups'. However, he stressed, 'this had hardly ever been a challenge to the Greek public service. Unlike its French or British counterparts, the Greek administration –its senior ranks included- had never been a magnet or a career of choice for the country's social elites… [t]he need to make the Service…attractive to promising young graduates from top Schools internationally, and offer it the ability to take on and pursue the drive for modernization apparently gave way to other, more mundane and partisan concerns'.[44]

Apart from the issue of recruitment of promising graduates, a factor affecting the ability of civil servants to perform their duties adequately was training. In the case of tax officers, the lack of appropriate training was a recurring object of complaint, as will be shown in the following chapters. Actually, the most appropriate commentator for such an issue is the representative body of tax officers. Charalampos Nikolakopoulos, a former President of the trade union of Greek tax officers, the National Union of Tax Officers,[45] was interviewed for the purposes of this monograph.

According to Nikolakopoulos, who became a member of the tax services in 1983, the state offered newly appointed tax officers training that lasted about 40 days. It provided them with basic knowledge that they should have in order to perform their duties. Apart from this, tax officers would have to make do with the seminars occasionally organised by the Ministry of Finance. These, however, were not very easy to attend. Relations of clientelism spilled over in this case too, as tax officers' chances to join such training seminars were, to a large extent and as

[44] Ibid.

[45] Nikolakopoulos was the President of the National Union of Tax Officers from 2011 to 2014. He has also served as the Treasurer in the local association of tax officers of Attica and the Cyclades from 1993 to 1997 and President of the same association from 2002 to 2002. Explaining how representation of tax officers functioned and still functions in trade union terms, Nikolakopoulos noted that, in general, civil servants' representation is done in three levels. On the primary level there are local associations of civil servants, that is, prefectural, intra-prefectural and multi-prefectural local associations, all of which are members in the secondary-degree body, which is called the Union. In the case of tax officers it is called the National Union of Tax Officers (Panellinia Omospondia Ergazomenon stis DOY, POE-DOY). The National Union of Tax Officers is a member to the third-degree body, the Civil Servants Supreme Administrative Council (ADEDY). Namely, a tax officer cannot become a member of the National Union of Tax Officers or ADEDY without also being a member of a first-degree body, that is, a local association of tax officers.

Nikolakopoulos notes, dependent on patronage relations between them and trade unionists, as well as trade unionists and politicians:

> The Ministry of Finance occasionally organised training seminars, which, however, were not compulsory, and, mostly, could not be attended by all tax officers. There were always a limited number of seats and those that had the chance to attend them were either those that pressed very much for it, or those which, through the back door, had managed to have access to the centres of power. In such cases, relations with the trade unionists always played a role. And it is true that some trade unionists functioned, unfortunately, as members of the various 'party armies', helping the tax officers who voted the party that those trade unionists supported to have access to these seminars. Specifically, the Head of the unit in which a tax officer belonged would suggest whether the tax officer should attend a seminar or not. The Head could reject an officer's application to attend a seminar for various reasons. One reason could be the heavy workload of the department in which the tax officer belonged. Another one could be the bad relations of the Head with that specific officer. But there were also those cases in which the Head prioritised the applications of those tax officers who were the Minister's acquaintances. The Heads were, in their majority, the partisan friends of the various Ministers, and were replaced when governments changed, or whenever the Minister of Finance got replaced.[46]

Nikolakopoulos' views are important, not only because he served as the representative of Greece's trade union of tax officers, but also because the points he raises with regard to the body of tax officers are not easily found in the relevant literature. However, the inadequate training of tax officers was not the only disadvantage of the tax system. The next pages will be focusing on some of the system's structures that made the distribution of the tax burden highly unfair, contributing, as a result, to tax evasion, for some 'the epitome of the Greek malaise'.[47]

[46] Charalampos Nikolakopoulos, interview data.

[47] Yiannis Palaiologos, *The 13th Labour of Hercules* (Athens: Estia, 2014), p. 52, in Greek.

Key Information on the Greek Tax System

Although at a 'somewhat slower pace'[48] than other European or OECD countries, the post-Second World War period in Greece witnessed a gradual increase of the state's total tax revenues. Specifically, their rate over total GDP increased from 15.9% in 1948 to 34.3% in 1995.[49]

An examination of the distribution of the tax burden among social classes throughout the period 1960–1998 suggests that whereas, in 1960, salaried employees and pensioners contributed 28% of the total tax burden, in 1998 such a contribution had increased to 58.4%.[50] Such an increase probably reflected a respective increase in population shares: according to census data, salaried employees and pensioners were, in 1961, 17.21% of the population, whereas in 2001 they comprised 45.8% of the population.[51] Also, up to 1975 industrialists and merchants bore a larger part of the tax burden in comparison to salaried employees. Freelance professionals also paid fewer taxes than salaried employees. Yet the difference in the tax burden between the latter two classes was more or less stable. From 1975 however, salaried employees started paying more taxes than both industrialists and merchants and freelance professionals.[52]

Tatsos wrote that it is important to examine whether such changes reflected an actual increase of the tax burden of the salaried employees post-1975 or other factors, such as an increase in their number.[53] In spite of noting this, in his analysis he mainly focused on fiscal drag, that is, the phenomenon of the inevitable increase of the tax burden due to inflation 'even when taxpayers' real income remains stable or even gets reduced'.[54] Tatsos noted that fiscal drag affected the distribution of the tax burden, but, focusing particularly on the period 1980–1995, he suggested that

[48] Tatsos, *Shadow Economy*, p. 277.

[49] Ibid.

[50] Source: Ministry of Finance data, in Tatsos, Shadow Economy, p. 293.

[51] Hellenic Statistical Authority, *Statistical Yearbook of Greece*, issue 1962, pp. 26; 50; 50, issue 2005, p. 184 and issue 2009–2010, pp. 42; 108.

[52] Tatsos, *Shadow Economy*, pp. 290; 223.

[53] Ibid., p. 290.

[54] Ibid., p. 302.

all professional classes were affected by inflation and not only salaried employees.[55]

However, an examination of the data presented by Tatsos in conjunction with occupation data from the censuses of 1961 and 1981 indicates that salaried employees bore a disproportionately large part of the tax burden. For example, in the 1980s, when farmers contributed around 0.2% of the total tax burden, they comprised around 10% of the country's population.[56] Twenty years before, when they were 23.3% of the population, they again paid less than 1% of total taxes. Also, between 1960s and 1980s pensioners' population increased almost fivefold,[57] and their contribution to the total tax burden more than doubled. Such an increase was similar to that of salaried employees, the population of which, however, had seen a much more modest increase in the course of those twenty years—specifically, they comprised 14.4% of the population in 1961 and 17.7% of it in 1981.

To draw similar conclusions about entrepreneurs' per capita tax burden is not that straightforward. For example, the census provides information for people that worked in industrial enterprises, without however making explicit references on their role, that is, without mentioning whether or not they participated in those companies' ownership. In other words, it is not possible to know whether a person belonging to that category was an ordinary employee of an industrial company, an executive, an owner, or had a combination of those roles. It is important to note however that, as Tatsos's analysis shows, entrepreneurs' total tax burden had a significant long-term decline. It is equally important to remember that in Greece and up to the late 1980s, the share of taxes on income, profits and capital gains (but also that of total tax revenue) over GDP, as Charts 2.1 and 2.2 show, was significantly lower than the OECD average.

Such data reinforce the point which was made in the Introduction: the main problem of Greek entrepreneurs as far as the system of taxation was concerned, was, most probably, not the level of taxes they paid, however much they might complain about this.

Another key characteristic of the Greek tax system, not only in the immediate post-war years but, throughout the period examined here, was

[55] Ibid., pp. 302–308.

[56] This is according to the 1981 census.

[57] In 1961, pensioners were 2.81% of the population whereas in 1981 13.3% of it.

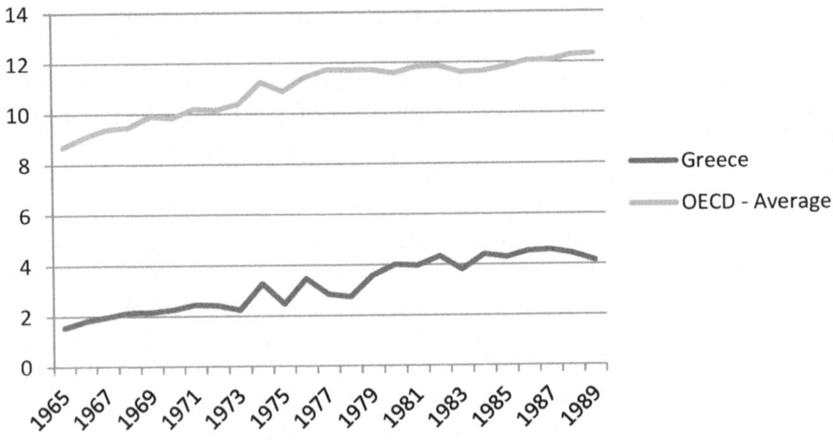

Chart 2.1 Taxes on income, profits and capital gains, % GDP (*Source* Revenue Statistics, OECD.stat, https://stats.oecd.org/Index.aspx?DataSetCode=REV [accessed 13/12/2015])

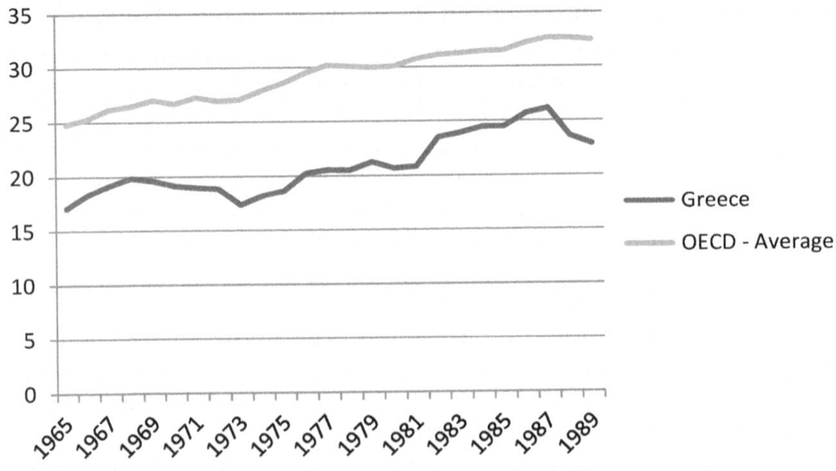

Chart 2.2 Total tax revenue, % GDP (*Source* Ibid.)

that it was heavily based upon indirect taxes. The bias that the Greek governments had toward indirect taxation should be attributed, according to Thanasis Giouras, to two reasons. The first one was the incapability of the tax auditors to capture the tax accruing from business income and the income of the wealthier classes. This again indicated that the main disincentive the tax system posed for Greek entrepreneurs was not the level of taxes they paid. The second reason why the governments favoured indirect taxes was, Giouras notes, that they provided a way to tax consumption that was financed through invisible receipts.[58]

The fact that direct taxes were, as a source of revenue, much less significant than indirect ones, had implications for the tax system's fairness. This is because direct taxes are generally more progressive than indirect ones and, precisely because of their progressivity, they contribute to the fairer distribution of the tax burden, being thus considered an effective tool for the redistribution of income.[59] Theory also suggests that direct taxes should increase as a country's level of economic development rises. This hypothesis is supported by the empirical literature for other countries, but not in the case of Greece.[60] It is also particularly telling that, up to 1965, that is, in a period when the country experienced its fastest growth rates, the share of income taxes (which are direct ones) in total tax revenues was constantly decreasing.[61] The situation is even worse today: the rate of income tax over total tax revenues is currently in Greece at the same, or even a lower level than what it was more than a century ago in countries such as Germany and the United Kingdom.[62]

This analysis leads to a very important point raised by the literature, according to which the increase in the level of economic development that Greece experienced in the post-war period was not reflected in the tax system. Due to this reason, today the Greek tax system has many characteristics that are met only in countries which are in the initial stages of economic development. It has, for example, a small share of profit

[58] Thanasis Giouras, *Taxation and Politics, Political-Economic Problematic and Financial Thought* (Athens: Sakis Karagiorgas Foundation, 2000), p. 327, in Greek.

[59] Tatsos, *Shadow Economy*, pp. 278–279.

[60] Ibid.

[61] Source: Ministry of Finance data, in Tatsos, Shadow Economy, p. 293.

[62] Ibid., p. 282.

taxation to total tax revenues. Also, certain social groups and professions are taxed in more favourable terms than others.[63]

A further weakness of the Greek tax system has been that, as an analysis of the evolution of the rate of tax revenues over GDP shows, in the years when national elections took place the otherwise upward trend of this rate got, in some strange way, reversed. This probably indicated the various governments' efforts to be more lenient in terms of collecting taxes, in order to satisfy the body of voters and increase the chances of their re-election to power. Or, as Tatsos has put it, it indicated, not only the incoherency in the exercise of tax policies, but also that the way the Greek tax system functioned was 'adjusted to the political circumstances and demands'.[64]

The tax system was often used for political electioneering rather than as a means for the redistribution of income and the implementation of policies that would benefit society. This undoubtedly affected the legitimacy of the tax system and contributed to evasion, which is probably the most serious fiscal problem in Greece today.[65]

When examining the issue of tax evasion in more detail, it should be noted that the first relevant studies in Greece appeared in the late 1980s. For this reason, and because the share of tax revenues over GDP has always been unstable,[66] it is not easy to have a clear view about the evolution of the phenomenon prior to the late 1980s. This is so even after examining the Ministry of Finances' annual reports for the execution of the budget. For example, the ratio of the difference between asserted and collected personal income taxes over the total amount of direct taxes collected could be considered indicative of the level of evaded taxation on personal income.[67] This ratio, as the data from the Ministry's reports suggest, decreased from 1955 to 1965, increased from 1965 to 1975 and had a downward trend from this point and up to 1990. As far as corporation tax is concerned, the corresponding ratio (the share of the difference between asserted and collected corporate income taxes over the total amount of direct taxes collected), was decreasing from 1955

[63] Ibid., pp. 280–282.

[64] Ibid., p. 277.

[65] Ibid., p. 74.

[66] Ibid., p. 277.

[67] 'Greece, Selected Issues', p. 24.

to 1965 but kept increasing from this point and up to 1990.[68] It could be therefore hypothesised that tax evasion on corporate income was the reason why the total amount of tax evasion increased significantly from the late 1970s.[69] This however does not seem to be accurate, given that corporation tax was a relatively small share of taxation.

In general, current literature indicates that Greece today is a country with significantly high levels of tax evasion. According to two 2012 studies, annual unreported income in the country exceeds €28 billion, and the shadow economy's share over GDP throughout the period 1999–2010 amounted to approximately 27%, compared to an OECD average of 20.2%.[70] A more recent study suggested that 43%-45% of self-employed income in Greece evades taxation.[71] With regard to the character of evaded taxes, Tatsos notes that the majority of evasion is detected on personal income taxation. This, he notes, is due to the nature of personal income taxes, which, for example, being direct taxes, are 'particularly visible' to the taxpayers and therefore 'spur…their reactions'.[72] Apart from this, not only is there a difficulty in defining what precisely taxable personal income is, but the distinction between personal and business expenses is not always clear. On the whole, personal income taxation is a highly convoluted tax, something which, in combination with the tax services' administrative problems, as Tatsos notes, leads to even higher levels of taxation.

Actually, when trying to focus more closely on the causes of tax evasion in the country, one realises that the Greek tax system is replete with features that make it highly unfair, something which explains the characterisation of tax evasion as 'the most massive and most tolerable expression of anti-social and illegal behaviour' in the country.[73] One of the reasons why the tax system has been considered unfair is the unequal distribution of the tax burden. It is generally difficult to have a clear view

[68] Ministry of Finance, *Annual Reports for the Execution of the Budget*, various issues, in Greek.

[69] Kalyvianakis et al., pp. 275–279.

[70] 'Greece, Selected Issues', p. 20.

[71] Artavanis, Nikolaos, Morse, Adair and Tsoutsoura, Margarita. 'Measuring Income Tax Evasion Using Bank Credit: Evidence from Greece', *Quarterly Journal of Economics*, 2016.

[72] Tatsos, *Shadow Economy*, p. 186.

[73] Manesiotis, in Tatsos, *Shadow Economy*, p. 74.

about such a distribution, because the allocation of income in the various income brackets is uncertain, as the only available data, derived from the assessment of personal income tax returns, are considered inaccurate. It is also difficult to define the level of taxes imposed upon each specific income bracket, because of the tax shifting that takes place and of course tax evasion. However, there have been studies indicating that throughout the period 1964–1984 the distribution of the tax burden was regressive, as for the three higher income brackets this burden was significantly lower than that of the three lower ones.[74]

Such an unequal distribution of the tax burden[75] led to economic inequalities; in other words, 'the tax system made income distribution more unequal than it was before the application of taxation'.[76] It seems that the situation did not change in the post-1984 period, because there were not any significant improvements in the tax legislation. Tatsos notes that it is actually possible that post 1984 the inequalities caused by the tax system grew larger.[77]

To the unequal distribution of the tax burden throughout the period under consideration led also taxes in favour of third parties, a category of taxes that were usually imposed upon transactions and which were characterised by the economists George Break and Ralph Turvey as '[one] of the most distinctive features of the [G]reek tax system'.[78] Revenue from such taxes was obtained by various organisations, professional classes or lobbies with great negotiating power, 'of a political, economic or trade-union nature'.[79] There existed 1500 such bodies in 1951[80] and 1800

[74] Ibid., p. 287.

[75] The unequal distribution of the tax burden is also an outcome of the unbalanced relation between direct and indirect taxes, as already mentioned.

[76] Tatsos, *Shadow Economy*, p. 287.

[77] Ibid.

[78] Ibid., p. 309.

[79] Ioanna Glykou, *State and Tax Policy, an Historical and Theoretical Approach and the Case of Greece* (Athens: Sakoullas, 2009), p. 177, in Greek.

[80] Frangos, in Giouras, p. 330.

taxes in favour of third parties in 1967.[81] According to current estimates, their number ranges from 350 to almost 1000.[82]

Apart from making the distribution of the tax burden even more unequal, taxes in favour of third parties made the tax system less transparent and of course increased the sense of unfair treatment shared by the taxpayers who paid them.[83] The fact that the finances of the recipient bodies were usually not taken into account in the state's budget[84] but also the lack of any control in terms of the way the bodies used such funds[85] has been described as a blow in the relationship between the taxpayer and the state. More specifically, it has been argued that the existence of such third parties, which 'interfered in the relation of "trust" between citizens and the state, urging both sides to deceive one another',[86] was an expression of the disintegration of the Greek society.

Other characteristics of the tax system that made it unfair by contributing to the unequal distribution of the tax burden, thus also increasing incentives for tax evasion, were the preferential tax regime of the farmers[87] but also the series of tax rebates that provided significant tax relief for the higher income classes and small or no relief for

[81] Manolis D. Xanthakis, *Tax Regime, Shadow Economy and Tax Evasion in Greece* (Athens: Papazisis, 1993), p. 33, in Greek.

[82] 'At Least 350 Taxes in Favour of Third Parties Have Been Targeted by the Government and the Troika'. http://www.unitedreporters.gr/news/GR/Forologika_themata/forologika_themata/Sto_stohastro_kyvernisis_kai_troikas__toylahiston_350_foroi_yper_triton [accessed 5.2.2014], in Greek.

[83] Tatsos, *Shadow Economy*, pp. 308–309.

[84] Giouras, p. 329.

[85] Glykou, p. 177.

[86] Giouras, p. 330.

[87] For more information on the tax treatment of farmers see G. V Dertilis, *Ineffectual of Effective? Taxes and Power in the Neo-hellenic State* (Athens: Alexandria Publications, 1993), pp. 26; 48–49, in Greek. The starting point of this research is the mid-1950s, which saw the introduction of laws that, as will be explained in the following chapter, changed considerably the landscape of the Greek tax system. These laws were the legislative orders 3323/1955 and 3843/1958, concerning individual and legal entities taxation respectively. The legislative order concerning individual income taxation established a 'very high tax-free threshold, which virtually exempted agricultural income from any kind of taxation' (Dertilis, p. 40). Dertilis notes that the participation of agricultural income in the state's total tax revenues amounted to less than 1 per cent until the decade of the 1990s (ibid.).

the medium and lower ones.[88] Throughout the period 1960–1998 the per capita tax exemptions and rebates given to the financially stronger classes of industrialists, traders and freelance professionals increased much more rapidly than those given to other classes, such as pensioners and salaried employees.[89] Of course, this also indicates the point mentioned before: That the main problem for Greek entrepreneurs with regard to the tax system was not the money they spent on paying their taxes but the system's complexity, arbitrariness and poor organisation.

Referring also to the current times, Tatsos has noted that among the reasons for the high level of tax evasion in Greece is the proliferation and complexity of tax legislation and the ineffective organisation of the tax bureaus.[90] The retired tax officer who was interviewed for this research noted that one of the characteristics that made tax legislation complicated, something which was a big issue for tax officers too, was the way the texts of laws were written. For example, in case part of a law was repealed, the wording used was of the following type: 'Subparagraph x of paragraph y of law z is abolished', where x, y and z were numbers. The fact that there was no full description of the provisions of the law that were referred to, made it difficult to understand which specific part of the law changed, and in what way'.[91]

The structure of the Greek economy is yet another factor: the country has fewer salaried employees per capita than the majority of other European ones as well as a large number of farmers, the income of whom has traditionally evaded taxation, to a very large extent.[92] The chronically high levels of inflation and the insufficient indexation of taxes have also led to a continuous increase of the tax burden 'prompting even more the taxpayers to seek ways to reduce their tax burden'.[93]

A further reason that increases tax evasion in Greece is, according to a recent IMF report, the '[h]igh dissatisfaction with government services and public goods. If the individual does not perceive that he gets anything

[88] Tatsos, *Shadow Economy*, pp. 295–297.

[89] Ibid., pp. 299–300.

[90] Ibid., p. 75.

[91] Retired tax officer requesting anonymity, interview data.

[92] Tatsos, *Shadow Economy*, p. 75.

[93] Ibid., p. 186.

in return from the government, the incentives not to pay taxes are high'.[94]

Conclusion

The analysis in this chapter has shown that in Greece, throughout the years this research covers, clientelistic and patronage relations were more important than formal state structures. The tax system was regressive, favoured certain social and professional groups and lacked the necessary legitimacy.

It has also been shown that the share of taxes paid by entrepreneurs was gradually decreasing. This, however, did not persuade them to invest more. Therefore, the fact that they did not invest more should be attributed not to the amount of taxes they paid, but to other aspects of the tax system. The analysis in the following chapters will show that such aspects had to do with issues such as the tax system's complexity, the tax legislation's continuous changes but also the tax officers' arbitrariness and lack of necessary training.

As will be shown in the following pages, such issues discouraged investment in manufacturing industry, Greece's most dynamic sector for a substantial part of the period under consideration here, and contributed to the increase of tax evasion. In other words, the analysis here will confirm Baumol's point according to which, when institutions such as the tax rules do not function properly, productive forms of entrepreneurship suffer whereas 'unproductive' and 'destructive' forms of it, such as tax evasion, thrive. However, it will also be shown that, in the Greek case, this was not so because of the level of taxes, as Baumol's theory suggests, but due to a different set of characteristics of the tax system.

Bibliography

Interviews

Charalampos Nikolakopoulos (President of the National Union of Tax Officers from 2011 to 2014, Treasurer in the Association of Tax Officers of Attica and the Cyclades, from 1993 to 1997 and President of the Association of Tax officers of Attica and the Cyclades from 2000 to 2002).

[94] 'Greece, Selected Issues', p. 26.

Retired tax official who asked to remain anonymous.

Official Publications

Hellenic Statistical Authority, *Statistical Yearbook of Greece*, issue 1962, pp. 26; 50; 50, issue 2005, p. 184 and issue 2009–2010.

Ministry of Finance, *Annual Reports for the Execution of the Budget*, various issues, in Greek.

Web Resources

'At Least 350 Taxes in Favour of Third Parties Have Been Targeted by the Government and the Troika'. http://www.unitedreporters.gr/news/GR/Forologika_themata/forologika_themata/Sto_stohastro_kyvernisis_kai_troikas__toylahiston_350_foroi_yper_triton [accessed 5.2.2014], in Greek.

Papantoniou, M., 'Greece Marks 61 Years After Suffrage', *Greek Reporter*, 28.5.2013. http://greece.greekreporter.com/2013/05/28/greece-marks-61-years-after-suffrage/.

Revenue Statistics, OECD.stat, https://stats.oecd.org/Index.aspx?DataSetCode=REV.

'The Right of Voting in Greece', *Kyros-Education*, 18.2.2002. https://kyros.wordpress.com/2012/02/18/δικαίωμα-ψήφου-στην-ελλάδα/.

Secondary Literature

Argyriades, D., 'Greek Exit from the Crisis—A Pressing and Much-Needed Public Service Reform', *Social Sciences*, 2 (2013).

Artavanis, Nikolaos, Adair Morse and Margarita Tsoutsoura, 'Measuring Income Tax Evasion Using Bank Credit: Evidence from Greece'. *Quarterly Journal of Economics*, 2016.

Close, D. H., *Greece Since 1945* (Great Britain: Pearson Education Limited, 2002).

Coombs, C. A., in N. Mouzelis, *Modern Greece, Facets of Underdevelopment* (London: The Macmillan Press Ltd., 1978).

Dertilis, G. V. *Ineffectual of Effective? Taxes and Power in the Neo-Hellenic State* [*Ατελέσφοροι ή τελεσφόροι: φόροι και εξουσία στο νεοελληνικό κράτος*]. Athens: Alexandria Publications, 1993 (in Greek).

Eliades, E. A., 'Stabilization of the Greek Economy and the 1953 Devaluation of the Drachma' Staff Papers, *International Monetary Fund*, 4, 1 (Sep., 1954).

Freris, A. F., *The Greek Economy in the Twentieth Century* (London and Sydney: Croom Helm, 1986).

Giannaris, N. V., *Greece and Yugoslavia, an Economic Comparison* (New York: Praeger, 1984).

Giouras, Thanasis. *Taxation and Politics, Political-Economic Problematic and Financial Thought* [*Φορολογία και Πολιτική. Πολιτικο-οικονομική προβληματική και δημοσιονομική σκέψη*]. Athens: Sakis Karagiorgas Foundation, 2000 (in Greek).

Glykou, Ioanna. *State and Tax Policy, an Historical and Theoretical Approach and the Case of Greece* [*Κράτος και φορολογική πολιτική: μια ιστορική και θεωρητική προσέγγιση και η πε- ρίπτωση της Ελλάδας*]. Athens: Sakoullas, 2009 (in Greek).

Kazakos, P., *Between State and Market* (Athens: Patakis, 2001), in Greek.

Kostis, K. *State and Enterprises in Greece, the history of 'Aluminium of Greece'* (Athens: Polis, 2013), in Greek.

Makrydimitris, A., *The Administration in Crisis, Texts on Administration and Society* (Athens: Nea Sinora-Livanis, 1996), in Greek.

Meynaud, J. *Political Forces in Greece, vol. I*, trans. by P. Merlopoulos (Athens: Savvalas, 2002).

Michas, N. A., 'Economic Development, Social Mobilization and the Growth of Public Expenditures in Greece', *American Journal of Economics and Sociology*, 39, 1 (January 1980).

Palaiologos, Y., *The 13th Labour of Hercules* (Athens: Estia, 2014), in Greek.

Psalidopoulos, M., *Desperate Supervisors, American Consultants in Greece, 1947–53—From Paul A. Porter to Edward A. Tenenbaum* (Athens: Metamesonikties Ekdoseis, 2013).

Rose-Ackerman, S., and Palifka, B. J., *Corruption and Government—Causes, Consequences, and Reform* (New York: Cambridge University Press, 2016).

Sbarounis, A. J., in T. C. Kariotis, 'The Economy: Growth Without Equity', in *Greece in the Twentieth Century*, eds T. A. Couloumbis, T. Kariotis and F. Bellou (Athens: Hellenic Foundation for European and Black Sea Studies, 2004).

Sutcliffe, A. *An Economic and Social History of Western Europe Since 1945* (London and New York: Longman, 1996).

Sotiropoulos, D. A, *The Tip of the Clientelist State—Organisation, Staffing and Politicisation of the Higher Echelons of the Central Administration in Greece, 1974–2000* (Athens: Potamos, 2001).

Tsoukalas, K., *State, Society, Labour in post-war Greece* (Athens: Themelio, 2005), in Greek.

Tatsos, Nikos, *Shadow Economy and Tax Evasion in Greece* [*Παραοικονομία και φοροδιαφυγή στην Ελλάδα*]. Athens: Papazisis, 2001 (in Greek).

Vetsopoulos, A. 'Efforts for the Development and Stabilization of the Economy during the Period of the Marshall Plan'. *Journal of Modern Greek Studies*, 27, 2 (October 2009).

Xanthakis, M. D., *Tax Regime, Shadow Economy and Tax Evasion in Greece* (Athens: Papazisis, 1993), in Greek.

CHAPTER 3

A 'Sibylline Authority' in a Growing Economy, 1955–1967

Introduction

The period examined in this chapter has been characterised as the golden years of the Greek economy, because of the rapid growth rates, the increase in productivity, the low inflation, but also, the significant increase of industrial investment. Still, even in this period of remarkable progress, there were factors of uncertainty in the economy that created difficulties for Greek business. From the late 1950s and up to about the mid-1960s, uncertainty came mostly from the emerging competition due to the Agreement of Association with the then six countries of the European Community. For the rest of the period, uncertainty was mainly the result of the unstable political situation that led to the fall of the government and ultimately, in spring 1967, to the imposition of a military dictatorship.

An additional factor of uncertainty was the tax system, and more precisely, the way the tax system functioned. Weaknesses such as the system's complexity, bureaucratic procedures and insufficient organisation, but also the frequent changes of legislation and the arbitrary, poorly trained and sometimes also corrupt tax officers, although not being the number one problem of the economy, appear to have discouraged investment. This was indicated by the various complaints voiced by entrepreneurs and representatives of business, but also politicians. For example, in a 1962 Parliamentary discussion Petros Garoufalias, an MP from the centrist party Centre Union noted that 'it is not enough to

Z. Pittaki, *Exploring the roots of systematic tax avoidance in Greece*, Palgrave Studies in Economic History,
https://doi.org/10.1007/978-3-030-71979-1_3

address private initiative with either pleas or threats…for its indolence with regards to …investment…We also have to provide it with a tax system that, at least, will not discourage investment'.[1] In the same vein, in 1965 the Minister of Economics stressed that problematic relations with tax authorities created issues of trust that even made it difficult for the state to implement its developmental policies. There were efforts to improve the situation, such as the tax reforms of the mid and late 1950s, but these did not appear to have had any long-lasting effects. This was because the measures taken in the following years were fewer in number and not particularly effective. Indeed, these were mostly recommendations, and were introduced sporadically, without being part of a wider plan for the reformation of the system.

For entrepreneurs, a poorly organised, confusing, obscure but also arbitrary and potentially abusive tax mechanism made taxes highly unpredictable. As relevant literature points out, tax uncertainty adversely impacts upon investment.[2] Therefore, it seems reasonable to suggest that, although not as manifest as in subsequent periods, the problems in the function of the tax system discouraged entrepreneurs from investing in Greek industry, even in the context of very rapid growth of the 1950s and 1960s. This chapter proceeds as follows: after an overview of the basic characteristics of the economy there is an analysis of developments in the tax system and the industrial sector from the mid to the late 1950s. Then the focus turns on the period from the late 1950s to the eve of dictatorship, exploring how developments in the economy, the socio-political situation as well as various weaknesses of the system of taxation appeared to create difficulties for the development of industry.

[1] 'The Government Squeezes National Income', *Eleftheria*, 3.8.1962, pp. 1; 4.

[2] For an empirical examination of the adverse effects of tax uncertainty upon investment see indicatively Kelly D. Edmiston 'Tax Uncertainty and Investment: A Cross-Country Empirical Examination', *Economic Inquiry*, 42, 3 (July 2004), 425–440. For a theoretical study of the effects of tax policy uncertainty on investment see Kevin A. Hassett and Gilbert E. Metcalf, 'Investment with Uncertain Tax Policy: Does Random Tax Policy Discourage Investment?', *The Economic Journal*, 109, 457 (July 1999), pp. 372–393.

1955–1967: A Brief Overview of the Economy

The years covered in this chapter witnessed a continuous increase in Greece's GDP growth rate, the per capita annual increase of which was 5.8% during the decade 1951–1960.[3] Also, there were not any significant inflationary pressures up to 1972; it is characteristic that for the majority of the period 1955–1972, the inflation rate rarely exceeded 5%, something which was not the case for a significant part of the interwar period.[4]

There was also a continuous increase in the productivity of labour[5] and shipping and tourism became important sources of revenue for the Greek economy.[6] Such a positive environment benefited industry, investment in which saw a significant increase. During the period 1957–1964 the average annual rate of increase of fixed capital investment in manufacturing was 13.6%.[7] More importantly, there was a slow but steady shift in the focus of industrial interests. Specifically, in 1955 more than 60% of production in the manufacturing sector came from low-technology traditional sectors like foodstuffs, textiles and clothing.[8] However, the state exerted serious efforts to attract the attention of investors from abroad; it

[3] E. Ioakimoglou and J. Milios, 'Capital Accumulation and Over-Accumulation Crisis: The Case of Greece (1960–1989)', *Review of Radical Political Economics*, 25, 2 (June 1993), p. 81.

[4] Source: Drakatos, p. 151 and Psalidopoulos, Monetary Management, p. 148.

[5] George K. Bitros, 'Greece: How and Why Things Turned Upside Down', in *Essays in Applied Economics and Finance*, ed Giannis Katsoulakos (Athens: Athens University of Economics and Business, 2013), p. 21, in Greek.

[6] With regards to developments in tourism, see, indicatively, George Galanos, 'The Greek Tourism Industry and the Challenge of the Economic Crisis', in *Greece's Horizons—Reflecting on the Country's Assets and Capabilities*, eds Pantelis Sklias and Nikolaos Tzifakis (Athens: Konstantinos Karamanlis Institute for Democracy, 2013), p. 134 and Ilias Ioakeimoglou, 'The Greek Economy 1960–2007, Development, Productive Structure and Labour Market', http://www.ine.otoe.gr/Upl/pdf/Greece_IneOtoe.pdf [accessed 15/2/2014], p. 12, in Greek. As far as the shipping industry is concerned, see indicatively Gregory J. Grigoropoulos 'Shipping and Sustainable Economic Development: The Case of Greece', in *Greece's Horizons*, pp. 121–129.

[7] Drakatos, p. 53.

[8] H. Louri and I. Pepelasis- Minoglou, 'A Quantitative Exploration on the Determinants of (De-) Industrialisation: the Case of Greece', *International Review of Applied Economics*, 15, 4 (2001), p. 404.

offered important incentives for this purpose, such as special tax exemptions and capital, interest and profits repatriation.[9] As a result, in the beginning of the 1960s foreign investment capital started to flow into the country.[10] Still, the development of the industry was sustained on indigenous capital, as, until 1966, 87% of industrial investment was funded by domestic funds.[11]

Regardless of their origin, one of the most important characteristics of the investment funds of the period was that they were channelled to 'new' manufacturing sectors such as the chemical and metallurgical industries. Indeed, these years witnessed a shift of investment from low-technology consumption goods to capital goods.[12] Thus, in the mid-1960s a series of big industrial units were established, such as the country's aluminium producing company called the Aluminium of Greece, the Esso-Pappas chemical and oil refining industries, and the Chemical Industries of Northern Greece in Macedonia. Manufacturing is considered to be 'the most dynamic factor behind the increase of the total product' during this period.[13]

A series of other developments benefited industry greatly, such as the establishment of organisations and bodies like the Investment Bank in 1962, the National Bank for Industrial Development in 1963 and the Greek Investment Bank in 1964.[14] A significant event for industry was also the signing, in 1961, of the Agreement of Association with the then six countries of the European Community, a development that exposed Greece to the first post-war 'wave of internationalisation'.[15] The Agreement set out the elimination of tariff barriers against Greek products in the European Community countries within 11 years, and, respectively,

[9] C. Tsoukalas, *The Greek Tragedy* (Harmondsworth, Penguin, 1969), p. 138.

[10] Nikos Mouzelis, 'Capitalism and Dictatorship in Post-war Greece', *New Left Review*, I (March–April 1996), p. 66.

[11] Michalis Psalidopoulos, *History of the Bank of Greece, 1928–2008* (Athens: The Bank of Greece, 2014), p. 212, in Greek.

[12] Ibid.

[13] Drakatos, p. 62.

[14] Ibid., p. 60.

[15] Bitros, p. 22.

the elimination of tariff barriers Greece was imposing on imported products from EEC countries within 22 years.[16] There have been various views with regards to the impact of the Association. For example, it has been argued that the terms of the agreement were favourable to Greece[17] and that the association contributed to the orientation of Greek exports towards the European Community countries.[18] However, at least for the first years following Association, there was not any substantial increase in the Greek exports, given that very few products were 'available and suitable in order to be channeled to the large European markets'.[19]

At the time there were also political events that brought significant fluctuations in the economic climate, increasing uncertainty, for example, the coming to power of a centrist political party in the early 1960s, after 11 consecutive years of right-wing governments. This event introduced a period of political unrest, due, to a large extent, to the bad relations between the leader of the centrist government and the royal family, which supported the Right.

Additionally, from the mid to the late 1950s the state made significant efforts to reform the tax system and reduce its complexity by simplifying the procedures of filing a tax return. Furthermore, there were also efforts to modernise and improve the organisation of the tax bureaus and to normalise relations between taxpayers and tax officers. This involved the imposition of measures that controlled the authority of the latter and their tendency to be arbitrary in their decisions. The evidence that will be presented shortly indicates that such developments seemed to encourage investment in manufacturing industry. This was not the case from the end of this period and up to the eve of dictatorship, which was characterised by a scarcity of similarly important initiatives in the tax system.

From the Mid to the Late 1950s: Developments in the Tax System and in the Industrial Sector

During the first years of the period covered in this chapter, Greece managed to recover the losses it suffered during the war and became

[16] Psalidopoulos, *History*, p. 42.

[17] Bitros, p. 23.

[18] Psalidopoulos, *History*, p. 42.

[19] Drakatos, p. 74.

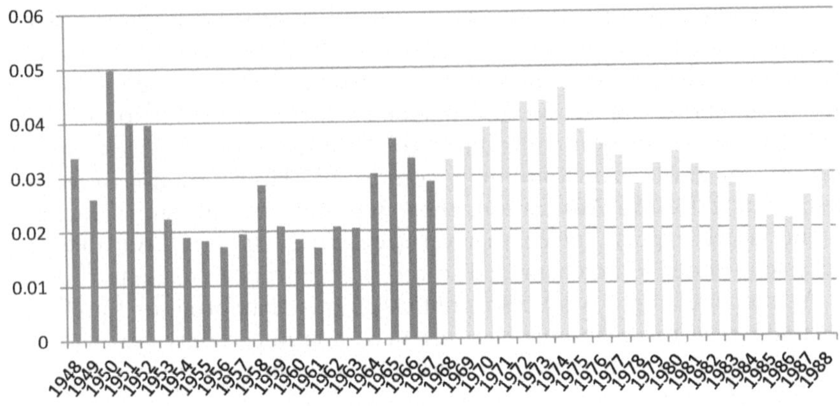

Chart 3.1 Manufacturing, gross private investment in fixed capital, % GDP (1948–1967) (*Source Long-term Statistical Series of the Greek Economy*, pp. 27; 10)

again part of the international economy.[20] A series of developments that preceded this period contributed to this end, such as the Korean war (1950–1953) that benefited the Greek shipping industry.[21] Additionally, foreign aid funds kept on flowing to the country even after the discontinuation of the Marshall plan aid in 1952.[22] Equally, the Papagos government monetary reform of 1953 led to the devaluation of the drachma by 50% and associated it to the Bretton Woods system of fixed exchange rates.[23] All these developments gave to the economy an impetus that contributed to the progress that followed. As Chart 3.1 shows,[24]

[20] See for example Vetsopoulos, p. 296; Michas, p. 39 and Freris, p. 143.

[21] Psalidopoulos, *History*, p. 204.

[22] Bitros, p. 8.

[23] See Psalidopoulos, *History*, p. 204 and also Dimitris Skalkos, 'The Devaluation of the Drachma in 1953 and Economic Development', *Capital*, 16.7.2013. http://www.capital.gr/news.asp?id=1835769 [accessed 10.10.2014], in Greek.

[24] This chart, as well as several others following, displays more years than are being addressed in the chapter in order for the reader to have an idea of the long-term development of the depicted item. The different colours serve the purpose of highlighting different periods. For example, in Chart 3.3 the focus is on the period 1948–1967, hence the brighter colouring in the columns concerning these years. In the same vein, Chart 3.4

the share of investment in manufacturing over GDP was particularly high during the period from the late 1940s to the early 1950s:

What also reflected the general progress in the economy was the fact that, as Chart 3.2 shows, from 1956 to 1959 there was a considerable rise in the number of new industrial units established annually.

Chart 3.3 shows that there was also a considerable rise in the number of already existing industrial units that were extended, from 1957 to 1959.

As far as the system of taxation is concerned, it underwent a series of reforms in the mid to late 1950s. It was set within a wider framework of restructuring of the economy. Right-wing governments attempted to do this, at a time when, in the initial phase of the Cold War, economic development was considered to be a means of averting the spread of leftist ideas.[25] These reforms were important in terms of simplifying the process of filing a tax return, both for business and individual taxpayers, increasing the amount of tax revenue collected, modernising the ways tax services functioned and reducing tax officers' tendency to be arbitrary when performing their duties.

The mid-1950s saw the introduction of new legislation that set the taxation of income on a unified basis, considered today 'the most important post-war tax law', one that marked 'the tax future of Greece for the decades that followed'.[26] Specifically, in the 1955 annual reception held by the Federation of Greek Industrialists (FGI), the Minister of Coordination of the government described the enactment of law 3323/1955 concerning individual taxation as an effort to ease the complexities of the tax system.[27] The new legislation was introduced to replace law 1640/1919,[28] the articulation of which was based on French corporate tax law.[29] The critiques of this previous law related to its structural

is focusing on the 1955–1967 period, that is why the columns corresponding to these years are more brightly coloured than the rest of them.

[25] Kostis, p. 53.

[26] Giouras, p. 322.

[27] Vovolini Archive, *Viomichaniki Epitheorissis*, Vol. 22, May 1955, p. 18.

[28] Stephanos Mich. Sellas, *The Greek System of Taxation* (Athens: Papazisis, 1989), p. 38, in Greek.

[29] Christina Florou, 'Comparative Evaluation of the Methods Used to Determine the Aggregate Net Income of the Greek Stock Companies' (Unpublished doctoral thesis, Aristotle University of Thessaloniki, 2009), p. 13, in Greek.

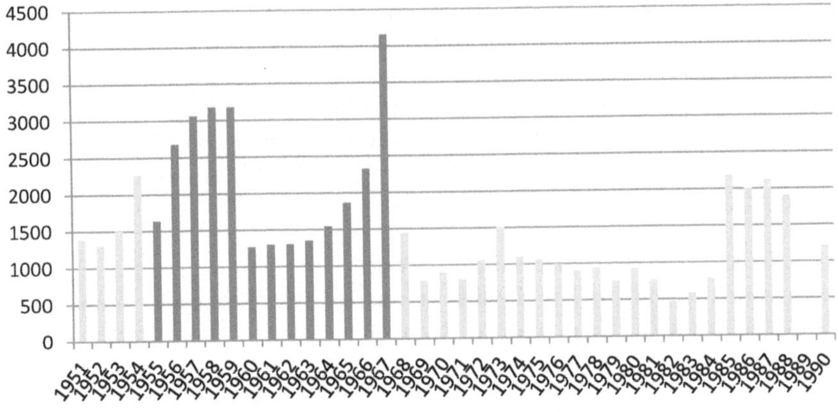

Chart 3.2 Number of new factories and workshops of industrial and handicraft enterprises established (1955–1967) (*Source* Hellenic Statistical Authority, *Statistical Yearbook of Greece*, various issues[30])

[30]The exact wording for years 1951–1959 was 'Number of permits issued for the foundation and expansion of industrial factories and handicraft workshops', for years 1960 and 1961 'Number of permits granted for the establishment, enlargement and operating of factories and workshops of industrial and handicraft enterprises', for years 1962–1985 'Operation permits issued to new and extended factories and workshops of industrial and handicraft enterprises', and for years 1986–1990 'Operation permits or exemption certificates issued to new or extended factories and workshops'. No data were found for 1989. Also, in the issues concerning the period 1967–1984 it was mentioned that according to Compulsory Law 207/4.12.1967 owners of industrial and handicraft establishments with mechanical equipment not exceeding 10 Horsepower for Greater Athens and 15 Horsepower for the rest of the country were exempt from an operation permit. In the issue concerning 1985 it was mentioned that 'Included are only foundations of industrial-handicraft establishments for which special license of the Ministry of Industry, Energy and Technology is required. For continental Attica (which includes Greater Athens) and the islands Salamina and Aegina, a license is required for the installation of any mechanical equipment, while for the rest of the country for the installation of motors of 15 Horsepower and over'. In the issues concerning the period 1986–1990 it was noted that by the Presidential Decree 84/1984 on the continental Attica and the islands of Salamina and Egina, a license was required for the installation of any mechanical equipment, while for the rest of the Country from 15 Horsepower and over. In the same issues it was noted that an exemption certificate was issued to all new establishments, excluding those located on the continental Attica, Salamina and Egina, for the installation of mechanical equipment of up to 15 Horsepower. For the years 1986, 1987, 1988 and 1990 the number of companies for which exemption certificates were issued was 2059, 1566, 1561 and 1217 respectively (no relative values were found for 1989).

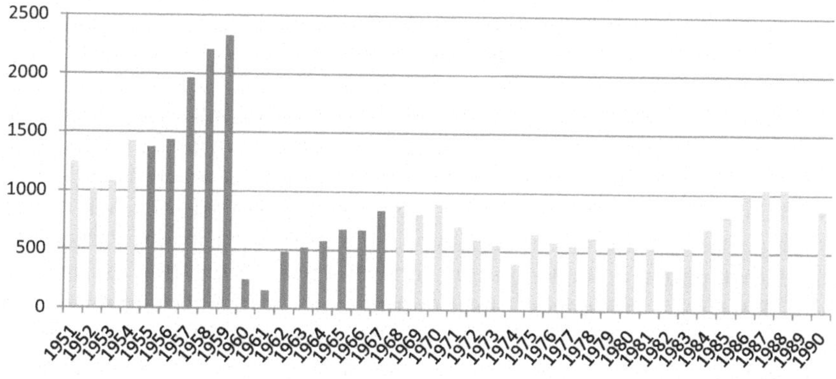

Chart 3.3 Number of extended factories and workshops of industrial and handicraft enterprises (1955–1967) (*Source Statistical Yearbook of Greece*, various issues[31])

weaknesses, such as the complexity and the great number of tax returns—specifically, up to seven—that had to be filed each year by taxpayers but also, the 'institutional disadvantages resulting from the defective tax auditing procedures'.[32] In such a climate, the legislation introduced in 1955 was presented as a means of simplification of the whole procedure of filing a tax return, and also a way to increase the degree of tax fairness, because of the relatively high-tax rates for high-income thresholds it introduced.[33] In their 1964 monograph on the Greek tax system, Break and Turvey described income taxation in the following way:

> The tax scale is expressed as a scale plus a surcharge, the revenue from the latter being assigned to OGA (farmers' social insurance). Since this surcharge is itself subsequently deductible, tax rates are not effectively as high at first sight be thought. The marginal rate starts at 3% and does not

[31] See previous footnote.

[32] Giouras, pp. 317–318.

[33] Glykou, p. 148.

> get much beyond 60% for the very rich. But in addition to the graduated tax there is a flat 3% on unearned income imposed for reasons of equity.[34]

Generally, the new tax legislation met different degrees of acceptance among the political world of Greece of the time. The majority of the MPs hailed it as a 'revolution', but there were also some characterising it as a 'coup d'état'.[35] Among those who supported the law was the MP of the ruling party, Theodoros Sarantis, who, in a discussion in the Parliament noted that under unified taxation and with the aggregation of income from all sources, the process of submitting a tax return became much less time-consuming, not only for the taxpayers, but also for the tax officers, increasing also in this way the efficiency of the latter when performing their duties:

> [E]ach taxpayer will have to submit only one tax return and go through only one taxing procedure…anyone can understand how much this will free tax officers from a pointless preoccupation, [allowing them] to devote themselves in going after tax evaders'.[36]

The introduction of the new law was accompanied by further measures of modernisation of the tax system, aiming particularly at the improvement of the organisation of the tax administration and the reduction of tax evasion.

In a circular that would 'regulate the internal and external functioning of the tax offices', signed by the deputy minister of Economics Leonidas Dertilis, it was set that each tax office would be divided in departments, each one of which would consist of two distinct bureaus; the first one would focus on internal operations, whereas the second one on 'the audit and inspection of the firms functioning or the taxpayers dwelling within the tax office's jurisdiction'. This department would be in turn divided into regional sectors, each one of which would be audited by a specific audit team. In addition, in every tax office a special department focusing on the audit of 'very important' firms would be created; at least once

[34] George F. Break and Ralph Turvey, *Studies in Greek Taxation* (Athens: Centre of Planning and Economic Research, 1964), p. 39.

[35] Giouras, p. 319.

[36] Index of Parliamentary Discussions 1946–1967, Minutes from the Sitting of the Special Committee, 6/26.7.1955, pp. 56–62.

every fifteen days, there would be meetings between the director of the tax office and the heads of the various departments in which the 'discovered tax evasion schemes and the respective proposed solutions' would be discussed.[37] Apart from this, another circular published by the Ministry of Economics stressed that, for the first year of the imposition of the new law 'the directors of tax bureaus should sufficiently justify...fine impositions', while also recommending that they be 'particularly lenient' in cases of omissions, oversights, etc.[38]

However, the introduction of the 1955 legislation attracted also an important amount of critique. For example, according to a newspaper article published at the time, the law was introduced after a 'most brief and most insufficient discussion'.[39] The same point was raised in a 1957 article of the *Bulletin of Tax Legislation* where it was noted that the law was published two months after the beginning of the economic year 1955–1956, following the established practice according to which 'to a strange coincidence - not to say tactic - all major tax laws in...[the] country are published late, as a rule, after the beginning of the economic year which they consider'.[40] Furthermore, critiques noted that the legislation of 1955 increased the tax burden imposed upon middle-income classes, the 'backbone'of the country's 'civil regime'.[41]

However, at the same time, and according to the notes of Michalis Stasinopoulos, a member of the Council of State in the 1950s, the 1955 legislation exempted a large number of low-income owners from the responsibility to pay taxes:

> It is characteristic...that while [with the previous law] the tax returns filed per year were almost 760 thousands, those that were filed during the first

[37] 'There Will Be a Continuous Monitoring of the Taxpayers', *Empros*, 03.12.1955, p. 1.

[38] 'Significant Leniency Is Recommended When Fines Upon Income Tax Are Imposed', *Empros*, 10.12.1955, p. 1.

[39] This is from an article entitled 'The Scopes of the Rearrangements', contained in a newspaper cutting found in the archive of the company CHROTEX. From the layout of the cutting and in comparison to other articles found in the same archive it seems very likely that the article was published in 1957 in the newspaper *I Naftemporiki*.

[40] *The Bulletin of Tax Legislation*, 11, 11, 23.01.1957, p. 46.

[41] Again from the article 'The Scopes of the Rearrangements' mentioned in footnote no. 40.

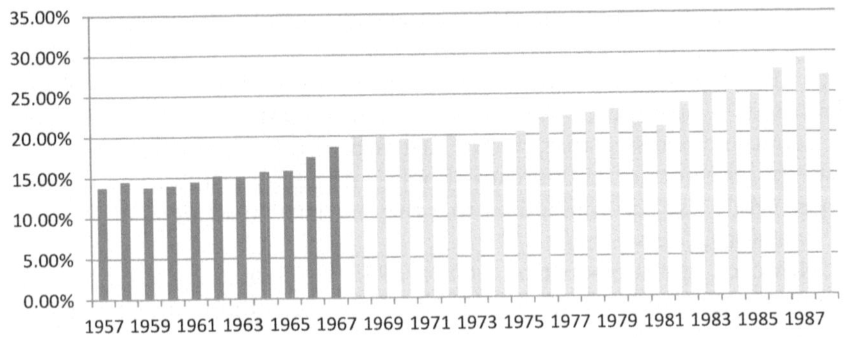

Chart 3.4 Tax revenue, % GDP (1955–1967) (*Source Long-term Statistical Series of the Greek Economy*, pp. 13; 86–87)

> year of enactment of the new law, [taking also into consideration] those that were filed after an audit took place, were only 246 thousands.[42]

Another development the new law brought about was an increase of tax revenue. Indeed, the years following the introduction of the new legislation saw an increase in the amount of tax revenue as a share of GDP, as Chart 3.4 indicates.

The reforms of the 1950s considered also taxation of business. In the 1955 reception held by the FGI mentioned above, the Minister of Coordination announced that another law was to follow soon. Its aim would be the 'consolidation of the terms under which firms are taxed', and, in other words, the introduction of the law 3843 regarding corporate taxation.[43] Entrepreneurs complained that their views with regard to this law were not sufficiently taken into consideration by the government. For example, in the 6 September 1957 Board Meeting minutes of the Union of Corporations and Limited Liability Companies, it was noted that the president of the Union referred to a series of amendments[44] that needed to be made with regard to the new law under scrutiny by Parliament. Amendments had been proposed by the Union also during the drafting of the law, without however being implemented. According to the minutes, it

[42] Vovolini Archive, File 30, Eftaxias Family, sub-file 1, Evidence no. 61, p. 2.

[43] Vovolini Archive, *Viomichaniki Epitheorissis*, Vol. 22, May 1955, p. 18.

[44] The minutes contained no information on what these amendments should be.

was decided that the Union would submit a new memorandum with the proposed amendments. Apart from this, the Union would 'formulate a protest regarding the content of the draft law'.[45]

This very same issue was mentioned again in the meeting of 7July 1958, in which the president noted that out of all the Union's pending issues, the most important was the one relating to this specific draft law. This time, it was mentioned that a memorandum already submitted by the Union regarded the removal of articles that were 'particularly burdensome' for corporations.[46] It was decided that a new memorandum would be addressed to the Legislative Committee of the Parliament.[47]

Such concerns reflected the stance of a significant part of the Greek business community, given that they were expressed by an important business union of the country. However, in spite of all the critique, the law was passed in late September 1958.[48] It had the form of a legislative decree and was subjected to a number of minor additions and alterations in 1959.[49] The law contained 21 articles.[50] It stated that unlike the 1955 law regarding individual income taxation, corporate income would be taxed on the basis of a flat tax rate of 35%.[51] Yet, as was the case with individual income, the tax was imposed on the aggregate income of the company, accruing from all possible sources. Specifically, such sources could be of the following seven kinds: constructions, for-profit companies, leased land, securities, agricultural businesses,

[45] Union of Corporations and Limited Liability Companies, Board Meeting Minutes 26.01.1953–27.10.1965, 6.9.1957, p. 37.

[46] No information was found with regards to which specific articles were considered burdensome.

[47] Union of Corporations and Limited Liability Companies, Board Meeting Minutes 26.01.1953–27.10.1965, 7.7.1958, p. 41. No evidence regarding whether such a memorandum was actually sent to the Committee or not has been found.

[48] See 'e-forologia', *Online Bank*, Legislative order 3843/1958. http://www.e-forologia.gr/lawbank/document.aspx?digest=48DBD85F893B6FC0.1D031AEA53&version=1958/09/3 [accessed 03.10.2014], in Greek.

[49] Sellas, p. 122.

[50] Ibid.

[51] The tax rate remained 35% until 1973 (see Vasilios Manesiotis, 'Tax Structure Change During Economic Development: The Case of Greece' [Unpublished doctoral thesis, Northwestern University, 1985], p. 50).

wage-income services and freelance services.[52] Again, the fact that income would be taxed on an aggregate basis had significant positive implications: it meant that, if a company made a loss from a specific source of income, its total taxable income would be reduced. A further implication was that instead of seven tax returns per year, companies would have to file only one, covering their total income from all possible sources.[53] As for the legal entities that were subjected to this law, these were of the following types: indigenous corporations, public, municipal and communal for-profit companies, partnerships and their unions, as well as foreign companies operating in Greece and every other type of for-profit foreign organisation.[54] However, entities such as state organisations, public, municipal and communal for-profit organisations (for specific kinds of incomes that were considered to be tax exempt), as well as churches and charitable organisations, were not subject to this law, and were thus exempt from corporate taxation.[55] It should be noted at this point that this study considers laws 3323/1955 and 3843/1958 to be the two pieces of legislation that truly introduced reforms in the tax system. As will be shown in the next chapters, the rest of the legislation that was introduced throughout the period under consideration was not of similar importance.

Another significant characteristic of the 3843/1958 law is that it provided tax exemptions for profits that would fund investment projects.[56] Actually, the 1950s and 1960s saw an introduction of a large number of similar tax incentives laws. For example, there was the law 3213/1955 that provided '[e]xemption from taxes, dues and other charges…of the portion of capital stock in excess of 5 million drachmas for new corporations capitalised at over 15 million drachmas or for existing corporations increasing their capitalisation to more than 15 million drachmas'. In addition, it would mean 'freezing, for a period to up to 15 years from start-ups, of all taxes…in effect at the time of the approval of an

[52] Georgios N. Stathopoulos, *Taxation of Indigenous and Foreign Companies* (Athens, Federation of Greek Industries, 1964), p. 7, in Greek.

[53] Ibid., pp. 7–8.

[54] Ibid., p. 9.

[55] Ibid.

[56] Psalidopoulos, *History*, p. 41.

application to invest'.[57] Or, law 3765/1957 that provided that under specific criteria, mergers of corporations as well as conversions of sole proprietorships and partnerships into corporations would be exempt from capital gains taxes, property transfer taxes, stamp taxes upon revenues and all types of third party taxes.[58]

According to Break and Turvey, the most important tax incentives of the period were introduced with law 4002/1959 that provided tax exemptions for productive investment made by large industrial and handicraft enterprises until the end of 1964.[59] The exact character of the exemption was the following: 'Investment expenditure may be deducted from undistributed profits which, in the case of partnerships, limited liability companies, etc., means net profits less the proprietors' withdrawals. The amount deducted may not exceed 50% of the undistributed profits in Attica, 60% in the provinces and 90% in the islands'.[60] The law also provided a 50% deduction of the taxable profits of mining enterprises as well as quarry enterprises exporting at least 50% of their production, to cover expenses relating to investments of new productive facilities, irrespective of the location of such enterprises.[61] As a matter of fact, as Chart 3.5 suggests, the years following the introduction of this law saw an increase in investment in mining and quarrying industries as a share of GDP.

More broadly, the incentives such laws provided allowed firms to 'recover the original cost of their new investments relatively quickly' and provided serious reductions of the cost of taxes.[62] For example, by 1962, under law 4002/1959 Greek corporations were claiming deductions of DRS 91 million. This amount was equal to 15% of their total taxable profits.[63] Also, as Table 3.1 suggests, whereas, in 1959, tax allowances provided by two of the laws mentioned here (4002/1959 and 3213/1955) and also law 2176/1952 concerning provincial and

[57] Break and Turvey, pp. 246–247.

[58] Ibid., p. 243.

[59] Ibid., p. 41.

[60] Ibid.

[61] Ibid., p. 240.

[62] Ibid., p. 197.

[63] Ibid., p. 198.

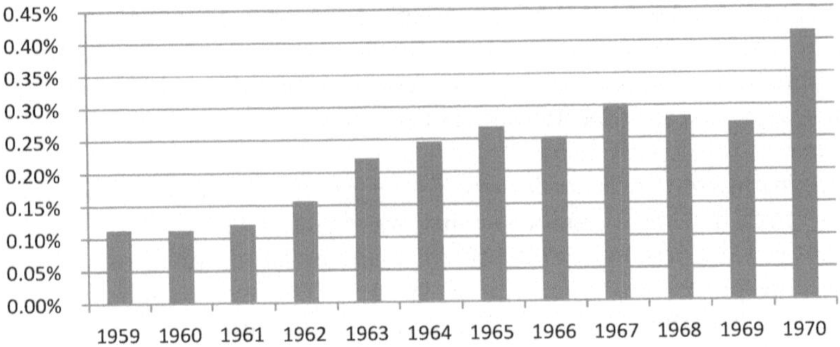

Chart 3.5 Mines and quarries, gross private investment in fixed capital, % GDP (1959–1970) (*Source Long-term Statistical Series of the Greek Economy*, pp. 27; 10)

Table 3.1 Ratio of total special allowances to taxable profits

1959	*1960*	*1961*	*1962*
12%	16%	22%	28%

*Allowances under laws 4002/1959, 3213/1955 and 2176/1952.
Source Break and Turvey, p. 199

island firms,[64] were equal to 12% of the total taxable profits of indigenous corporations, three years later, their absolute magnitude had become four times bigger, amounting to 28% of such corporations' total taxable profits.

Generally, the tax incentives of the time were important in terms of their number, but also in terms of the reduction of tax burden they allowed. According to a relevant 1964 study, tax incentives serving 'the curtailment of consumer demand needed to shift resources into developmental activities' and giving 'important monetary rewards to those who invest' were 'already so well developed in Greece that opportunities for further expansion [were] extremely limited'.[65]

[64] Ibid.

[65] Ibid. p. 195.

However, implementation of such tax incentives faced obstacles that came from the system itself. Tatsos for example stressed that incentives' application required, in most of the cases, 'undue bureaucratic procedures'.[66] Such procedures had to do, to a large extent, with the complexity in the structure of the tax system. For example, according to the proceedings of the first national accounting congress in 1957, the country suffered from '[the] unquestionably serious problem of the application of tax justice', which functioned under a 'labyrinthine' regime.[67] This problem of high complexity related, it was noted, to the unsuitability and incompetence of the bodies responsible for handling tax disputes.[68] Similarly, in his speech in the second congress of the Chambers of Commerce and Industry of Greece, the president of the Chamber of Commerce and Industry of Thessaloniki referred to an OEEC[69] report for Greece which mentioned that '[t]here is no hope that firms will reach the apex of their efficiency...with no clear, specified and effective dissemination of information. In Greece many factors oppose this. The most important one is the State's strict and detailed inspection of the accounting books of firms, which forces industry to engage in dull paperwork, which is not met in...industrially advanced countries'.[70]

Of course, the problem with the inspection of the accounting books of firms was not only that it forced them to engage in dull paperwork, but also that it was a responsibility of the tax authorities to inspect. On this matter, what distinguishes the mid to late 1950s period from the one starting from the late 1950s and ending with the beginning of dictatorship is that in the former, the state's policies to ameliorate frictions between taxpayers and tax officers and to enhance the latters' professional capabilities seemed to be more effective.

[66] Nikos Tatsos, *Public Finance in Greece* (Athens: Sbilias, 1991), pp. 233–234.

[67] CHROTEX Archive, 'Tax Courts', *I Naftemporiki*, 28.02.1957, p. 6.

[68] Ibid.

[69] OEEC stands for the Organisation for European Economic Co-operation, renamed to Organisation for Economic Co-operation and Developmen (OECD) in 1961.

[70] Vovolini Archives, *Viomichaniki Epitheorissis*, Vol. 26, Proceedings of the 2nd Congress of the Chambers of Commerce and Industry of Greece, 20–23.10.1957, pp. 53–54. The full report was published in the newspaper *O EconomicosTahidromos* ('An official report of the OEEC experts reveals: Greek Industry is poorly organised', 10.10.1957, pp. 8–9).

Such policies were necessary, as the complaints regarding the role of tax officers were numerous. For example, there were complaints relating to the tax officers' ability to adequately perform their duties: 'The directors of the tax offices, being, in their majority, ignorant of accounting, increase the profits of [the audited books], totally arbitrarily and unjustifiably', argued one of the entrepreneurs' representatives in 1957.[71] The issue of knowledge and training of tax officers was raised in research studies of the period too. For example, Petros Pougouras and Christos Kyttaris, while noting that one of the first teachers of accounting in Greece claimed that 'less than one-tenth of [tax] officers know how to conduct comprehensive audits',[72] argued that the number of competent tax auditors was important and continuously increasing.[73] However, a different perspective was offered in a subsequent study speaking, not of total ignorance, but of mediocrity. Specifically, the study was written by George Langrod, a French Professor and consultant for the OECD. Langrod was well-known in Greece[74] and had been invited by the Greek government in 1963 in order to provide advice and technical assistance on the reorganisation of the public administration.[75] In his study he focused on the broader Greek public sector and stressed the Administration's 'failure to understand the need for further training' and 'the self-satisfaction of many high-grade civil servants in spite of the flagrant mediocrity of the results'.[76]

Apart from issues of training and knowledge, tax officers were also criticised for an excessive eagerness to increase the amount of taxes they collected. For example, it was noted in an economic magazine of the time that 'cash euphoria' had always been their primary aim, given that

[71] Ibid., speech of A. Nikolopoulos, president of the Athens Traders Association, p. 73.

[72] Petros K. Pougouras and Christos A. Kyttaris, *Tax Control of Commercial and Industrial Enterprises* (Athens, 1957), pp. 9–10, in Greek.

[73] Ibid., p. 10.

[74] Demetrios Argyriades, 'Ethics and Governance from a Comprehensive Perspective: How Are We Going to Face the Multiple Challenges of Our Times', Panteion University of Political and Social Sciences, Centre of Governance and Sustainable Development. http://www.dee.gr/mediaupload/publications/20100618_ithiki_kai_diakibernisi.pdf [accessed 7.7.2015], p. 2, in Greek.

[75] Georges Langrod, *Reorganisation of Public Administration in Greece—A Report* (Paris: OECD, 1965), pp. 11, 84–94.

[76] Ibid., p. 38.

they had...'claims over the...surplus of collected revenue'.[77] In a subsequent newspaper article however, this so-called 'euphoria' was explained in somewhat different terms. Specifically, it was noted that if the revenues collected during a specific year in a tax office were less than that of the previous one, this would be considered a personal failure of the director, a failure for which he would be held responsible. This, naturally, created a pressure for increased revenues. And, unfortunately, despite the hiring of scientific personnel, 'the mindset of tax bureaus did not change...the new employees, instead of raising the standards of audit...were carried away by the established mindset, which regard[ed] the taxpayer solely as a source of revenue for the State'.[78]

Also, the way tax officers performed their duties was often described to be unnecessarily aggressive. Significantly, this was acknowledged by members of the government. For example, according to a 1959 study entitled 'Measures against tax theft' found in the personal archive of Konstantinos Papakonstantinou, a Minister of Economics in the 1958–1961 Karamanlis government,[79] the legislative order 3848/1958 on business income taxation set that the audit reports leading to the rejection of accounting books would be examined by Advisory Committees.[80] It was noted, however, that such committees' decisions almost always coincided with the audit reports that rejected the books. Apart from this, the reports that the committees issued were lengthy and 'written in a pointlessly adversarial spirit'. It was stressed in this study that this had to change and that strict measures such as the rejection of accounting books should be avoided:

> A timely intervention is needed before honest taxpayers... become very upset and start resorting to acts of tax fraud or non-keeping of accounting books. The auditors and the members of the Advisory Committees have to understand that rejection of the accounting books...is an event that

[77] Vovolini Archive, *Viomichaniki Epitheorissis*, Vol. 25, March 1958, p. 16.

[78] 'The Organisation of the Tax Agencies Is Erratic and Inefficient', *O EconomicosTahidromos*, 23.06.1960, p. 6.

[79] The 'Konstantinos G. Karamanlis' Foundation, 'Historical Archive', *Konstantinos Papakonstantinou*. http://www.ikk.gr/Default.aspx?tabid=236 [accessed 26.10.2014], in Greek.

[80] No further information about such Advisory Committees has been found, with regards, for example, to their composition.

> causes great suffering to the taxpayers, and should take place in totally extraordinary cases.[81]

There was not any clarification with regard to what those extraordinary cases might be, but it seems that the reference was to cases in which the mistakes and/or omissions in the accounting books indicated tax evasion. Also, from the wording of the study, it seems that the problem with such advisory committees was that they did not seem to serve the role they had been created for: to check and control the tax auditors. Instead, for the most part, their decisions were in accordance to those of the tax auditors and they did not act as a check or balance.

In the same study, it was also noted that control of the works of the tax services was 'shadowy and in most cases non-existent', and that, therefore, the establishment of inspection agencies of the various tax offices was necessary.[82] Sometimes there were additional complaints about extortionary tactics used by tax officers during audits. For example, cases such as the one of two tax officers who were brought into custody with the accusation of blackmailing a factory owner 'in order to extort DRS 6,000 from him…through the issuing of a favourable audit report'[83] made appearances in the press. In newspaper articles, sometimes tax officers were described as people that had the ability to 'burn' the taxpayer:

> [The tax collector] is the one who assesses [the taxpayer's] profits, audits his books and estimates how much he has to pay. If he wants to, he can make an estimation of 10 million. If he wants to, he makes one of 1 million. If he wants he accepts the accounting books, if [not] he rejects them. Therefore, the easiest thing for him is to blackmail the taxpayer.[84]

Indeed, tax officers' arbitrariness was an issue that not only appeared in the press, but was openly discussed by entrepreneurs too. For instance, in the 1957 congress of the Chambers of Commerce and Industry of

[81] The 'Konstantinos G. Karamanlis' Foundation, Konstantinos Papakonstantinou Archive, File 202A', Findings of the Economics Committee, 1959–1961, Notes on Tax Evasion, Measures against tax theft, p. 4.

[82] Ibid., p. 9.

[83] 'The Two Tax Officers That Were Blackmailing a Factory Owner Have Been Taken into Custody', *Ta Nea*, 27.04.1956, p. 6.

[84] D. Psathas, 'The Tax Collectors', *Ta Nea*, 12.02.1955, p. 1.

Greece the president of the Chamber of Commerce and Industry of Epirus noted that the tax system allowed for compromises to take place between taxpayers and tax officers. Such compromises were achieved after the two parties negotiated with regard to the tax that would have to be paid. Of course, the very fact that such negotiations did take place increased the degree of arbitrariness of the tax system in general, and, more specifically, the arbitrariness in the behaviour of the tax officers. Even worse, such negotiations and compromises were deemed necessary by the taxpayers, it was noted, because taking legal actions would prove useless. In more detail, in the president's words, any taxpayer in such an occasion would think of the following way:

> If I take legal actions, would it ever be possible for me to expect any further gain, especially from a second-degree court that is chaired by a...[Judge] who has no knowledge of such matters and an Economic Inspector who is undoubtedly a mouthpiece, if not an extension, of the inclinations and the aims of the Tax Officer?[85]

In the same vein, the press of the period commented negatively on a new tax measure[86] that was proposed for the fight against tax evasion and that would give tax officers a 'sibylline authority'. The measure concerned individual taxation and regarded the introduction of irrefutable presumptions of wealth. Specifically, with the new measure, 'having a car, [and] a refrigerator, paying a rent...[would be considered] not indications, but irrefutable proofs of wealth'. In any case where a taxpayer was in possession of such goods he would have to pay a tax that would be determined by the director of the tax office. It was uncertain however what the result of such determination would be, that is, how much tax the taxpayer would be asked to pay, hence the use of the term 'sibylline'.[87]

Similarly, there were frequent references in the press about the 'extremities and abuses' during tax audits. In one such article, focusing specifically on the compulsory use of accounting books and records, it was noted that

[85] Vovolini Archive, *Viomichaniki Epitheorissis*, Vol. 26, 1959, Proceedings of the 2nd Congress of the Chambers of Commerce and Industry of Greece, 20–23.10.1957, pp. 268–269.

[86] No information has been found about whether the measure was actually implemented or not.

[87] 'In Deep Water', *Empros*, 02.08.1958, p. 3.

'to date, no measure has been taken in order to guarantee that the tax collectors would…respect them'. It was also mentioned that in a meeting between the Minister of Economics and representatives of the 'productive classes'[88] the president of the Traders Association asked for measures that would punish the tax collectors in cases of 'defective' audits. This would 'reduce the shoddiness with which they examine the accounting books of firms, causing confusion and inconvenience to taxpayers'.[89]

However, it is important to stress that not all complaints about tax officers are related to blackmailing purposes and other extortionary tactics. An entrepreneur that was interviewed for this research implied that the problems he faced in his relationship with the tax officers, which made him 'suffer', had to do with issues of idiosyncrasy and mode of thought:

> At around 1956-1957… industries were split into standardised and non-standardised [that is, industries producing products with uniform and non-uniform characteristics, respectively].The standardised ones paid a 6% tax 'for the support of the soldiers', whereas the non-standardised ones paid 1%.[90] I owned a tubes and pipes making factory, which was a standardised industry, so we paid a tax of 6%. However, next to this factory I also owned an organised machine centre, which was non-standardised, therefore for this one I should be paying a tax of 1%. The director of the tax office would not agree with this. I took the case to the courts and won. However, the director, which, I should like to note, was a good officer, would not accept the court's decision. That is, I had auditors visiting [me] with the director's instructions to not accept what I was saying. The deputy director of the tax office used to tell me that the director had been stuck up with this issue and that there was nothing that could be done. When the director

[88] The term 'productive classes' probably had different meanings for different stakeholders. For the Chamber of Commerce and Industry of Athens, it seems that the term was attributed to entrepreneurs, governors and executives of Banks, but also members of the Parliament and ministry executives (*Bulletin of the Chamber of Commerce and Industry of Athens*, 1, January 1965, pp. 14–15).

[89] *O Economikos Tahidromos*, 31.12.1959, p. 10.

[90] This tax probably related to the Compulsory Law 1836/1951, entitled 'On modification and codification of the legislation regarding the protection of those who resigned from the army and participated in the cause against members of gangs'. No information about the logic of the differentiation in the tax rates of the standardised and non-standardised industries has been found. What seems to be the case is that the non-standardised industries were taxed at a lower rate because they had lower profit margins.

> retired, the deputy took his post, and followed exactly the same tactic. At the end, I appealed to the State Council and got my money back. He was a good officer, he just had his quirks...I have suffered a lot from them, but I don't think the tax officers of this period were bad officers.[91]

It seems, therefore, that tax officers' arbitrariness was often due to the fact that they simply had the power to invent their own rules and impose their own will on those that they audited. However, what differentiated the period from the mid to the late 1950s to the one that followed (late 1950s to dictatorship) was that the state seemed to be more effective in terms of addressing the criticism regarding the tax authorities.

Specifically, the sources indicate that in the mid to late 1950s the state implemented a significant number of measures in order to address the issues relating to the behaviour of tax officers and, particularly, their role during tax audits. For example, in 1955, the Minister of Economics Andreas Apostolides,[92] referring to incidences in which tax officials 'taking advantage of their position extort money from taxpayers', declared that relevant court cases would be given priority over others, in an effort to combat corruption. It was also declared that 'the tax authorities...would place under their protection those filing complaints against tax collectors receiving bribes...so that [taxpayers] feel no fear in pressing charges against [those] extorting bribes'.[93] In the same spirit, one year later, it was noted in the press that the Minister of Economics, apart from giving instructions to the directors of the tax offices as to how they should perform their duties in cases of dispute resolutions with the taxpayers, characterised as 'unacceptable' the fact that 'tax officials don't always show the appropriate interest in order to even out differences [with the taxpayers]'.The Minister stressed that during the process of dispute resolution, the taxpayer should have at his disposal all necessary information gathered by the tax authorities and be given answers about

[91] Entrepreneur no. 2 requesting anonymity, interview data.

[92] Lampros Eftaxias was appointed a minister of Economics from the Papagos government, in 15 December 1954. After Papagos' death in 4 October 1955, the government was assigned by the Crown to Konstantinos Karamanlis, who set Andreas Apostolides as a minister of Economics and (temporarily), Coordination. 'The General Secretariat of the Government', *Alexandros Papagos Government*. http://www.ggk.gov.gr/?p=1194 and 'Konstantinos G. Karamanlis Government'. http://www.ggk.gov.gr/?p=1206 [accessed 15.10.2014], in Greek, and Meynaud, pp. 124–125.

[93] 'Mr Apostolides on Bribery', *Empros*, 12.11.1955, p. 16.

any questions he might have.[94] In the same year, the Minister of Coordination Dimitrios Helmis announced specific policies undertaken by the government, among which was the establishment of 'a series of measures in favour of the taxpayers, such as the impossibility of the easy rejection of the accounting books, [except from] cases of fraud'. There would also be provisions that would allow taxpayers to re-submit incomplete tax returns.[95]

Also, in 1957, the government withdrew (for the sake of further study and elaboration, as it was noted), a bill that had attracted public opposition because of the increased powers it gave the tax auditors. In general, new legislation, that is, draft bills or law amendments and additions, was proposed either by the government, or one or more Ministers, or by any other member of the Parliament. Bills were deposited in the Parliament's legislative department and were then forwarded for further processing and examination or for discussion and vote by the various competent committees of the Parliament. After that, bills were forwarded for discussion and vote by the full plenary of the Parliament.[96]

The bill referred to here was entitled 'On penal sanctions against tax law offenders'. It was proposed in early September 1957 and would allow tax officers to conduct audits in both the business and house premises of the taxpayer, while also imposing increased penalties on those refusing to be audited. If the taxpayer complained, the auditors would have the authority to have him arrested for a maximum of 24 hours. The bill, according to a statement of the Minister of Coordination Dimitrios Helmis, was proposed in order to contribute to the government's efforts to combat tax evasion.[97] Yet, it was withdrawn only a few days after it was proposed, amidst a flood of complaints characterising it as draconian,[98] and stressing that the penalties it set aimed to 'invent and establish a…tax evaders seeking mechanism…a kind of Holy Inquisition aiming to

[94] 'Recommendations from the Ministry of Economics to the Tax Services', *Empros*, 10.11.1956, p. 4.

[95] *Bulletin of the Chamber of Commerce and Industry of Athens*, May 1956, 4, pp. 18–19.

[96] Hellenic Parliament, 'The Institution'. http://www.hellenicparliament.gr/Vouli-ton-Ellinon/O-Thesmos/ [accessed 1.12.2015], in Greek.

[97] 'Will the Draconian Law Be Withdrawn?', *Eleftheria*, 05.09.1957, p. 1.

[98] 'The Draconian Tax Measures Should Be Withdrawn', *Eleftheria*, 06.09.1957, pp. 1; 6.

verify tax conscience'.[99] Again tax conscience was used here to denote the moral attitudes of taxpayers' towards tax evasion. The choice of the words here is important; the phrase 'Holy Inquisition' suggests that people were fully aware that tax evasion was an unlawful act. At the same time, however, it was justified, that is, their conscience allowed it, due to the way that the tax system functioned. Moreover, the fact that the government reacted almost immediately, stating that the bill would be 'withdrawn till the Minister of Economics returns from [a] trip abroad', indicated that its introduction was probably the result of a misunderstanding among the members of the government. [100] The bill's withdrawal also indicates that in spite of the need to curb tax evasion, the government recognised that it was important to contain the arbitrariness of the tax authorities.

Even more so, two years later, it was stressed in a law expert's article that according to the article no.52 of the law 3323/1955 (modified and completed by the legislative order 3765/1957), it was a criminal offence for the director of a tax bureau to issue a tax assessment notice containing false data. The matter had to do with the ease with which, sometimes, tax officers rejected accounting books and records. Specifically, rejection or acceptance of accounting books was regulated by article 53 of the Tax Code and articles 34 and 36 of law 3323/1955.[101] Accounting books and records could be rejected if the entries in them were proven to be inaccurate and not representative of the real economic situation of the taxed firm.[102] Such inaccuracy could be the result of errors or omissions which would make it impossible to assess the firm's taxable income on the basis of the data presented.[103] The point of the article was that the examinations that tax officers performed in such cases should be done with very careful consideration. In more detail, the following were mentioned:

[99] 'The Draconian Tax Bill on the Tax Officers' Investigative Capacities Was Withdrawn', *Ta Nea*, 06.09.1957, p. 1.

[100] Ibid. The fact that no further information has been found with regards to the bill indicates that it was not proposed again by the government.

[101] *The Accountant*, 23, April 1974, p. 365.

[102] *The State Gazette*, Tax Code, issue 1, no. 116, 5.5.1956, p. 1274.

[103] *The Accountant*, ibid.

> [S]ome times, the various tax bureaus, either because of lack of knowledge or because of neglect while performing their tasks, or because of over-zealousness, or, last, for their own ends, are trying to reject the taxpayer's accounting books through non-existent offences...If the director of a tax bureau finds that the audit he ordered is not accurate, or that it refers to false offences, [he] should not issue a tax assessment notice. The... [opposite] is a criminal offence..[A]ccording to article 242 of the Penal Code 'any civil servant with a duty to issue or create public documents, in cases in which he falsely certifies, in such a document, incidences having...legal implications, is punished with incarceration for at least a year'.[104]
>
> Apart from such measures, research studies of the time identify that this was a period when the Ministry of Economics offered tax officers tutorial classes on accounting and tax law taught by university professors, inspectors of the ministry and directors of tax offices.[105]

It seems therefore that during the mid to late 1950s the state made significant efforts not only to contribute to the professional development of tax officers, but also to set specific limits that would protect the taxpayers from their potentially arbitrary judgement when determining taxable income. Such measures and also the efforts for simplification of the tax legislation and modernisation of the internal organisation of the tax bureaus probably reduced the difficulties that the tax system was causing to business. It seems, in other words, that the measures undertaken in this period reduced the unpredictability and thus the uncertainty of the tax system, making business planning easier. It seems that this played a role—of course within the framework of general economic growth of the period—to the creation of an economic environment that was friendlier to entrepreneurial initiative.

However, from the late 1950s the situation in the system of taxation changed importantly. There seemed to be a scarcity of equally significant improvements in the system of taxation, but also, certain socio-political events increased the degree of uncertainty in the economy. Such developments will be analysed in more detail in the next section.

[104] *Bulletin of the Chamber of Commerce and Industry of Athens*, February 1959, 2, p.26.

[105] Pougouras and Kyttaris, p. 21.

From the Late 1950s to the Eve of the Dictatorship: An Industrial Downturn Amidst Social, Political and Economic Uncertainty

From the late 1950s there was a relative slowdown in the pace of industrial development. As the relevant charts in the previous pages showed, 1958, 1959 and 1960 saw a continuous reduction in the level of investment in manufacturing. Also, from 1960 to about 1963 there was a sharp decline in the number of new industrial units established annually and, in 1960 and 1961, in the number of already existing industrial units extended. Of course, the charts also indicate that in 1963 and 1964 there was an increase of investment in manufacturing, as well as a gradual increase, from 1962 onwards, in the number of new industrial units and those extended. Even so, there were signs of stagnation in the overall performance of industry: according to the 1967 annual statement of the Governor of the Bank of Greece, there was a decline in the rate of increase of industrial investment that was characterised 'unjustifiable'.[106] Also, a 1962 report of the Economic Development Financing Organisation stressed that 'in spite of the continuously improving conditions of the Greek economy and the strong encouragement offered by the State in furthering economic development projects', the private sector had not shown 'the requisite initiatives'; it had not played a 'sufficiently important part in meeting national exigencies'.[107]

This reality reflected the fact that the private sector was experiencing a number of difficulties even in the framework of substantial economic growth of this period. The tax system, although not the main problem of the Greek economy at the time, was one of such difficulties, as the coming pages will show. However, before focusing on this issue, there will be an analysis of other factors that affected the general economic, social and political climate. These matters had a compound impact upon business and private initiative in general during this period.

[106] Bank of Greece, *Statement Made by Governor Xenophon Zolotas at the Annual Meeting of the Bank of Greece, 20 April 1967* (Athens: The Bank of Greece, 1967), p. 8.

[107] Historical Archives of the Piraeus Bank Group Cultural Foundation, Economic Development Financing Organisation Archive, *Report of Activities Up to December 31, 1961*, p. 12.

To begin with, it is possible that the private sector's reluctance to invest reflected a general slowdown in the economy from the late 1950s. Indeed, whereas a large part of the literature examining the development of the Greek economy post-Second World war treats the broader period from the 1950s to the 1970s as one of positive developments in the economy,[108] there are also perspectives indicating that the end of the 1950s saw an economic growth slowdown (see Table 3.2). The late 1950s were marked by 'intense crisis-like phenomena' such as the deterioration of the trade balance post-1955.[109] As the following table shows, the rate of increase of the national income in 1959 was lower than that of the years 1955, 1956 and 1957. There was also significant instability in the GDP growth rate between 1961 and 1963. It seems reasonable to suggest that such developments related also to the international recession of 1958, expressed as a reduction in the prices of raw materials and a slowdown in the output in various industrialised countries.[110]

It is also possible that the slowdown of investment reflected a generalised climate of uncertainty caused by various other events. One such event could have been the 'long negotiations concerning the country's association with the European Economic Community',[111] which ended up with an agreement in 1961.[112] Specifically, the Greek government

[108] For example, for Drakatos the years from 1957 to 1973 where characterised by general growth and progress in the productive activities (pp. 49–74). Kazakos considers the period 1953–1967 as one that saw the country's transition from a stage of reconstruction to one of development (pp. 163–265). In the same vein, Psalidopoulos characterises the broader period 1957–1971 as one of 'investment upsurge' (*History*, p. 212). As for Korres and Chionis, they note that there were signs of recovery in the economy since 1948 and regard the 1960s and 1970s as decades that were marked by improvements in the country's basic economic magnitudes (Georgios M. Korres and Dionysios P. Chionis, *Greek Economy, Economic Policy and Analysis of the Basic Macroeconomic Magnitudes* [Athens: Stamoulis, 2003], p. 29).

[109] Yiannis Milios, 'The Greek Economy in the 20th Century'. http://users.ntua.gr/jmilios/Oikonomia_Eikostos1ab.pdf [accessed 20.12.2014], p. 15, in Greek.

[110] International Monetary Fund, *Annual Report 1959*. http://www.imf.org/external/pubs/ft/ar/archive/pdf/ar1959.pdf [accessed 14.12.2014], p. 2 and *Annual Report 1960*, https://www.imf.org/external/pubs/ft/ar/archive/pdf/ar1960.pdf [accessed 14.12.2014], p. 1.

[111] G. Vlahopapadopoulos, *The Effectiveness of Tax Incentives in Greece and Suggestions for their Reform* (Athens: Centre of Planning and Economic Research, 1967), p. 37, in Greek.

[112] Bitros, p. 22.

Table 3.2 GDP growth rate (%), 1950–1967

1950	*1951*	*1952*	*1953*	*1954*	*1955*	*1956*	*1957*	*1958*	*1959*	*1960*	*1961*	*1962*	*1963*	*1964*	*1965*	*1966*	*1967*
6.25	8.28	0.29	13.06	3.1	6.81	8.7	6.02	3.99	4.01	3.11	11.28	0.58	10.07	7.54	9.25	5.35	4.65

Source *Long-term Statistical Series of the Greek Economy*, p. 10

officially submitted a request for Association in June 1959,[113] but the negotiations initiated in 1958.[114] In other words, it took three years for the Agreement to get signed (1958–1961).[115] Moreover, it was not until November 1962 that the Agreement came into force.[116] Also, in spite of the fact that, as noted in the beginning of this chapter, Association with the Community countries contributed to an opening of the Greek economy, the prospects of the intensification of competition increased uncertainty even more after the signing of the Agreement. The climate was aggravated by the fact that entrepreneurs seemed to consider that the state had an obligation to support indigenous companies from international competition. For example, in 1966 the guild of hat making craft industries sent a letter to the Ministries of Industry and Commerce expressing complaints about the influx of hats imported from abroad paying 'minimum' duties: '[A]ll craft industry owners and employees are horrified to see the economic destruction they are led to because of the uncaring attitude of the State…all advanced States are trying in every possible way to fund, support and mostly promote their craft industries…but unfortunately this policy is not followed in our own country'.[117]

Industrialists also complained that their views were not taken into consideration during the Association negotiations. Indicative of this was an article that appeared in the *Bulletin of the FGI* five years after the signing of the Agreement. In it, it was noted that the Prime Minister stressed the importance of cooperation between 'the state, the productive classes, employers and employees'for the development of the economy. For the Federation, the timing of these words raised 'bitter considerations', as it was noted that 'at long last', the government had decided to put forward a cooperation agenda which the Federation had been calling for since the beginning of the Association Agreement. It was also noted that the productive classes could not play the role of the leader in such a

[113] Ministry of Foreign Affairs of Greece, 'The Country's Course in the European Union'. http://www.mfa.gr/exoteriki-politiki/i-ellada-stin-ee/i-poreia-tis-elladas-stin-europaiki-enosi.html [accessed 05.10.2014], in Greek.

[114] Psalidopoulos, *History*, p. 205.

[115] Ibid.

[116] Ibid.

[117] The Hellenic Literary and Historical Archive, The guild of hat making craft industries, 'Memorandum to the Ministries of Commerce and Industry', 16.03.1966.

cooperation, given that, 'apart from all other defects', they had 'no kind of influence over the state'and were 'not being heard by the governments, no matter how hard they tried'.[118]

Such accusations, however, do not seem fair; the work of Nicholas Moussis, who served in the European Commission up to 2000, suggests that the views and demands of Greek industrialists with regard to Association were expressed during negotiations, and also largely satisfied,[119] and that the reasons why they expressed discontent were deeper.[120] Specifically, he notes that the FGI was always in favour of the Association,[121] however, its attitudes 'varied from almost complete satisfaction...to almost total denial of the usefulness of the Agreement and the way it was concluded'.[122] When the Agreement was signed, some of the members 'could not contain their pleasure and spoke enthusiastically about the Association'.[123] Other members, however, 'or the same ones at second thought, conceived it to be more advisable to emit some cries of protest from time to time in order to show that they had been dragged into the scheme'. In this way, '[i]f the experiment proved to be a failure and was fatal for many of its members, the organization would not be the one to be blamed for it'.[124] It is also possible, as he notes, that 'when...the impact of the first reductions of tariffs began to be felt by [the FGI's] inefficient members...[it] begun protesting about its "unfair" treatment'.[125]

The stance of industrialists also denotes that there were asymmetries in the information regarding the terms of the Agreement but also uncertainty with regards to the actual impact of the Association itself. Indicative of the climate of uncertainty was the fact that, during the negotiations and

[118] *Bulletin of the FGI*, 5,105, 15.11.1966, pp. 1–2.

[119] Nicholas S. Moussis, *Greek Industrialists and the Association of Greece with the Common Market* (Brussels, 1967), pp. 137–138.

[120] Nicholas Moussis' Phd thesis focused on the FGI and Greece's association with the EEC. Moussis worked in the European Commission from 1967 to 2000 ('Europedia', *Author*. http://www.europedia.moussis.eu/author/?lang=en [accessed 11.11.2014]).

[121] Moussis, p. 136.

[122] Ibid., p. 132.

[123] Ibid., p. 142.

[124] Ibid.

[125] Ibid., p. 143.

one year before the signing of the agreement in April 1960, in a general assembly of the members of the FGI, the then president of the Federation characterised association with the EEC as a 'fire test' for the Greek industry.[126]

Apart from this, there have been various different views about what the Association's implications were for the wider economy. For example, the 1966 article from the *Bulletin of the FGI* mentioned above noted that some members of the government, and also Heads of various organisations, were reluctant or even negative when commenting about the country's prospects four years after the Association Agreement was signed. It was also stressed in the article that one of the officials even suggested that the Agreement should be 'reestablished on a new basis'.[127] With regard to the Federation's views per se, it was noted that the Agreement did not bring about 'even a small reduction of the distance between the economies of the Six and that of Greece', and did not have any positive effects in terms of the growth rate of the Greek economy'.[128] There was also the fear of foreign competition. For example, in a relevant newspaper article it was noted that the country's 'gradual tariff disarmament' that association with the EEC meant, would cause 'boundless freedom of imports' and an inability to protect domestic production from foreign competition.[129]

Of course, the Association had also positive aspects. For example, the signing of the Agreement was accompanied by a funding package of $125 million, of which Greece had collected the $69 million until 1967.[130] Also, as noted before, the conditions with regard to the gradual tariff reductions were favourable for Greece. Apart from this, Association indeed contributed to an opening of the Greek economy to the international markets. Still, it seems that during the period which saw the elimination of tariff barriers between Greece and the EEC countries, the Greek economy did not manage to increase its exports enough so as

[126] Federation of Greek Industrialists, *The Greek Industry in 1959* (Athens: Federation of Greek Industrialists, 1960), p. 6, in Greek.

[127] *Bulletin of the FGI*, 5,105, 15.11.1966, p. 4.

[128] Ibid.

[129] CHROTEX Archive, 'The Exports Problem', *O EconomicosTahidromos*, 15.04.1965, p. 1.

[130] Korres and Chionis, p. 384.

to dynamically participate in the international competition.[131] According to Bitros, it seemed that the Greek authorities' primary aim was not to increase the country's exports, but to make it able to withstand the competition within the European Community.[132]

However, the Association procedures were not the only factor of uncertainty during the 1960s. Another factor of uncertainty—in fact, destabilisation—was the political turmoil that led, in April 1967, to the dismantling of democracy and the imposition of a military dictatorship regime that ruled the country for seven consecutive years.[133]

To understand the political turmoil of the 1960s, one should go back to the late 1950s. It was then that, as the sociologist Nicos Mouzelis notes, the Right started losing its electoral power in the countryside and the towns. Indicative of such a development was 'the spectacular 1958 election gains of the left-wing party EDA[134]... [which made it] for a time the major opposition in parliament'.[135] Such developments made the Right mobilise its para-state mechanisms, and specifically IDEA,[136] a group of rightist officers within the Greek army established in 1944; IDEA intervened in the electoral process in order to ensure that similar electoral results would be avoided in the future.[137] Indeed, in October 1961 Karamanlis' right-wing government announced the holding of early elections, in the hope, according to Meynaud, that 'the international tension of the time (especially the rise of the Wall between the two Berlins) would lead the Greek electorate to a renewal of their mandate'.[138] The elections ended up with a win for Karamanlis, which, according to Mouzelis, was secured by the para-state mechanisms

[131] Bitros, p. 23.

[132] Ibid., p. 24.

[133] Stathis Efstathiades, 'The Backstage of a Coup That Paved the Road for Democracy Through a...DICTATORSHIP', *To Vima*, 16.97.2000. http://www.tovima.gr/politics/article/?aid=124233 [accessed 15.10.2014], in Greek.

[134] EDA stands for Unified Democratic Left (Eniaia Dimokratiki Aristera).

[135] Mouzelis, 'Capitalism', p. 71.

[136] IDEA stands for Sacred Bond of Greek Officers (Ieros Desmos Ellinon Axiomatikon), see ibid., p. 58.

[137] Ibid., pp. 58–59; 71.

[138] Meynaud, p. 136.

mentioned above.[139] In such a framework, the opposition complained about the legitimacy of the elections, declaring that 'it would not recognise the government of the electoral coup'.[140] Apart from this, a series of cases of fraud and acts of violence against followers of the opposition parties were brought to justice, 'turning Greece into a big electoral court'.[141] According to Meynaud, the volume of evidence supporting the opposition's accusations was impressive.[142] The political crisis that emerged ended up with Karamanlis' resignation in June 1963 and with the calling of another round of elections that took place on 3 November and brought Georgios Papandreou, the leader of the centrist party Centre Union, to power.[143] This introduced a considerable change in the Greek political scene, as it meant the assumption of the government from a non right-wing political party for the first time after 11 years of right-wing governments (1952–1963).[144] The fact, however, that the new government had not achieved a strong majority in the Parliament, led Papandreou to ask for another round of elections, that took place on 16 February 1964. This time, the Right suffered a serious defeat and the Centre Union emerged as the solid winner of the elections, acquiring an 'unprecedented'[145] 53% of the voting share.[146]

Kazakos wrote that in the early 1960s people thought that political changes that would promote structural reforms in the society and the economy had to be done. What signalled such changes was, for some, the arrival in power of Papandreou's Centre Union.[147] The new government focused on increasing the working classes' purchasing power and reducing inequalities,[148] as, some of the measures undertaken were the provision of income support to farmers and the increase of civil servants' wages.

139 Mouzelis, 'Capitalism', pp. 71–72.

140 Meynaud, p. 143.

141 Ibid., pp. 143–144.

142 Ibid., p. 144.

143 Ibid., p. 146.

144 Ibid., p. 179.

145 Mouzelis, 'Capitalism', p. 72.

146 Meynaud, p. 154.

147 Kazakos, pp. 250–251.

148 Ibid., p. 252.

Table 3.3 Share of income tax of legal entities over total direct taxes

1960	*1961*	*1962*	*1963*	*1964*	*1965*
9.56%	10.18%	10.28%	10.54%	10.70%	12.66%

Source Hellenic Statistical Authority, *Statistical Yearbook of Public Finance 1966* (Athens, 1967), p. 49. The term legal entities stands for corporations, partnerships, associations, etc

More generally, the new government aimed to exercise certain Keynesian-type policies, with the introduction of more lax monetary policies and the increase of the level of public expenditure.[149] In such a framework, internal and external debt increased and the danger of inflation became one of the arguments of the opposition when attacking the government's policies.[150] However, in spite of the increase in public expenditure, the fiscal balance tended to get restored by the significant increase in productivity.[151] Also, as Table 3.3 indicates, the share of total tax revenues to GDP increased in 1964 and 1965.[152] As far as business was concerned, there was an increase in the share of income tax from legal entities to the total direct taxes of the state (Table 3.3).

In fact, however, what distinguished these years were not the economic policies the new government implemented, but the political unrest caused by the accession to power of Papandreou's party. His party saw, during this period, the emergence of 'a strong left wing' within it.[153] The unrest was to a large extent related to the tumultuous relations between Papandreou and the then royal family, which was powerful enough to '[intervene] in any aspect of the Greek political reality'.[154]

[149] 'Drachma for 60 Years', in *Four Interviews of Xenophon Zolotas in Economicos Tahidromos* (Athens: Economicos Tahidromos, 1988), pp. 14–15.

[150] Kazakos, p. 253.

[151] Ibid., p. 259.

[152] The Centre Union was in power from February 1964 to July 1965 ('The General Secretariat of the Government', *Governments from 1909 to date.* www.ggk.gov.gr/?page_id=776&sort=time [accessed 10.01.2015], in Greek).

[153] Mouzelis, 'Capitalism', p. 72.

[154] Dimitrios Stebilis, '21 April 1967: The Ending of a Chronic Political Crisis and the Beginning of a Dark Period', *History—Theoretical Texts, Documents of the Revolutionary Movement.* http://istorika-ntokoumenta.blogspot.co.uk/2013/06/21-1967.html

Specifically, current appreciations of the political status quo of the period point out that Papandreou's winning was 'a big shock for the Palace'.[155] The journalist Stathis Efstathiades[156] notes that 'the King[157] was not the typical kind of monarch, but a party leader…his party was not the conservative National Radical Union, neither the previous…National Rally or the Progressive Party[158] …The King's and the royal court's party was, in general terms, the Right'.[159] This tension-filled climate led, apart from the increase of the political heat between Papandreou and Karamanlis' parties, to the severing of the unity in the former's party.[160] According to Papandreou's son, who would later become a Prime Minister too, such a breakdown in the unity among the members of the Centre Union was 'funded' by Tom Pappas, a Greek-American entrepreneur who established the Esso-Pappas industries in the early 1960s.[161] Interestingly enough, according to Robert Keeley, the then US Embassy Charge d' Affairs, Pappas was the person who once complained about the difficulties

[accessed 20.12.2014], in Greek. The article has also been published in the newspaper *The Road of the Left*.

155 Efstathiades. The polity of Greece during the period 1952–1967 was a Constitutional Monarchy ('Hellenic Parliament', *Constitutional History* [accessed 14.10.2014]).

156 Efstathiades has been an accredited correspondent of the newspaper *To Vima* in Washington and the United Nations since the decade of the 1960s ('The Hellenic Centre for European Studies', *Stathis Efstathiades*. http://www.ekem.gr/index.php?option=com_content&view=article&id=77&Itemid=61 [accessed 20.12.2014], in Greek.

157 I.e. the Former King Constantine II of Greece. For a brief reference on the history of the ex-royal family in Greece see, indicatively, Aisha Labi, 'Throneless Abroad', *Time*, 03.06.2002. http://content.time.com/time/world/article/0,8599,2050238,00.html [accessed 15.10.2014].

158 The National Rally was a right-wing party established by General Alexandros Papagos, who won the elections and became a Prime Minister in November 1952. Upon his death in October 1955, the Crown designated Konstantinos Karamanlis as a Prime Minister. Karamanlis had served in the Papagos government as a minister of Public Works (Meynaud, pp. 120–125, and 'The General Secretariat of the Government', *Alexandros Papagos Government*) and formed his own party, the National Radical Union, in January 1956 (Meynaud, p. 273). As for the Progressive Party, this was established by the right-wing politician Spyros Markezinis in February 1955. Markezinis had also served in the Papagos government, as a minister of Coordination, from November 1952 to April 1954 (Meynaud, p. 269).

159 Efstathiades.

160 Ibid.

161 Markos Karasarinis, 'The Person Called "Esso"', *To Vima*, 30.07.2012. http://www.tovima.gr/vimamen/guys/article/?aid=468973 [accessed 15.10.2014], in Greek.

he had establishing his industries in Greece using the following phrase, which suggests the presence of crony capitalism in the Greek economy: 'I had to buy-off four governments within five years in order to make this'.[162] Regardless of whether such allegations were true or not, it is a fact that on July 1965 the King designated the right-wing politician Georgios Athanasiadis-Novas, president of the Parliament at the time, as Prime Minister, and two members of Papandreou's party as Ministers of National Defence and Public Order. This event triggered a time of serious political upheaval, called the period of 'apostasy'; it is characteristic that from 15 July 1965 to 3 April 1967, five different people assumed leadership of the government.[163] The events of this period, not only increased even more the political turmoil, but also spurred social upheaval, reflected in articles appearing in left-wing newspapers of the period:

> The apostates [are] spineless servants of the Crown, the foreigners and the Right...[they] disapprove of the policies of the Centre which were [once] run by themselves, replacing them with the policies of the National Radical Union. They are imposing new taxes, according to the wishes of the National Radical Union. They are dismissing civil servants, according to the wishes of the National Radical Union, in order to hire those that they want...And while they are imposing new taxes upon the people, they exempt...Tom Pappas from any taxes and duties.[164]

Such an atmosphere of generalised unrest had an impact on the industrial sector, as was acknowledged also by the government that succeeded that of Papandreou. Specifically, in 1967 the Ministry of Coordination recognised that during 1965, the climate of uncertainty caused by the political turmoil but also credit constraints had had a negative impact on the rate of increase of investment. A relevant report noted that in spite of the continuation of investment projects by large industries such as Esso-Pappas and Aluminium of Greece, investors' 'hesitation to assume investment initiatives' had become manifest: the rate of increase

[162] Ibid.

[163] 'The General Secretariat of the Government', *Governments from 1909 to Date* [accessed 15.10.2014].

[164] The 'Konstantinos G. Karamanlis' Foundation, Ioannis Mpoutos Archive, File 6, 'Decadence', *I Avgi*, 09.01.1966, p. 1.

of investment was 11.2%, significantly lower than that of the year 1964 (18.9%).[165]

Moreover, in the statement of the Governor of the Bank of Greece made in the annual meeting of the Bank on 20 April 1967—that is: one day before the imposition of the dictatorship—it was stressed that, in spite of the fact that the post-war performance of Greece placed it 'among the top countries in the international growth league tables',[166] 1966 saw a reduction in the rate of increase of investment in both manufacturing and construction.[167] The rate of increase of industrial investment as a whole declined, it was mentioned, in spite of the fact that there were ample profit opportunities in the sector. Also, it was noted that annual reports of previous years had predicted the oncoming reduction in the rate of investment in industry but 'no measures were taken to meet it'.[168] Therefore, the report continued, the decline in industrial investment should be attributed to 'the reduced potential for further expansion of existing firms and domestic investors in Greece and to the inadequacy of government agencies, specifically set up for this purpose, to stimulate substantial new investment'.[169] Apart from this, it was noted that the structural readjustments the economy needed had not taken place 'at the necessary and desired pace'.[170]

As the previous pages have shown, the economic and social characteristics of the period, but also its intense political heat, made up a tapestry of uncertainty. This, it appears, discouraged business initiative and therefore also industrial investment. A further factor that appeared to cause uncertainty, and, as the critiques indicated, needed a structural reform, was the system of taxation. It seems that the weaknesses of the tax system created difficulties for business, as Baumol's theory suggests. The remaining part of this chapter will analyse a series of such weaknesses.

[165] Ministry of Coordination, *National Accounts of Greece 1948–1965* (Athens: State Printing Office, 1967), p. 27–28 [in Greek].

[166] *Statement Made by Governor Xenophon Zolotas*, p. 8.

[167] Ibid., p. 3.

[168] Ibid., p. 17.

[169] Ibid.

[170] Ibid., p. 8.

Weaknesses in the System of Taxation from the Late 1950s to the Eve of the Dictatorship

From the late 1950s the various administrative problems burdening the tax system became increasingly pressing. According to a 1960 newspaper article, in spite of the manning of the various tax bureaus with graduates from economic and law departments, no positive measure had been undertaken as far as the internal organisation of the tax services was concerned. On the contrary it was stressed that 'the occasionally imposed reforms, apart from their erratic character, have always had negative effects in the efficiency of the service'. It was also noted that the number of the members of staff manning each tax office varied from three-four up to three hundred employees. As a result, 'nine tenths of the tax offices have less than ten employees, the director of the tax office included'. Such a differential composition most of the time had adverse effects, in organisational terms, as there existed many tax offices with only 'one-two employees and a janitor'. Most of such small tax offices spent only one-third of the working time on 'productive work', whereas all remaining time was usually spent on 'managing correspondence, or on collecting, classifying and sending out useless, most of the times, statistical data'.[171]

The recognition of such problems by the members of the tax services themselves was by no means a rarity. In a similar article written in 1963 by a tax official it was noted that 'undoubtedly, since their establishment until today, tax offices are functioning without any program and...organisation. Both the internal and external work is managed...in a casual and unscientific way'. It was also noted that the tax offices' organisation was a permanent problem and that the members of the tax services had to 'run a marathon...in order to cover within a limited amount of time a disproportionate and continuously increasing workload'. Due to this reality, the quality of tax officers' work had fallen, it was stressed, and there was a danger that 'especially the young employees become addicted to work of such a quality'.[172]

[171] 'The Organisation of the Tax Agencies is Erratic and Inefficient', *O Economicos Tahidromos*, 23.06.1960, p. 6.

[172] Nik.Politakis, 'Organisation of the Tax Services', *The Tax Review*, 2, 9, 162–163, 1 April 1963, pp. 295–296.

The analysis of the problematic reality tax officers faced when trying to perform their duties within their services was particularly telling:

> It is not possible in almost any tax office to easily and safely find a tax file…in most cases the taxpayers' files are found on or out of the filing cabinets, on the desks, on the chairs, on the floor, inside the employees' drawers and sometimes in their houses. One understands how difficult it is and how much time is needed for a file to be found under such circumstances. If we add to all of this the frequent reassignment of posts amongst the members of staff, then the drama acquires the…extent of torture.[173]

The lack of organisation was prevalent in the tax services' external works too: 'the same anarchy and sloppiness is present also in the audits…there is a large number of cases in which one fiscal year is audited, whereas another one is not…one fiscal year is audited on the basis of some specific criteria whereas the next one on totally different criteria, while the firm's circumstances have not changed'.[174]

The organisational problems not only of the tax bureaus, but of the Greek civil services in general, were also acknowledged in the report prepared by Langrod, in which he noted that 'within ministries…[t]here is an absence of any theoretical consideration or dependence on principles; empiricism pure and simple is the rule, and the half-measures taken are often merely piecemeal'.[175]

A further weakness came from the relations of patronage affecting the hierarchical structures of the system. For example, the matter of who would be appointed directors of the large tax offices in the capital and the provinces, depended, as some argued, [176] on the political party in power and their appointment was not the result of relevant competitions for the posts. It was noted that recently patronage had become even more pervasive: 'Unbelievable bargains are said to be taking place amongst party executives, in order for their own protégés to obtain key

[173] Ibid.

[174] Nik.Politakis, 'Organisation of the Tax Services' (part 2) *The Tax Review*, 2, 9, 164, 20 April 1963, p. 360.

[175] Langrod., p. 34.

[176] 'The Organisation of the Tax Agencies is Erratic and Inefficient', *O EconomicosTahidromos*, 23.06.1960, p. 6.

positions'. As a result, there was 'as usual, a crowding-out of the really capable ones and an ascent of those who had the necessary means'.[177] Langrod's analysis, again in a wider perspective, acknowledged but also attempted to explore the reasons behind the relations of nepotism and patronage between politicians and civil servants:

> Whereas the Constitution of 1911, the Statute of 1951 and the Constitution of 1952 as in force at present...with a view to obliterating all traces of the "spoils system," established the basic principle of a career for life for civil servants, giving administrative staff established status on the one hand and security of tenure on the other, they did not succeed in cutting out political influence, or giving psychological stability to the government servants. In point of fact, for all the solemn legal guarantees, the civil servant lacks confidence; he always feels he is threatened by the effects of changing political considerations, and this leads him to look for support elsewhere, thus breeding servility and uncertainty.[178]

Another object of criticism for the tax system was, in a fashion similar to the period from the mid to the late 1950s, the issue of complexity. In a meeting with the Minister of Economics in 1965, the president of the Chamber of Commerce and Industry of Piraeus, Nikos Svoronos,[179] noted that 'sometimes, the procedures and prerequisites for some pieces of legislation are so complex that the entrepreneur waives his right to use them, resulting in a non-fulfillment of the scope of the legislation'.[180] Langrod's report indicates that such a complaint was probably not an exaggeration:

> It would take a whole book to describe, by impartially analysing the facts observed, the unimaginable difficulties which a member of the public encounters in the course of activities which deserve every attention and help from the powers-that-be...an investigation of the Greek administrative methods proves the truth of "Parkinson's Law"; the guidance given to the individual is especially harassing; there are often numbers of useless

[177] Ibid.

[178] Langrod, p. 47.

[179] He was probably referring to legislation that was adopted for the promotion of investment.

[180] *Bulletin of the Chamber of Commerce and Industry of Athens*, 1, January 1965, p. 16.

> formalities; endless delays, sidestepping of the law, old-fashioned methods; and great uncertainty as to the results.[181]

Additionally, and unlike the period examined in the first part of this chapter, from the late 1950s to the imposition of the dictatorship there was a scarcity of measures controlling tax officers' behaviour in the process of assessing and collecting tax liabilities. In fact, problems relating to the role of the tax officers appeared to grow larger, as there were critiques arguing that the incidences showing that part of the body of the tax officers did not inspire confidence to the taxpayers had increased.[182] On the whole, the fact that the relevant complaints came not only from entrepreneurs, but also from politicians and ordinary citizens, as well as the consistency in the pattern of such complaints suggested that the problem was general and did not affect only business.

In the case of entrepreneurs, a memorandum sent in March 1960 to the Ministry of Economics by the Chamber of Commerce and Industry of Heraclion, was accompanied by a letter that was written by a lawyer and addressed to the president of the city's Court of First Instance. This letter enumerated a number of cases showing, according to its author, 'the [members of the] tax services' efforts to secure their careers as civil servants through increasing taxable income to completely unrealistic levels'.[183] A few years later, in his speech in the fifth Congress of the Chambers of Commerce and Industry of Greece, the counsellor of the Chamber of Commerce and Industry of Imathia commented on the politicians' urge for a spirit of trust to be created among taxpayers and tax collectors, with the following words:

> We are all aware of the…orders of the ministry of Economics, through which tax officers are requested to cultivate a spirit of cooperation and understanding between tax collectors and taxpayers. But which one of us

[181] Langrod, p. 38.

[182] This was noted in a 1960 Parliamentary speech by Konstantinos Mitsotakis, that will be presented in more detail below (pp. 92–93). Mitsotakis was an MP of the Centre Union at the time, who also became a minister of Economics in 1964–1965 Papandreou's government ('The General Secretariat of the Government', *Georgios Papandreou Government*. http://www.ggk.gov.gr/?p=1239 [accessed 10.11.2014], in Greek).

[183] The 'Konstantinos G. Karamanlis' Foundation, Konstantinos Papakonstantinou Archive, File 12A, F01348, Spir.Lizardos, 'Tax Evasion', *I Naftemporiki*, 11.03.1960, p. 7.

> has ever seen something like that, who doesn't know about the abuses and very often, the blackmailing tax officers do, creating a climate of permanent disputes? But how could there be no such abuses..., when the promotion of tax officers depends, on the one hand, on the number of accounting books they reject and on the other, on how much privileged the posts they hold are? [How could there be no such abuses when tax officers] are never going to be subject to any kind of sanctions for any kind of abuse, no matter how great it is, when determining the taxable income?[184]

Actually, it seems that problematic relations with the tax officers even reduced the scope and efficiency of the tax incentives. In the same congress, the President of the Chamber of Commerce and Industry of Heraclion, referring to three tax incentives laws aiming particularly to the development of regional industries (legislative orders 942/1949, 2176/1952 and law 321/1955), stressed that 'the benefits stemming from the incentives laws should be of a permanent nature, without being subject to cancellation and without depending on the judgment of tax auditors with regards to the sincerity of the regional industries' accounting books'.[185]

A broadly similar view was presented through studies of the period. Nikolaos Moscholios, for example, noted that whereas on one level the introduction of tax incentives seemed enough to increase industrial investment with the development of new projects or the extension of the already existing ones, a closer examination indicated that such instruments' attractiveness depended on other factors that were usually of higher importance. Examples of such factors were the social and economic environment that would 'give a sense of certainty or high probability that the business will survive'.[186] Such an environment could not be simply achieved through tax incentives, but through a stable tax system that would guarantee economic stability and fair income distribution.[187] It was noted that in spite of the fact that tax incentives were expected to

[184] Vovolini Archive, *Viomichaniki Epitheorissis*, Vol. 32, 1965, Proceedings of the 5th Congress of the Chambers of Commerce and Industry of Greece—8th theme of the agenda, 14-17/6 1964, p. 318.

[185] Ibid., p. 171.

[186] Nikolaos Mich. Moscholios, *Tax Incentives, Comparative Research, Greece-European Economic Community* (Athens, 1967), pp. 3–4. The book was found in the Library of the Historical Archive of the National Bank of Greece.

[187] Ibid.

contribute significantly to the country's industrialisation, they were over time proven to have had much less effect than anticipated.[188]

Apart from the critique coming from representatives of business, citizens' letters of complaint often appeared in newspapers too. The tone of such letters was usually rather direct, vividly conveying discontent because of the problematic relations with tax officers. For example, one letter written by a professional, described how 'the prevailing atmosphere in the office of the director of the tax service [resembled that of] paying ransom':

> The director reads the report, writes something down and then, turning to the taxpayer says 'I will reduce it by 40%'. If the taxpayer insists, as I did, he might achieve an even greater reduction. The little people know that they are right, but, not wanting to get involved in tax fights with the State, at the end, give in. It brings sadness to see that the State has ended up making tax officials negotiating for a ransom from the taxpayers…when I left the tax office I met an old lady…who had gone through the torture of compromise for a property transfer tax saying 'may God punish you, antichrists'.[189]

The 'torture of compromise' affected also business, and relevant references appeared in politicians' speeches too:

> Even for the slightest reason, the accounting books of merchants and industrialists get rejected…, and instead of a tax of, say, DRS 10,000, the tax auditor, through the rejection of the books, imposes a flat tax of DRS 100,000, and then asks the owner of the industry to compromise…The reduction of any kind of tax rates has no effect when, through another door, that of classifying the tax payer to a higher tax bracket than the one he really belongs, the State oppresses the taxpayer and exercises over-taxation.[190]

Politicians stressed that such a situation made citizens lose their confidence in the state. For example, in a Parliamentary discussion in March 1960 about a draft bill put forward by the Karamanlis government regarding measures against tax evasion, Stefanos Stefanopoulos, an MP

[188] Ibid., p. 7.

[189] 'It Is Not Taxes, It Is Ransom', *Ta Nea*, 20.10.1962, p. 6.

[190] 'The Government Squeezes National Income', *Eleftheria*, 3.8.1962, pp. 1, 4.

from Papandreou's Centre Union, addressing the Minister of Economics, spoke of cases of 'outrageous abuses which made citizens suffer'.[191] Such abuses were perpetrated by members of the public administration, Stefanopoulos noted, and the fact that there seemed to be no subsequent punishment had shaken the citizens' trust in the State.[192] In a similar vein, Konstantinos Mitsotakis, also an MP of Centre Union, noted that the role of tax officers was indeed problematic, as it created a sense of mistrust among taxpayers. This mistrust led to low levels of tax conscience, that is, tolerance of tax evasion because tax mechanisms were considered illegitimate and unfair. It was necessary for the state to address this issue:

> [We] should admit that the quality of part of the body of tax officers is so low that today they do not inspire confidence to the taxpayers. The number of [such] incidences has lately increased and there is a danger that the public will have the impression that bad tax officers are the rule and [not]... the exception...if we want this country to obtain tax conscience and if we want to combat tax evasion, we should start with the tax officers.[193]

Mitsotakis acknowledged again the issues of trust arising from the problematic relations with the tax authorities some years later, when he was the Minister of Economics of the government. In a meeting with the executive board of the Chamber of Commerce and Industry of Athens in January 1965, he noted that it was necessary for both the State and the citizen to stop regarding each others as enemies, and for the tax system to inspire 'understanding and trust'.[194] In this context, Mitsotakis stressed the following:

> Even nothing more remains from my passing from the ministry of Economics, it would be enough for me if I could help dissolve this mutual distrust which literally blocks the exercise of any policy, because...it is...

[191] The 'Konstantinos G. Karamanlis' Foundation, Konstantinos Papakonstantinou Archive, File 12A, F01348, 'The Parliamentary Discussion on the Tax Bill', *I Naftemporiki*, 11.03.1960, p. 6.

[192] Ibid.

[193] Ibid., p. 8.

[194] *Bulletin of the Chamber of Commerce and Industry of Athens*, 1, January 1965, p. 9.

> unthinkable and unacceptable to have the State disputing with the citizen and the citizen to treat the State as an enemy.[195]

The whole situation was aggravated by the fact that, whereas, in the period from the mid to the late 1950s the relevant measures undertaken in order to address tax officers' arbitrariness were numerous and relatively severe, and had been backed up by specific laws in some cases,[196] in this period the state did not seem particularly willing to exert similarly significant efforts. More precisely, it seems that, from the late 1950s to the eve of dictatorship what the state mostly did was at best to issue recommendations, and, at worst, to merely express hopes. For example, in 1960 the Ministry of Economics issued a circular in which it was stressed that tax audits should be conducted 'with courtesy and respect for the audited citizen, whose views and explanations should be listened to with attention'. It was also noted that any audit should be conducted only after a written order from the director of the tax bureau, and that the auditors should demonstrate their professional identity cards to the taxpayers under investigation.[197] Also, a 1961 note from the 'Special Audit Team for the Implementation of the Tax Code' presenting measures for the reduction of tax evasion, contained 'a strict reminder of the orders for respect of the validity of professionals' accounting books'. What was also recommended was 'a limitation of the audits only to those companies that... do not appear to be presenting their actual economic results'.[198]

Aside from these few initiatives, the state did not seem particularly eager to implement measures that would improve administration, not only in the tax services, but in the public sector more generally. Conveying the atmosphere of the time, Ioannis Photopoulos, who served as an official of

[195] Ibid.

[196] For example, as already mentioned, according to article no.52 of the law 3323/1955 (modified and completed by the legislative order 3765/1957), it was a criminal offence for the Head of a tax bureau to issue a tax assessment notice containing false data.

[197] 'Tax Officers Will Conduct Audits only After a Written Order by the Heads of the Tax Offices', *Empros*, 19.3.1960, p. 16.

[198] The 'Konstantinos G. Karamanlis 'Foundation, Konstantinos Papakonstantinou Archive, File 202A', Findings of the Economics Committee, 1959–1961, Notes on Tax Evasion, Measures against tax theft, The Special Audit Team for the Implementation of the Tax Code, 'Note on the measures that should be assumed against tax evasion', p. 1.

the Central Service of the Ministry of Economics during the period 1965–1981, argued that Langrod's recommendations regarding the system of public administration were never implemented by the Greek authorities.[199] Dimitrios Argyriades, who worked with Langrod in the 1960s, offered a slightly different perspective on this matter. He considered that the latter's report led to a series of studies conducted during the period 1963–1967, which provided an analysis of the problems of the Greek administrative system. Argyriades also noted that after the publication of the report civil servants were sent abroad for further training. He did not, however, mention the number of such civil servants.[200] Apart from this, Argyriades acknowledged that the efforts to promote research in the field of administration 'soon encountered unexpected obstacles'. He explained that this was due to the authorities' inability to understand the difference between basic education and lifelong learning as well as due to an unwillingness to realise that Administration could be the object of scientific research.[201] Indeed, the situation would become even worse in the coming years. For example, as will be shown in the next chapter, the policies implemented during the 1967–1974 dictatorship led to a further disruption of the tax administration mechanisms.

On the whole, the period from the late 1950s to the eve of dictatorship was one with a scarcity of measures that could improve the organisation of the tax services, ease the complexities of the tax legislation but also improve tax officers' behaviour, setting, perhaps, more limits to their tendency to be arbitrary when performing their duties. There also seemed to be a lack of greater training that would improve their professional capabilities.

Conclusion

The present chapter showed how weaknesses of the system of taxation such as its complexity, bureaucratic rigidities and problematic role of tax officers created difficulties for the industrial sector during 1955–1967, a period that was otherwise one of rapid economic development for Greece. These years saw the enactment of laws that introduced reforms in the

[199] Ioannis Photopoulos, interview data.

[200] Argyriades, 'Ethics and Governance', p. 2.

[201] Ibid., p. 3.

tax system in terms of simplifying the process of filing a tax return and increasing the amount of tax revenue collected. However, the new laws did not seem to introduce any long-lasting improvement in the organisation of the tax bureaus. From the late 1950s to the eve of dictatorship, the state did not seem willing to undertake initiatives that would significantly improve relations between taxpayers and tax officers by containing the arbitrariness or offering substantial training in order to enhance officers' professional capabilities. Additionally, because of the already pressing problem of tax evasion, there was a significant amount of mutual distrust between the state and the taxpayers, therefore also between the state and business. In such a context, it seems that the tax authorities presumed business people were tax evaders and business people considered that the authorities often treated them as such. In terms of the administrative burdens of the tax system, the period from the mid to the late 1950s saw improvements in the organisation of the tax bureaus. An example of such improvements was the division of each tax office into departments. However, there was a scarcity of similar measures in the period from the late 1950s to the eve of the dictatorship.

The evidence that was presented in the previous pages suggests that such kind of problems were likely to have discouraged investment in manufacturing industry. As will be shown in the following chapter, in the period of dictatorship 1967–1974, and in spite of the declarations of the junta regime, no measures towards the modernisation of the system were introduced. On the contrary, the tactics of the regime led to a deepening of the disruption in the tax services. This was mainly done through the dismissals of civil servants that were considered disloyal to the regime and the dismantling of services that played a significant role in controlling the function of the tax bureaus, such as the Central Service of the Ministry of Economics.

Bibliography

Primary Sources

CHROTEX Archive

'Tax Courts', *I Naftemporiki*, 28.02.1957, p. 6.

'The Exports Problem', *O EconomicosTahidromos*, 15.04.1965, p. 1.

'The Scopes of the Rearrangements', contained in a newspaper cutting found in the archive.

Historical Archives of the Piraeus Bank Group Cultural Foundation

Economic Development Financing Organisation Archive, *Report of Activities up to December 31, 1961*, p. 12.

Index of Parliamentary Discussions 1946–1967

Minutes from the Sitting of the Special Committee, 6/26.7.1955, pp. 56–62.

Professor Michalis Psalidopoulos Personal Archive

Bulletin of the Federation of Greek Industrialists (FGI) (1966–1988).

The Hellenic Literary and Historical Archive (ELIA)

The guild of hat making craft industries, 'Memorandum to the Ministries of Commerce and Industry', 16.03.1966.

The 'Konstantinos G. Karamanlis' Foundation, Various Archives

The 'Konstantinos G. Karamanlis' Foundation, 'Historical Archive', *Konstantinos Papakonstantinou* <http://www.ikk.gr/Default.aspx?tabid=236> [accessed 26.10.2014], in Greek.

Konstantinos Papakonstantinou Archive, File 12A, F01348, 'The Parliamentary Discussion on the Tax Bill', *I Naftemporiki*, 11.03.1960, p. 6.

Konstantinos Papakonstantinou Archive, File 202A', Findings of the Economics Committee, 1959–1961, Notes on Tax Evasion, Measures against tax theft, The Special Audit Team for the Implementation of the Tax Code, 'Note on the measures that should be assumed against tax evasion', p. 1.

Konstantinos Papakonstantinou Archive, File 202A', Findings of the Economics Committee, 1959–1961, Notes on Tax Evasion, Measures against tax theft, p. 4.

Konstantinos Papakonstantinou Archive, File 12A, F01348, Spir.Lizardos, 'Tax Evasion', *I Naftemporiki*, 11.03.1960, p. 7.

Ioannis Mpoutos Archive, File 6, 'Decadence', *I Avgi*, 09.01.1966, p. 1.

Union of Corporations and Limited Liability Companies Archive

Board of Directors Meeting Minutes (1957–1989)

Vovolini Archive

File 30, Eftaxias Family, sub-file 1, Evidence no. 61, p. 2.

Viomichaniki Epitheorissis, Vol. 22, May 1955, p. 18.

Viomichaniki Epitheorissis, Vol. 26, Proceedings of the 2nd Congress of the Chambers of Commerce and Industry of Greece, 20–23.10.1957, pp. 53–54.

Viomichaniki Epitheorissis, Vol. 25, March 1958, p. 16.

Viomichaniki Epitheorissis, Vol. 26, 1959, Proceedings of the 2nd Congress of the Chambers of Commerce and Industry of Greece, 20–23.10.1957, pp. 268–269.

Viomichaniki Epitheorissis, Vol. 32, 1965, Proceedings of the 5th Congress of the Chambers of Commerce and Industry of Greece—8th theme of the Agenda, 14-17/6 1964, p. 318.

Newspapers, Magazines and Serial Publications

a) Newspapers

Capital (just two new articles i found online), Dimokratia* (also an online new article), Eleftheria, Empros, Imerisia (and new online), I Avgi, I Kathimerini, I Naftemporiki, O Economicos Tahydromos, Makedonia, Rizospastis, Ta Nea, To Vima, To Vima tis Kyriakis (in Greek).

b) Magazines and Serial Publications

The Accountant, Tax Review, The Bulletin of Tax Legislation, Bulletin of the Chamber of Commerce and Industry of Athens.

Interviews

Entrepreneur no. 2 requesting anonymity.

Photopoulos, I.

Official Publications

Bank of Greece, *Statement made by Governor Xenophon Zolotas at the Annual Meeting of the Bank of Greece, 20 April 1967* (Athens: The Bank of Greece, 1967), p. 8.

Federation of Greek Industrialists, *The Greek Industry in 1959* (Athens: Federation of Greek Industrialists, 1960), p. 6, in Greek.

Hellenic Statistical Authority, *Statistical Yearbook of Greece*, various issues.

Hellenic Statistical Authority, *Statistical Yearbook of Public Finance 1966* (Athens, 1967), p. 49.

International Monetary Fund, *Annual Report 1959*. http://www.imf.org/external/pubs/ft/ar/archive/pdf/ar1959.pdf [accessed 14.12.2014], p. 2 and *Annual Report 1960*. https://www.imf.org/external/pubs/ft/ar/archive/pdf/ar1960.pdf [accessed 14.12.2014], p. 1.

Long-Term Statistical Series of the Greek Economy, pp. 27; 10.

Ministry of Coordination, *National Accounts of Greece 1948–1965* (Athens: State Printing Office, 1967), p. 27–28 [in Greek].

The State Gazette, Tax Code, issue 1, no. 116, 5.5.1956, p. 1274.

Web Resources

Argyriades, D. 'Ethics and Governance from a Comprehensive Perspective: How Are We Going to Face the Multiple Challenges of Our Times', Panteion University of Political and Social Sciences, Centre of Governance and Sustainable Development. http://www.dee.gr/mediaupload/publications/20100618_ithiki_kai_diakibernisi.pdf, in Greek.

'e-forologia', *Online Bank*, Legislative order 3843/1958. http://www.e-forologia.gr/lawbank/document.aspx?digest=48DBD85F893B6FC0.1D031AEA53&version=1958/09/3, in Greek.

'Europedia', *Author*. http://www.europedia.moussis.eu/author/?lang=en.

Hellenic Parliament, 'The Institution'. http://www.hellenicparliament.gr/Vouli-ton-Ellinon/O-Thesmos/, in Greek.

Ioakeimoglou, I., 'The Greek Economy 1960–2007, Development, Productive Structure and Labour Market'. http://www.ine.otoe.gr/Upl/pdf/Greece_IneOtoe.pdf, p. 12, in Greek.

Karasarinis, M. 'The Person Called "Esso"', *To Vima*, 30.07.2012. http://www.tovima.gr/vimamen/guys/article/?aid=468973, in Greek.

'Konstantinos G. Karamanlis Government'. http://www.ggk.gov.gr/?p=1206, in Greek.

Labi, A., 'Throneless Abroad', *Time*, 03.06.2002. http://content.time.com/time/world/article/0,8599,2050238,00.html.

Milios, Y., 'The Greek Economy in the 20th Century'. http://users.ntua.gr/jmilios/Oikonomia_Eikostos1ab.pdf, in Greek.

Ministry of Foreign Affairs of Greece, 'The Country's Course in the European Union'. http://www.mfa.gr/exoteriki-politiki/i-ellada-stin-ee/i-poreia-tis-elladas-stin-europaiki-enosi.html, in Greek.

Skalkos, D. 'The Devaluation of the Drachma in 1953 and Economic Development', *Capital*, 16.7.2013. http://www.capital.gr/news.asp?id=1835769, in Greek.

Stebilis, D., '21 April 1967: The Ending of a Chronic Political Crisis and the Beginning of a Dark Period', *History—Theoretical Texts, Documents of the Revolutionary Movement*. http://istorika-ntokoumenta.blogspot.co.uk/2013/06/21-1967.html, in Greek.

'The General Secretariat of the Government', *Alexandros Papagos Government*. http://www.ggk.gov.gr/?p=1194, in Greek.

'The General Secretariat of the Government', *Georgios Papandreou Government*. http://www.ggk.gov.gr/?p=1239, in Greek.

'The General Secretariat of the Government', *Governments from 1909 to Date* [accessed 15.10.2014].

'The Hellenic Centre for European Studies', *Stathis Efstathiades*. http://www.ekem.gr/index.php?option=com_content&view=article&id=77&Itemid=61, in Greek.

Secondary Literature

Bitros, G. K., 'Greece: How and Why Things Turned Upside Down', in *Essays in Applied Economics and Finance*, ed Giannis Katsoulakos (Athens: Athens University of Economics and Business, 2013), in Greek.

Break, G. F., and Turvey, R., *Studies in Greek Taxation* (Athens: Centre of Planning and Economic Research, 1964).
'Drachma for 60 Years', in *Four Interviews of Xenophon Zolotas in Economicos Tahidromos* (Athens: Economicos Tahidromos, 1988).
Drakatos, K., *The Big Cycle of the Greek Economy (1945–1995)* (Athens: Papazisis, 1997), in Greek.
Edmiston. K. D., 'Tax Uncertainty and Investment: A Cross-Country Empirical Examination', *Economic Inquiry*, 42, 3 (July 2004), 425–440.
Florou, C., 'Comparative Evaluation of the Methods Used to Determine the Aggregate Net Income of the Greek Stock Companies' (Unpublished doctoral thesis, Aristotle University of Thessaloniki, 2009), in Greek.
Freris, A. F., *The Greek Economy in the Twentieth Century* (London and Sydney: Croom Helm, 1986).
Galanos, G., 'The Greek Tourism Industry and the Challenge of the Economic Crisis', in *Greece's Horizons—Reflecting on the Country's Assets and Capabilities*, eds Pantelis Sklias and Nikolaos Tzifakis (Athens: Konstantinos Karamanlis Institute for Democracy, 2013).
Giouras, Thanasis, *Taxation and Politics, Political-Economic Problematic and Financial Thought* (Athens: Sakis Karagiorgas Foundation, 2000), in Greek.
Glykou, Ioanna, *State and Tax Policy, an Historical and Theoretical Approach and the Case of Greece* (Athens: Sakoullas, 2009), in Greek.
Grigoropoulos, G. J., 'Shipping and Sustainable Economic Development: The Case of Greece', in *Greece's Horizons*, pp. 121–129.
Hassett, K. A., and Metcalf, G. E., 'Investment with Uncertain Tax Policy: Does Random Tax Policy Discourage Investment?', *The Economic Journal*, 109, 457 (July 1999), 372–393.
Ioakimoglou, E., and Milios, J., 'Capital Accumulation and Over-Accumulation Crisis: The Case of Greece (1960–1989)', *Review of Radical Political Economics*, 25, 2, (June 1993), p. 81.
Kazakos, Panos, *Between State and Market* (Athens: Patakis, 2001), in Greek.
Korres, G. M. and D. P. Chionis, *Greek Economy, Economic Policy and Analysis of the Basic Macroeconomic Magnitudes* (Athens, Stamoulis, 2003), p. 29.
Kostis, K., *State and Enterprises in Greece, the History of 'Aluminium of Greece'* (Athens: Polis, 2013), in Greek.
Langrod, G., *Reorganisation of Public Administration in Greece—A Report* (Paris: OECD, 1965), pp. 11, 84–94.
Louri, H., and I. Pepelasis- Minoglou, 'A Quantitative Exploration on the Determinants of (De-) Industrialisation: The Case of Greece', *International Review of Applied Economics*, 15, 4 (2001).
Manesiotis, V., 'Tax Structure Change During Economic Development: The Case of Greece' (Unpublished doctoral thesis, Northwestern University, 1985).

Meynaud, J., *Political Forces in Greece, vol. I*, trans. by P. Merlopoulos (Athens: Savvalas, 2002).

Michas, N. A., 'Economic Development, Social Mobilization and the Growth of Public Expenditures in Greece', *American Journal of Economics and Sociology*, 39, 1 (January 1980), 31–48.

Moscholios, N. M., *Tax Incentives, Comparative Research, Greece-European Economic Community* (Athens, 1967). The book was found in the Library of the Historical Archive of the National Bank of Greece.

Moussis, N. S., *Greek Industrialists and the Association of Greece with the Common Market* (Brussels, 1967).

Mouzelis, N., 'Capitalism and Dictatorship in Post-war Greece', *New Left Review*, I (March–April 1996).

Pougouras, P. K., and C. A. Kyttaris, *Tax Control of Commercial and Industrial Enterprises* (Athens, 1957), in Greek.

Psalidopoulos, M., *Monetary Management and Economic Crisis—The Policy of the Bank of Greece, 1929–1941* (Athens: The Bank of Greece, 2011), in Greek.

Psalidopoulos, M., *History of the Bank of Greece, 1928–2008* (Athens: The Bank of Greece, 2014), in Greek.

Sellas, S. M., *The Greek System of Taxation* (Athens: Papazisis, 1989), in Greek.

Stathopoulos, G. N., *Taxation of Indigenous and Foreign Companies* (Athens, Federation of Greek Industries, 1964), in Greek.

Tatsos, N., *Public Finance in Greece* (Athens: Sbilias, 1991).

Tsoukalas, C., *The Greek Tragedy* (Harmondsworth, Penguin, 1969).

Vetsopoulos, A., 'Efforts for the Development and Stabilization of the Economy during the Period of the Marshall Plan', *Journal of Modern Greek Studies*, 27, 2 (October 2009), pp. 275–302.

Vlahopapadopoulos, G., *The Effectiveness of Tax Incentives in Greece and Suggestions for Their Reform* (Athens: Centre of Planning and Economic Research, 1967), in Greek.

CHAPTER 4

'No Mutiny Will Be Allowed': Dismantling Democracy and Delegitimising the Tax System, 1967–1974

Introduction

The dictatorship was a key period in Greek history, as the seven years it lasted were marked not only by the sociopolitical upheaval that followed the abolition of democracy, but also the Turkish invasion of Cyprus. This period saw, in its majority, high rates of growth[1]; also, no other government would be as 'generous' in terms of introducing measures in order to persuade entrepreneurs to invest in the indigenous industrial sector. Still, business was facing a series of difficulties. One such difficulty came from the tax system, the disruption of which deepened substantially during the junta.

In more detail, the growth of the period was sustained by measures such as the increase of public investment, the relaxation of credit constraints, but also the provision of particularly generous incentives for the promotion of investment. A key characteristic of this period was that the industrial sector's share of the national product reached its highest percentage and also that during 1971–1972 the country's rate of increase of industrial production was the highest among all OECD members.[2]

[1] See Table 4.1, p. 5.

[2] See p. 7.

Z. Pittaki, *Exploring the roots of systematic tax avoidance in Greece*, Palgrave Studies in Economic History,
https://doi.org/10.1007/978-3-030-71979-1_4

However, the increase of public investment and monetary expansion caused a gradual overheating of the economy, the growth of which eventually stopped. This adversely affected the industrial sector, which was facing difficulties due to the first oil crisis of 1973–1974 that led to a dramatic increase in inflation. Industry was adversely impacted also by the uncertainty caused due to the general destabilisation of the Greek society because of the dictatorship, the Cyprus events and the students' uprising in 1973.

In addition, the system of taxation continued to be a further difficulty for entrepreneurs and Greek society more generally. Bureaucratic rigidities, complexity of legislation and procedures were persistent problems burdening the tax system. The evidence suggests that apart from imposing severe fines against tax law offences and ardently declaring its willingness to modernise the public sector and eradicate corruption from it, the junta established a regime that was anything but modern and non-corrupt.

As a matter of fact, in this period the situation in the tax services worsened because there were a large number of dismissals of civil servants that were regarded to be disloyal to the junta. This contributed to the dismantling of the Central Service of the Ministry of Economics, which was responsible for controlling the function of tax bureaus. Under such conditions, it seems that during the dictatorship the tax system not only kept on posing difficulties to business and therefore to industry too, but also entered a phase of very rapid deterioration in the quality of its administrative structures. In the coming pages there will first be a brief analysis of the events that preceded and followed the overthrow of the government and the imposition of a military coup regime. Next the characteristics of the economy and the industrial sector during the period will be analysed, with a reference to some of the difficulties the latter was faced with. The remaining part of the chapter will analyse the difficulties specifically caused by the various weaknesses of the system of taxation.

Subverting Democracy

At around 2am in the morning of 21 April 1967, tanks rolled onto the streets of Athens. A group of middle-rank military officers comprised of four colonels and one brigadier, had overthrown the government and arrested the Prime Minister, the leaders of the opposition as well as members of the leadership of the Armed Forces.[3] The dictators presented their movement as a way out of the country's political deadlock created 'because of the responsible political forces' inability to reach a consensus'[4] but also as a means to avert the 'communist danger'.[5]

The next days were marked by arrests and displacements of thousands of citizens, mostly those who were supporters or members of left-wing parties.[6] Also, all political parties and youth organisations were dissolved.[7] As Andrew Freris notes, the dictatorship 'reopened all the political wounds of the civil war[8] and added a few of its own by widespread jailing, exiling, torturing and numerous deaths'.[9]

It seems that there were many reasons that led to the dictatorship which included the intensification of political unrest in 1965[10] that led to the fall of the Centre Union government and the fact that the Crown 'intervened in any aspect of the Greek political reality'[11] not hesitating, according to Vasileios Markezinis, even to bribe politicians in order to support the first 'apostate' government in July 1965.[12] Another cause was the strength of the role of the army after the winning of elections by General Alexandros Papagos in 1952 and the establishment of paramilitary groups within it.[13] Indeed, all seem to have contributed to the coup.

[3] Othon Tsounakos, 'The coup of 21 April 1967', in *Greece in the 20th Century, 1965–1970*, I Kathimerini – Epta Imeres (special issue) (Athens: I Kathimerini, 12.12.1999), p. 12

[4] Excerpt from the documentary 'The trial of the junta' (5′:58″-6′:37″), in Greek. The documentary was created in 1981 and aired in 17.11.2014 in NERIT, the state-owned public broadcaster in Greece.

[5] Tsounakos, 'The coup', p. 14.

[6] Ibid., and 'Chronology' in *Greece in the 20th Century, 1965–1970*, I Kathimerini – Epta Imeres (Athens: I Kathimerini, 12.12.1999), p. 6.

[7] Othon Tsounakos, 'Resistance Movements', in *Greece in the 20th Century, 1965–1970*, I Kathimerini – Epta Imeres (Athens: I Kathimerini, 12.12.1999), p. 19.

[8] 1944–1949.

[9] Freris, p. 162.

[10] Vasilios Markezinis, *Greece of Crises, A Personal Essay* (Athens: Livanis, 2011), p. 54.

[11] Stebilis.

[12] Markezinis, p. 56.

[13] Stebilis.

There have also been several views about the external forces that supported the dictatorship. It has been noted for example that the US government encouraged the coup, as it believed that, for developing countries such as Greece of the time, the army could function as a 'bulwark against an uncontrollable anti-Western nationalism', and also support various modernisation reforms.[14] However, according to a different perspective, mainly the Left argued that the US secret services, not only encouraged, but played a very 'active' role[15] in the incitement of the coup. This was because, according to this view, the United States aimed to cancel the forthcoming elections that would probably mean the defeat of Karamanlis' National Radical Union and the 'almost certain victory of the "insubordinate" Georgios Papandreou'.[16]

However, it seems possible that the coup would have been imposed even in the absence of support from abroad, as there was not any resistance from within the country. Actually the dictators took by surprise the leaders of the army, the Greek people,[17] but also the political world, which, in spite of having acknowledged the possibility of a junta, did not expect that it would ever actually happen.[18]

Economy and Industry During the Dictatorship

According to the historian Thanos Veremis, the dictators did not have a 'politically comprehensible ideology or sensible views about the form of the regime or the nature of their choices'.[19] However, the views they expressed with regard to the economic policies that they would follow

[14] Kazakos, p. 247.

[15] Tsounakos, 'The Coup', p. 14.

[16] Ibid.

[17] Ibid.

[18] 'Greece: The Junta 5 Years After the Coup', *The Harvard Crimson*, 21.4.1972. http://www.thecrimson.com/article/1972/4/21/greece-the-junta-5-years-after [accessed 23.7.2015].

[19] Thanos Veremis, 'Impromptu Ideologies', in *Greece in the 20th Century, 1965–1970*, I Kathimerini – Epta Imeres (Athens: I Kathimerini, 12.12.1999), p. 15.

probably seemed pretty clear, as they pronounced their eagerness to establish a state that would be smaller,[20] less regulated[21] and more 'open' to entrepreneurship.[22] Indeed, in the Bank of Greece Governor's Annual Report for 1967 presenting the basic principles of the five-year economic plan for 1968–1972 it was noted that 'private business initiative is considered to be the basic pillar of the process of economic development, evolving within a framework of free competition, having profit as its main motivation...The role of the State and other...public bodies...shall be strictly limited to offering services of economic and social infrastructure in order to assist private business activities'.[23]

Further on this issue, Ioannis Pesmazoglou wrote that the dictators considered entrepreneurs' support to be necessary for the establishment of the regime, and, for this reason, their stance towards the latter's requests and propositions was one of a 'relaxed laissez-faire'.[24] By this it was meant that the economic policies followed adhered to some (hence the use of the word 'relaxed') liberal principles, as the regime 'was more open to entrepreneurship and attributed less importance to the role of the state aside of its traditional functions (defence, public order, infrastructure)'.[25]

However, this was obviously an 'asymmetric' laissez-faire.[26] It functioned in a non-democratic framework which, through the imprisonment of thousands, made it impossible for large parts of the Greek society to actively participate in the economy. Still, the majority of the people adapted to the new reality,[27] at least in the first years of the dictatorship.

With regards to the general characteristics of the economy, after a temporary recession in 1967 (manifested through a reduction in the GDP growth rate), the first years of the coup saw a rapid increase of growth

[20] Kazakos, p. 268.

[21] Psalidopoulos, *History*, p. 249.

[22] Kazakos, p. 268.

[23] Bank of Greece, *Bank of Greece Governor's Annual Report for 1967* (Athens: Bank of Greece, 1968), p. 24.

[24] Ioannis Pesmazoglou, in Kazakos, pp. 268–269. Pesmazoglou was an economist and politician.

[25] Ibid., p. 268.

[26] Kazakos, p. 269.

[27] Ibid., p. 267.

Table 4.1 GDP growth rate (%), 1965–1974

1965 (%)	*1966 (%)*	*1967 (%)*	*1968 (%)*	*1969 (%)*	*1970 (%)*	*1971 (%)*	*1972 (%)*	*1973 (%)*	*1974 (%)*
9.25	5.35	4.65	5.68	9.32	8.31	7.97	9.13	8.32	1.81

Source: Long-term Statistical Series of the Greek Economy, p. 10

(see Table 4.1): 'the governments of the dictatorship attempted from the outset to give a new impetus to the economy and to secure their legitimacy or, simply, [the people's] tolerance'.[28]

One of the most important measures undertaken for this purpose was the increase in public investment.[29] It expanded from DRS 30 billion during 1963–1967 to DRS 61 billion in 1968–1972.[30] A significant part of this expansion was due to a substantial increase in military expenditure, the share of which in total public expenditure increased from 13.4% in 1965 to 20.6% in 1975.[31] Other measures were the provision of tax incentives,[32] a more detailed analysis of which will be presented later. There was also an increase in the number of incentives for investment mainly for building construction and tourism,[33] the two major factors of economic expansion during this period.[34]

In addition, the number of loans given to enterprises increased.[35] Indeed, in contrast to the strict credit policies of the 1950s,[36] during the dictatorship it became much easier to obtain a loan. Psalidopoulos

[28] Ibid., p. 268.

[29] Psalidopoulos, *History*, p. 249.

[30] Ibid., p. 226.

[31] G.A. Provopoulos, *The Public Sector of the Greek Economy, Recent Trends and Economic Repercussions* (Athens: Foundation for Economic and Industrial Research, 1985), p. 33.

[32] Psalidopoulos, *History*, p. 249.

[33] Kazakos, p. 268.

[34] Ibid., p. 271.

[35] Antonis Karakousis, 'A Tumultuous Decade', in *Greece in the 20th Century, 1970–1980*, I Kathimerini – Epta Imeres (Athens: I Kathimerini, 19.12.1999), p. 24.

[36] Psalidopoulos, *History*, p. 227.

notes that for the first time, 'the Bank of Greece prepaid [commercial] banks' medium-term loans for investment in industry, construction, tourism and shipping'.[37] Low-interest rate credit was also provided to wheat trade firms and companies undertaking public works. More generally, the procedures required for the provision of loans to commercial enterprises were simplified. Furthermore, liquidity assistance was provided to commercial banks and there was a reduction in the discount rate of the Bank of Greece.[38] The dictatorship's governments also made attempts to attract investors from abroad.[39] Their efforts were not without success, as the amount of foreign investment capital in 1972 was double that of 1966.[40]

However, it is important to note that in many cases, as far as the exercise of economic policy is concerned, the dictatorship was more successful in producing highly populist statements rather than in implementing plans that would actually benefit the economy. For example, in November 1968, the regime concluded an agreement with Aristotle Onassis, regarding 'the functioning of the State oil refineries and the establishment and exploitation of a third refinery'. The USD 400 million investment[41] was the largest Greece had seen up to that point, most conveniently serving the dictators' propaganda that the 'Revolution', as they called their regime, created a sense of stability that persuaded 'Greek capital throughout the world and the Greek spirit of entrepreneurship to come back to the...motherland in order to actively contribute to the realisation of Greece's leap of rapid economic development'.[42] In truth, what happened was that at some point, Onassis withdrew his interest and the functioning of the refinery was offered with favourable terms to the Niarchos Group. The Group assumed the obligation to 'make various other investments as a compensation for the advantages [it had been given]'.[43]

[37] Ibid., p. 250.

[38] Ibid.

[39] Kazakos, p. 268.

[40] The reference here is to the level of imported investment capital per year (ibid., p. 271).

[41] This is according to the press of the time.

[42] *Bulletin of the Chamber of Commerce and Industry of Athens*, November 1968, 11, pp. 703; 729.

[43] Psalidopoulos, *History*, p. 47.

Yet, it was 'extraordinarily late' in fulfilling such obligations, and it actually never did so. More to the point, after the fall of dictatorship the state bought the refinery back from the Niarchos Group for USD 12 million, and it released the Group 'from its other contractual obligations'.[44]

Apart from this, the dictatorship caused the isolation of Greece in Europe, with the limitation of the 1961 Association agreement to the mutual reduction of tariffs[45] and the freezing of other terms such as 'agricultural harmonisation and financial assistance'.[46] Also, the freezing of the Association Agreement led to a 'deprivation of…credit from the European Investment Bank and to generalised uncertainty'.[47] More broadly, with the dictatorship, relations between Europe and Greece entered a phase of 'controlled crisis', which led to Greece's secession from the Council of Europe in December 1969 'in order to avoid being found guilty of human rights violations'.[48]

More significantly, the growth of the Greek economy during the period was sustained 'mainly by the increase of public expenditure and the relaxation of credit rules'.[49] In other words, the dictatorship disregarded the principles of monetary stability and fiscal discipline that characterised pre-1967 economic policy.[50] As a result, there was an increase of credit as well as of expenditure for large-scale infrastructure works. This in turn increased the state's debt and interest repayments (from 7.8% of the budget in 1966 they rose to 12.4% in 1971), leading to a monetary expansion that caused the overheating of the economy.[51]

The situation deteriorated when the Bretton Woods system of fixed exchange rates collapsed in August 1971.[52] Specifically, the end of dollar convertibility to gold led to an 8% devaluation of the dollar by the end of 1971.[53] The Greek monetary authorities' decision was to keep the

[44] Ibid.

[45] Ibid., p. 42.

[46] Kazakos, p. 289.

[47] Psalidopoulos, *History*, p. 44.

[48] Ibid., p. 290.

[49] Ibid., p. 207.

[50] Ibid.

[51] Ibid., p. 44.

[52] Ibid.

[53] Ibid., p. 15.

existing peg between the dollar and the drachma unchanged (i.e. DRS 30 = USD 1.00), and so, the drachma was also devalued by 8%.[54] It has been argued that pegging the drachma with the dollar probably reflected the Greek governments' 'political priorities', at the time, but did not serve the economy's long-term interests, given that, even during this period of the freezing of the relations with other European countries, the latter absorbed the majority of Greek exports.[55]

In spite of the drachma's devaluation, the country's trade deficit increased (probably also due to the increase in the price of oil) and prices started rising.[56] In February 1972 the drachma was devalued again, following a new devaluation of the dollar.[57] Actually, this was the time when the rapid growth of the economy stopped (see Table 4.1).[58] Also, the first oil crisis in October 1973 led to a dramatic increase of inflation[59]: whereas, up to this point, it rose by 3–4% per year, in 1973 and 1974 it soared to 15.5 and 26.9%, respectively.[60]

Apart from this, according to Kazakos, there was a general sense of destabilisation in the Greek society, caused by the realisation that the political regime was becoming increasingly unstable and fragile.[61] More broadly, seven consecutive years under a military dictatorship had caused public discontent, which was expressed through events such as the students' uprising in the Athens Polytechnic School in November 1973.[62] After the uprising, Georgios Papadopoulos, the leader of the government up to this point, was overthrown 'by a coup from his own right wing'.[63] The coup was organised by Dimitrios Ioannides, formerly the head of the junta's secret police, who established a regime that 'lurched even further to the right'.[64] The social unrest created in such a climate increased

[54] Ibid., p. 271.

[55] Ibid., p. 273.

[56] Ibid., p. 44.

[57] Ibid., p. 45.

[58] Ibid.

[59] Ibid.

[60] Kazakos, p. 268.

[61] Kazakos, p. 287.

[62] Ibid., pp. 287–288.

[63] Thomas G. Gallant, *Modern Greece* (London: Arnold, 2001), p. 202.

[64] Ibid.

even more after the tragic events of July and August 1974, when Turkey invaded Cyprus. The two-phase assault resulted in the killing of more than 3,000 people, the expulsion of more than 180,000 Greek Cypriots from their homes and the occupation of almost 40% of the island, the richest and most developed part of it.[65] These events were a fatal blow for the junta regime, which fell three days after the invasion, on 23 July 1974.[66]

The generalised unrest created in such a framework of events, as well as the bursting of the bubble in the economy in 1973 and 1974, also affected industry. However, it should be noted that it was during the dictatorship that the industrial sector's share of the country's national product reached its highest percentage (28% for the years 1970–1974).[67]

Actually, according to an official announcement of the government on the basis of OECD data, for the twelve-month period February 1971–January 1972, Greece's rate of increase of industrial production was the highest among all OECD member states.[68] In more detail, during the years 1969–1973, there was an 'explosive' growth of building construction, mainly housing.[69] The expansion was partly a result of the sharp increase in migration from the countryside; more specifically, investment in housing comprised 30% of total investment in fixed capital. In any event, it was much higher than in countries such as Portugal (17%) and Spain (18%).[70] Growth in construction also contributed to a growth in manufacturing, as building constructions also needed materials such as cement, timber, etc.[71] An example of a manufacturing industry that benefited from the growth in housing was IZOLA, the two main sectors of

[65] The Republic of Cyprus, 'Press and Information Office', *The 1974 Turkish Invasion and Its Consequences.* http://www.moi.gov.cy/moi/pio/pio.nsf/All/6F5DD418DD053ED1C2256D6D001E7571?OpenDocument [accessed 28.12.2014].

[66] BBC, 'On This Day', *1974: Greek Military Rule Gives into Democracy.* http://news.bbc.co.uk/onthisday/hi/dates/stories/july/23/newsid_2515000/2515819.stm [accessed 28.12.2014].

[67] Source: B. R Mitchell, *International Historical Statistics: Europe 1750–2005* (New York: Palgrave Macmillan, 2007), p. 1038.

[68] *Bulletin of the FGI*, 20,238, 31.05.1972, Annex, p. 33

[69] Thanasis Kalafatis, 'Construction Fever', in *Greece in the 20th Century, 1965–1970*, I Kathimerini – Epta Imeres (Athens: I Kathimerini, 12.12.1999), p. 24.

[70] Psalidopoulos, *History*, p. 272.

[71] Kazakos, p. 270.

which were construction materials and home appliances. In the company's 1970 report of the Board of Governors, the progress made in both sectors was stressed, noting that the increase in sales in comparison to 1969 was 25%.[72]

However, as Psalidopoulos mentions, according to the Bank of Greece the growth in building construction 'could not be considered a favourable factor in the long run, because it [would result] in an unbalanced structuring of production factors'.[73] Recent literature has supported this view; for example, it has been noted that construction 'excessively absorbed entrepreneurial capacity and sources...at the expense of other activities'.[74] Even more so, when the crisis of 1973 emerged, manufacturing also entered a period of stagnation.[75]

Generally, in the 1967–1970 period there was an excessive amount of loan funds channeled to already existing enterprises, something that 'not only reduced the funds available for new productive activities and investments, but also slowed down, according to [the Governor of the Bank of Greece], the transition from family enterprises to...joint stock companies, which offer a wider and more stable basis for the development of entrepreneurial activity'.[76] In this framework, in the midst of the economic downturn in 1974 and a few months before the fall of dictatorship, the president of the Federation of Greek Industrialists, Ioannis Mitsos, referred to the inconsistency characterising the policies the regime undertook for the development of industry. Such policies, noted Mitsos, 'add to the already existing uncertainty because of the international developments, breed entrepreneurial reluctance, make investment planning...difficult, [and] impede export efforts...'.[77]

The deterioration of the economic environment can be indicated by the fact that, in spite of the significant growth of the period,[78] the rate of

[72] The Hellenic Literary and Historical Archive, IZOLA Files, Report of the Board of Governors for 1970, p. 6.

[73] Psalidopoulos, *History*, p. 272.

[74] Kazakos, p. 270.

[75] Ibid., p. 288.

[76] Psalidopoulos, *History*, p. 257.

[77] Georgia M. Panselina and Maria Mavroeidi, *The Federation of Greek Industrialists, 1907–2007 – A Century in the Service of the Idea of Entrepreneurship* (Athens: Economia Publishing, 2007), p. 424.

[78] With the exception of 1974 (see Table 4.1).

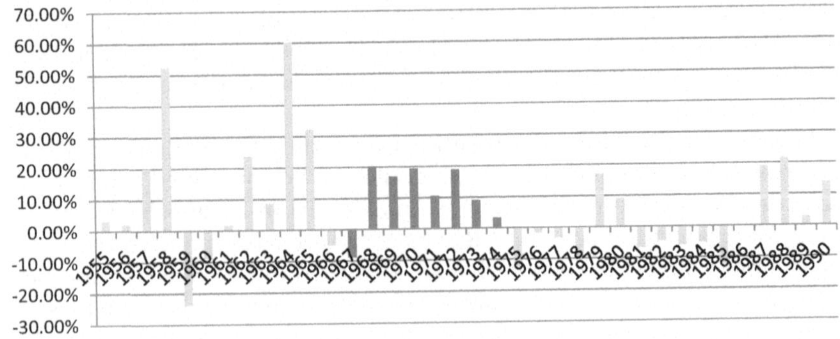

Chart 4.1 Annual rate of increase, gross private investment in fixed capital in manufacturing, 1967–1974 (*Source: Long-term Statistical Series of the Greek Economy*, p. 27)

increase of investment in manufacturing industry throughout dictatorship (1967–1974), although less volatile, was lower than previous years and significantly lower than 1964 and 1965 (see Chart 4.1).

Problems with credit probably contributed to the worsening of the economic environment. Indeed, in spite of the fact that, as noted above, the number of loans given to enterprises increased significantly during the dictatorship, the FGI still complained about the difficulty of securing a loan. This difficulty had to do, among others, with the level of collateral required as well as with the 'obsolete' criteria on the basis of which loan funds were given, i.e. the time-consuming procedures required for the provision of such loan funds.[79]

Many other factors could be examined too; for instance, according to Kazakos, although, in broad terms, the dictatorship followed liberal economic policies, many supporters of the regime envisioned models of development of a socialist type, in which, for example, business initiatives would be undertaken not by business people but by the army.[80] Yet, an additional difficulty was the system of taxation; the period of dictatorship saw particularly significant tax incentives for the promotion of industrial development, however, the system was suffering from a series of weaknesses. In spite of their declarations, the members of the coup did

[79] *Bulletin of the FGI*, 21, 243, 1972, p. 4.

[80] Kazakos, p. 275.

very little to modernise and improve the tax administration structures and reduce corruption. On the contrary, this period witnessed a dismantling of the tax services because of the dismissals of civil servants that were not on good terms with the regime. The rest of this chapter will examine in detail these and similar weaknesses of the tax system, which, as the evidence seems to suggest, was one of the factors posing difficulties to business and therefore also to the industrial sector. This point is in line with William Baumol's argument about how inefficient tax rules have a negative influence on entrepreneurship.

Developments in the System of Taxation During the Dictatorship and the Effect They Had on Industry

The first year of dictatorship saw the introduction of compulsory law 239/1967 (subsequently amended by compulsory law 285/1968). It implemented changes in taxation of individual income, some of which were the reduction of tax rates for all income classes. Aside from this, it also increased specific tax rebates and eliminated all special tax exemptions, 'apart from those that are completely justified on the basis of economic or social reasons'.[81] The purpose of these measures was, according to the report of the Governor of the Bank of Greece, 'the reduction of the tax burden imposed upon sincere taxpayers and the fight against tax evasion'.[82]

Some years later, in December 1971, the Minister of Economics Ioannis Koulis announced a series of similar tax measures that the government had decided to introduce. Among such measures were the elimination of tax exemptions 'for every legal or natural person…in case the exemption does not really serve, or does not serve anymore any economic or significant social purposes' as well as measures against tax evasion. Such measures evolved around the improvement of the 'means of tax control' and also set that each private car would be considered as a presumption of income. Specifically, it was stated that 'each private car…is considered an irrefutable presumption that the…taxpayer earned income equal to 15 times the…road taxes'. Nevertheless, the Minister

[81] *Bank of Greece Governor's Annual Report for 1967*, p. 67.

[82] Ibid.

Table 4.2 Direct taxes over total tax revenues (%), 1958–1975

1958	40.1	1967	40
1959	39.6	1968	40.7
1960	39.6	1969	40.8
1961	39.8	1970	41.7
1962	40.8	1971	43.5
1963	39.9	1972	44.1
1964	40.5	1973	43.2
1965	39.3	1974	47.7
1966	39.4	1975	43.1

Source: Bulletin of the Chamber of Commerce and Industry of Athens, January 1978, 1, p. 69

also announced reductions in the income tax 'leading to total tax reliefs of DRS 1,200 million'. Such reliefs would be translated to a reduction of personal income tax rates of up to 19.2% that would benefit 'both the lower income and urban middle income classes'. Tax reliefs and exemptions were also offered to the 'intellectual classes', that is, 'journalists, writers and artists',[83] probably in an attempt to gain their support.

It is possible that such reliefs and exceptions contributed to the reduction of tax revenue from 1972 to 1974 (see Chart 4.6), in spite of the fact that in the same period there was an important increase in the share of revenue from direct taxation, as Table 4.2 indicates.

The distinguishing characteristic of the system of taxation during the seven-year period of dictatorship was the number of tax laws offering incentives for the promotion of investment. It seems probable that such tax laws were suffering from the complexity that burdened the whole body of tax legislation. Still, the coup regime was, according to Kazakos, the least reluctant of all post-war governments in terms of implementing or increasing the scope of incentives through such laws.[84] For example, law 149 was introduced in 1967, extending until the end of 1970 a series of tax incentives introduced in past years 'for the promotion of the industrial development of the country'.[85] Also, 1967 saw the introduction of

[83] 'The Announcements of the Minister of Economics Mr. Koulis with Regards to the State Budget for 1972', *To Vima*, 12.12.1971, p. 7.

[84] Kazakos, p. 271.

[85] *Bank of Greece Governor's Annual Report for 1967*, p. 67.

compulsory laws 147/1967 and 148/1967[86] offering incentives for the further development of industry and tax incentives for the development of the capital market.[87]

More specifically, compulsory law 148/1967 regarded the promotion and improvement of the function of the capital market in order for it to 'fully contribute to the development of industrial and productive activities in general'.[88] According to the government, the expectation was that small and medium savers' trust would be the 'main driving force…for the promotion of industrial activities in the country', meaning that, by selling their stocks to the exchange market, companies would have more funds available for investment projects.[89] The state would also assist industries undertaking investment through covering part of their repayments of borrowed capital, by allowing them to use increased depreciation rates, but also by offering them 'special tax exemptions'. To this end, the full amount of industries' and mining enterprises' net profits would be tax exempt, provided that such profits would be used for the installation of new facilities or the increase of working capital.[90] In accounting terms, such profits would appear in the companies' balance sheets in the form of special tax-free reserves.

Commenting on laws 147 and 148 of 1967 the Minister of Coordination Nikolaos Makarezos stressed that their introduction served the further development of industry. This was necessary, noted Makarezos, because, in spite of the progress already made up to that point in the secondary sector, 'the achieved results, although important, do not meet the needs of the Greek economy, especially with regard to the request for increasing the speed of development in order to reduce as quickly as possible the distance between the living standards of our own people and that of the people of Western Europe'.[91]

[86] Law 148/1967 was modified and completed with legislative orders 34/1968, 232/1969 and 1314/1972. (Private information supplied, see also the issues of the *Code of the Greek Law Journal* (*Kodikas Nomikou Vimatos*), available in the library of the Athens Bar Association).

[87] *Bulletin of the Chamber of Commerce and Industry of Athens*, August–September 1967, 8–9, p. 535.

[88] Ibid.

[89] Ibid., p. 536.

[90] Ibid.

[91] Ibid.

Makarezos also noted that the views of the 'interested institutions, bodies and organisations' were taken into consideration in the wording of the two laws.[92] Indeed, in a public meeting with Makarezos and representatives of various other bodies and institutions, Dimitrios Marinopoulos, the then president of the FGI, noted that such legislation was 'a good start…the signal that will certainly lead to the promotion of…industrialisation. The…skilful exploitation of the new potential that is now at the disposal of the country's productive forces, depends on you and us, the industrialists. Our cooperation in developing the new productive strategy…is necessary'.[93]

In the same vein, during the announcement of the executive board's annual report for 1967 of the company IZOLA, its President Georgios Drakos, who had also served as the President of the FGI in 1958–1960 and 1962–1966,[94] noted that 'the government resulting from the recent political change undertook courageous economic measures', which were expected to affect the economy positively. What was also expected was the lifting of 'a very few tax measures [that are] not conducive to development'. This would bring, it was noted, 'the satisfactory development of private entrepreneurial initiative, which can flourish only in a framework of tax certainty'.[95]

Such declarations seem to indicate that what the FGI argues today, characterising its stance towards the coup regime as one of a 'tacit disapproval',[96] is not particularly accurate. Besides, the first time that a president of the FGI participated as a permanent member in the committee that was responsible for designing the state's five-year economic plans, was during the dictatorship, and specifically during the creation of the 1968–1972 plan.[97]

That relations between business and the junta were not bad has also been the conventional view in Greece. Still, having doubts about whether

[92] Ibid., p. 535.

[93] Ibid., p. 541.

[94] 'Federation of Greek Industrialists'. http://www.sev.org.gr/online/generic.aspx?id=12&mid=600&lang=gr [accessed 14.12.2014], in Greek.

[95] The Hellenic Literary and Historical Archive, IZOLA Files, Report of the Board of Governors for 1967 (no page number available).

[96] Panselina and Mavroeidi, p. 408.

[97] Ibid., p. 404.

the stance of industrialists towards the regime was indeed one of tacit disapproval does not imply that such a stance was one of an outright approval either. In fact, the matter requires an investigation that goes beyond the scope of the present research. For example, according to George Yannopoulos, apart from the army and the government of the United States, the junta was also supported by the 'economic and financial oligarchy of the country'.[98] However, when offering examples of such oligarchy, Yannopoulos referred to Tom Pappas, the Greek-American entrepreneur behind the establishment of the Esso-Pappas industries in the early 1960s (see pp. 90–91), Pechiney, the French group of companies that established the aluminium producing industry Aluminium of Greece in 1960 (see pp. 61; 91), as well as Greek ship owners.[99] Such examples could by no means be considered representative of the indigenous industrial class, or, even more broadly, the indigenous economic oligarchy of Greece.

More recent research has indicated that different industrialists had different views on the coup and that even within the FGI, there were different voices with regard to what the Federation's official stance towards the regime should be.[100] Also, it seems certain that industrialists' views were shaped by the various policies implemented by the regime. For example, in 1970 the FGI noted the 'understanding and goodwill demonstrated by the government in terms of the satisfactory resolution of [industrial issues]'.[101] On the other hand, the legislative order 1078/1971 entitled 'On tax and other measures for the support of regional development' caused the Federation's 'lively reaction' because it was introduced 'unexpectedly and without prior consultation with the FGI'.[102] Moreover, in 1972 law 147/1967 which offered 100% tax

[98] George Yannopoulos, 'The State of the Opposition Forces Since the Military Coup', in *Greece Under Military Rule*, eds Richard Clogg and George Yannopoulos (London: Secker & Warburg, 1972), pp. 173–174.

[99] Ibid.

[100] Christos Tsakas, 'Greek Business ahead of the European Challenge: State Strategy and Private Interests from the Association with the EEC to Democratic Transition' (unpublished doctoral thesis, University of Crete, 2015), pp. 111–113, in Greek.

[101] Panselina and Mavroeidi, pp. 414–416.

[102] Ibid., pp. 417–420.

exemption of the invested profits of industries and handicraft companies established in the centre of the country[103] expired.[104] Industrialists expressed their disappointment, speaking of 'an evil-eye fate that led to the reversal of a successful policy'.[105]

In more detail, the 31 January 1972 issue of the *Bulletin of the FGI* noted that the 'extremely effective' incentives that this law had introduced led, in the period 1968–1970, to a threefold increase of retained earnings, that were invested 'almost entirely in fixed assets and permanent working capital'. It also considered that whereas in 1965 the level of self-financing (as a result of retained earnings and depreciation reserves) represented 17.5% of the value of gross investment made by industries, it increased to 43% in 1969. The expiry of the law, would lead, according to the industrialists, to a 'suspension of investment with adverse effects in further industrialisation'.[106] However, as Chart 4.1, p. 107 shows, in the 1968–1970 period, which saw, according to the industrialists, a threefold increase of retained earnings, the annual rate of increase of investment was actually much smaller than that of 1965. This was so in spite of the increasing trend in the share of investment in manufacturing over GDP (see Chart 4.3, p. 117) and, among others, again seems to imply that the industrial sector was facing difficulties, even within the context of generous incentives.

As for the regime, they argued that there was no need for law 147/1967 to be extended, because the incentives it provided had already fulfilled the purpose for which they had been introduced.[107] On the contrary, it was noted that what was needed was 'a reform of the legislation of tax incentives in order to promote more intensively the economic development of the periphery'. In simpler terms, a more favourable tax treatment of the 'companies that are established in the less developed areas of the country' was needed.[108]

[103] Centre here means Piraeus and the wider region of Attica ('The Announcements of the Minister of Economics Mr. Koulis with Regards to the State Budget for 1972', *To Vima*, 12.12.1971, p. 7).

[104] *Bulletin of the FGI*, 20, 232, 29.02.1972, p. 2.

[105] Ibid., p. 2.

[106] *Bulletin of the FGI*, 20, 230, 31.01.1972, pp. 8–9.

[107] Ibid., p. 10.

[108] 'The Announcements', p. 7.

Actually, the dictatorship introduced a variety of other incentives too, such as legislative order 1312/1972, regarding new measures for the promotion of regional development.[109] 1972 also saw the introduction of legislative orders 1297/1972 on tax measures for the promotion of mergers and large business,[110] and 1313/1972, on tax measures for the promotion of tourism. In 1973 Royal decree 107 was published regarding the codification of the incentives law 4171/1961, whereas in March 1974 a new legislative order (331/1974) regarding tax incentives for the promotion of industrial production was introduced.[111]

As was the case with the laws 147/1967 and 148/1967, many of the laws just mentioned allowed firms to form special tax-free reserves. As Ulysses Kyriakopoulos, the president of the FGI during the period 2000–2006[112] stressed, the measure of tax-free reserves meant that 'as long as the company invested...part of its profits, it paid less income taxes. In the balance sheets of companies during the 1970s and 1980s there were...series of registers regarding the [tax free] reserves relating to various laws. Whoever asks any large and profitable Greek company he will be told that tax incentives were the best measure for the development of entrepreneurial activities'.[113] Indeed, such registers appear in the balance sheets of both IZOLA and CHROTEX.[114]

[109] This law was modified and completed with the legislative order 1377/1973. (Private information supplied, see also the issues of the *Code of the Greek Law Journal* (*Kodikas Nomikou Vimatos*), available in the library of the Athens Bar Association).

[110] For some, the introduction of such measures did not only serve economic purposes, but also reflected the regime's sociopolitical beliefs. This was argued by the retired tax officer that was interviewed for this research. Referring to Georgios Papadopoulos, the leader of the junta until 1973, the interviewee, noted the following: 'Papadopoulos used to say 'the big number of small family enterprises annoys us'. They were annoyed because the owners of such firms did not belong to governmental parties. Those belonging to the left, the communists, could not find a job in any big firm, so they had to make their own firms. This is why small firms annoyed the capital' (Retired tax officer requesting anonymity, interview data).

[111] Private information supplied, see also the issues of the *Code of the Greek Law Journal*.

[112] Interview data. Kyriakopoulos has been active in the Greek industry since the late 1970s. Apart from having been President of the FGI he has served, inter alia, as the vice president of Business Europe (ex UNICE) and as a member of the General Council of the Bank of Greece.

[113] Ibid.

[114] For information about the two companies see pp. 26–27.

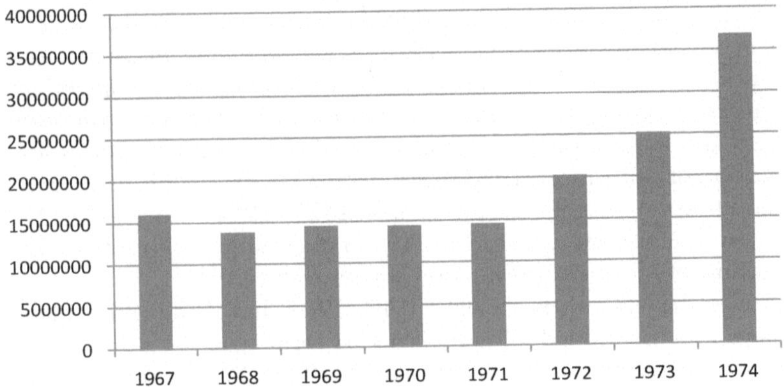

Chart 4.2 CHROTEX S.A., fixed assets' value, 1967–1974 (*Source* CHROTEX Archive, Board of Directors Meeting Minutes, various dates)

However, it is not straightforward to gauge the impact of the tax incentives for such firms. Specifically, with regard to CHROTEX[115] and according to information retrieved from the company's Board Meeting Minutes, in 1968 it indeed decided to buy new technical equipment for one of its factories.[116] It also announced its plans for the establishment of a representative office in Switzerland.[117] In August 1969 the company decided to invest again in new technical equipment,[118] and, one year later, to establish a new commercial company in Switzerland.[119] However, its balance sheets indicate that there was no increasing trend in the value of the company's fixed assets until 1970 (see Chart 4.2, p. 116). Also, in 1973, when it was ranked among the 200 largest industries in Greece, the company took advantage of law 148/1968 and formed a tax-free reserve.[120] However, it is not straightforward to assess to what extent this law contributed to the increase in the value of its fixed assets in 1974, given that this year saw a tremendous increase of inflation. In a

115 No relevant information could be found about IZOLA.

116 CHROTEX archive, Board Meeting Minutes, 17.04.1968, p. 107.

117 Ibid., p. 114.

118 Ibid., Board Meeting Minutes, 04.08.1969, p. 142.

119 Ibid., Board Meeting Minutes, 04.11.1970, pp. 158–159.

120 Ibid., Board Meeting Minutes, 31.03.1973, p. 206.

sense, the company's overall picture seems to imply that, just like the rest of the industry, it was faced with certain difficulties of the Greek economic environment, even during this period of incentives and high levels of investment.

On the whole, the broader picture of the performance of manufacturing during the dictatorship is complex. For example, as already mentioned, industry's share in the national product reached its highest level during the period (see Table 3.3). Also, as Chart 4.3 shows, the annual share of investment in manufacturing over the country's total GDP was continuously increasing during the period. It was, on average, larger than both the pre and post-dictatorship years—specifically, it was 3.86% during 1967–1974 in comparison to 2.69% during 1948–1966 and 2.98% during 1975–1988.

Moreover, as Chart 4.4 shows, the number of enterprises that extended factories and workshops during the dictatorship was larger on average than during the post-dictatorship period and also that of 1962–1966.

However, in spite of such progress, there were also signs that certain characteristics of the economy were posing difficulties to industrial investment. The charts that are illustrated here are merely contextual and cannot provide any direct conclusions of what the situation in the industrial sector was during the period, they offer, however, some relative

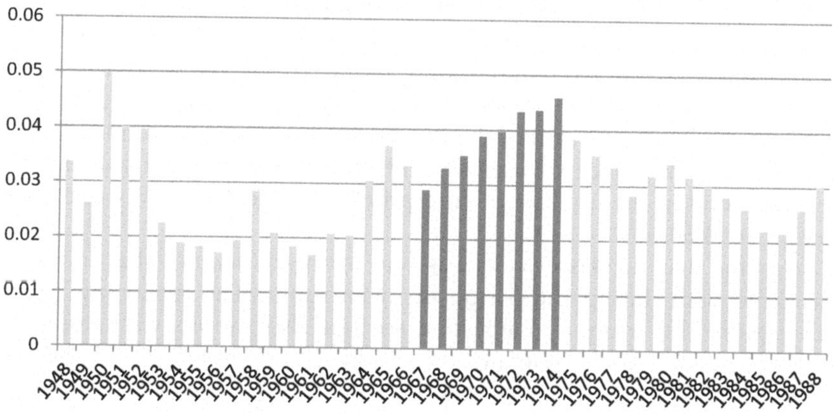

Chart 4.3 Manufacturing, gross private investment in fixed capital, % GDP (1967–1974) (*Source: Long-term Statistical Series of the Greek Economy*, pp. 10; 27)

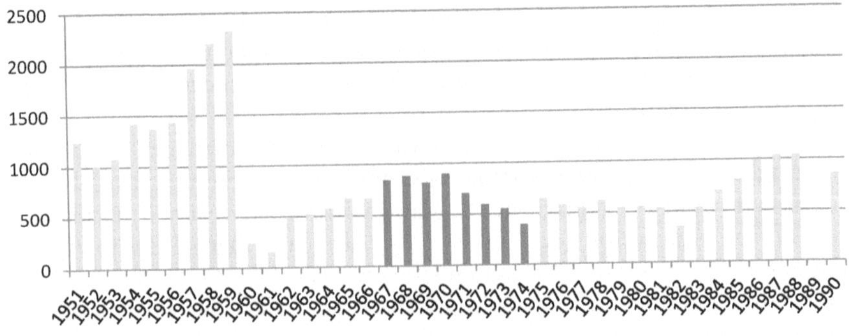

Chart 4.4 Number of extended factories and workshops of industrial and handicraft enterprises, 1967–1974 (*Source: Statistical Yearbook of Greece*, various issues[121])

indications. For example, Chart 4.4 shows that the number of companies that extended factories and workshops during dictatorship was lower than that of the period 1951–1959. Also, as Chart 4.5 shows, the first year of dictatorship saw the largest ever number of new factories and workshops established. On average, however, the number of new factories and workshops established throughout the dictatorship was lower than in the periods 1951–1959 and 1962–1966.[122]

Also, as already, throughout the dictatorship the rate of increase of investment in manufacturing was much more stable than the pre-dictatorship years, but yet significantly lower than in the years 1964 and 1965. Moreover, from 1970 to 1974, the last year of dictatorship, there was a continuous reduction in the number of enterprises' extended factories and workshops (see Chart 4.4), and, throughout the dictatorship, no positive trend in the number of enterprises' new factories and workshops (see Chart 4.5).

It seems that the tax system was one of the difficulties that industry was faced with during the period of dictatorship. The remaining pages will explore the critiques suggesting so, but also various weaknesses of the system, such as the bureaucratic rigidities and complexity of the tax

121 See Chapter 3, p. 42, footnote no. 26.

122 *Statistical Yearbook of Greece*, various issues.

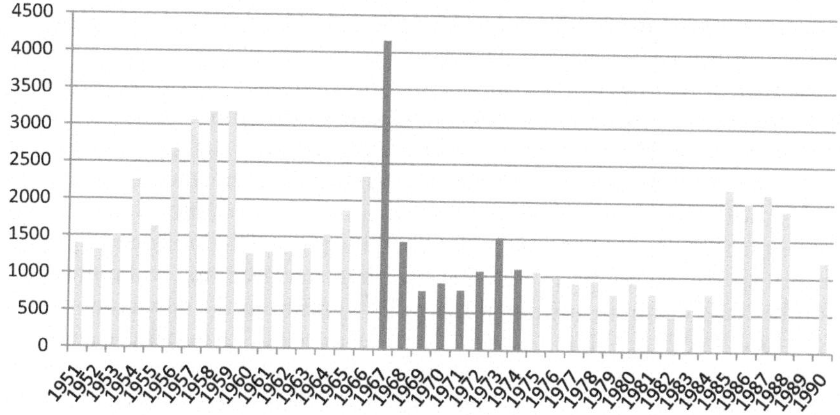

Chart 4.5 Number of new factories and workshops of industrial and handicraft enterprises established, 1967–1974 (*Source: Statistical Yearbook of Greece*, various issues[123])

procedures, the inadequate organisation of the tax bureaus, the confusion caused by tax legislation and the often problematic role of the tax officers.

It has to be noted that, especially in the initial phase of the dictatorship, the critiques regarding not only the tax system but any aspect of governmental policies were relatively few. This reflected not the scarcity of problems but the character of a regime whose leaders had shown a determination to control public expression of opinion: '[f]rom the moment that it was imposed,...the junta introduced preventive censorship in the Press, the literature, the cinema...From 1967 to 1969 censorship was harsh. Every newspaper article, every work of art should be approved by the military officers of the competent committee located in the Ministry of Press.... Writers cease[d] publishing their works in the censored press and stop[ped] printing their books'.[124] Censorship was also provided for in the new constitution the dictators introduced in 1968, which, apart from curbing the freedom of press, also virtually banned strikes and made

[123] See Chapter 3, p. 42, footnote no. 26.

[124] From the introduction of Iakovos Kampannelis' theatrical play 'Our Big Circus' ('Censorship During the Junta', 21.4.2013. http://chatzelenisgeorge.blogspot.co.uk/2013/04/blog-post_21.html [accessed 13.7.2014], in Greek.

'association and assembly…subject to the approval of the administration and the police'.[125]

In such a framework, the newspapers Kathimerini, Mesimvrini, Eleftheria, Athinaiki, Avgi and Dimokratiki Allagi discontinued their issues.[126] As for the media that still operated, they hosted the propaganda of the regime, which also, at the time, introduced severe measures against tax evasion but also civil servants' corruption. A few months after the imposition of the coup, the Deputy Minister of Economics Spyridon Lizardos, representing a government that declared its willingness to 'combat tax evasion in any possible way',[127] announced a new compulsory law (185/1967).[128] The law set the procedures of criminal prosecution against those who were accused of having broken 'paragraph 4 of the 5th article of the Tax Code and article 3 of the legislative order 3848/1958', by affecting the validity of accounting books. In more detail, the law, entitled 'On the imposition of penal sanctions against tax law offenders' stated that owners or managers of Greek companies and managers or representatives of foreign companies based in Greece being accused of such acts would be called before emergency military courts. Chief accounting officers of companies and 'any third person who in any way contributes to acts or omissions that constitute [the accounting books] inaccurate' would also face emergency military courts. The same applied for 'civil servants and any third person… [committing] crimes having to do with bribing'.[129]

It is not clear whether the severity of this law (or, more broadly, the cruel character of the regime) is what persuaded people to be more sincere when declaring their taxable income in the first years of dictatorship. It is noticeable however, that there was an increase in tax revenue in 1968 and 1969. According to the Bank of Greece Governor's annual reports for these years, the increase related to the rise of the national income and

[125] Yanis Yanoulopoulos, 'Greece: Political and Constitutional Developments 1924–1974', in *Greece in Transition, Essays in the History of Modern Greece 1821–1974*, ed John T. A. Koumoulides (London: Zeno, 1977), pp. 88–89.

[126] Robert McDonald, *Pillar & Tinderbox, The Greek Press and the Dictatorship* (New York: Marion Boyars, 1983), p. 28.

[127] *Bulletin of the Chamber of Commerce and Industry of Athens*, August–September 1967, 8–9, p. 457.

[128] Ibid., November–December 1967, 11–12, p. 646.

[129] Ibid., August-September 1967, 8–9, p. 457.

to the measures against tax evasion undertaken by the government, which contributed to the 'better capture of the tax base'.[130]

More significantly, according to Lizardos, the penal and administrative sanctions that the law provided for the types of offences mentioned above, such as imprisonment, imposition of large fines and loan-granting bans, were 'severe and economically devastating'.[131] For the cases of bribes, it was stated that 'any civil servant belonging to the Ministry of Economics, demanding or accepting gifts or other inappropriate benefits, or [demanding or accepting] the promise [of such gifts or other inappropriate benefits] in order for him to perform or omit a specific act relating to...tax matters, in the future or presently, will be punished with one year imprisonment'.[132]

The penalty of one-year imprisonment for similar offences had applied since the 1950s (see Chapter 3). However, it seems that in the authoritarian regime the junta had established, the threat of punishment was much more credible than in the past. Indeed, it has been noted in a relevant documentary that 'there were military courts from the first till the last day of dictatorship. Four and a half thousand trials, two trials per day'.[133]

More broadly, in an illiberal regime that did not hesitate to imprison, displace and even torture and put to death those it considered to be dissidents,[134] it seems that it was to everyone's interest to obey, or to appear as if obeying the law, and, generally, to try to avoid confronting the government and its disciplinary mechanisms. Tax officers could be no exception to the rule. Besides, the regime aimed to convince them about this, using strong language to condemn the instances of corrupt civil servants, and, for all other cases, employing a discourse comprised of a mixture of patriotic rhetoric, advice, warnings and veiled threats.

For example, a few months after the imposition of the coup, in a congress of tax officers organised in the Athens College of

[130] Bank of Greece, *Bank of Greece Governor's Annual Report for 1968* (Athens: Bank of Greece, 1969), p. 70 and *Bank of Greece Governor's Annual Report for 1969* (Athens: Bank of Greece, 1970), p. 69.

[131] *Bulletin of the Chamber of Commerce and Industry of Athens*, August–September 1967, 8–9, p. 457.

[132] Ibid., November–December 1967, 11–12, p. 647.

[133] 'The trial of the junta' (10′:47″-11′:00″).

[134] Freris, p. 162.

Commerce,[135] the regime's Minister of Economics Adamantios Androutsopoulos stressed in his speech that it was true that, 'maybe unfairly so, when the Greeks hear about civil servants having no integrity, they think of tax officers...We have to convince Greek taxpayers that this is not the case. Most important, we have to convince so ourselves'.[136] Acknowledging that lately there had been cases in which 'worthless civil servants fell short of their mission and of the Greek people's expectations', Androutsopoulos addressed tax officers with the following words:

> I would like you to do your job bearing in mind...the presumption that you are honest, that you have integrity and that you do all you can to perform your duties in the best possible way. Take initiatives. Being scared and avoiding responsibilities will not be forgiven...[r]egardless of your beliefs about...relations with the state, if any of you...do not have the moral strength to courageously perform your duties as civil servants,...if [you] do not want to remain on board the ship, you can state so. [Because], when in the middle of the sea, no mutiny will be allowed.[137]

Androutsopoulos also noted that the state's fiscal mechanisms should become quick and responsive to 'the new national circumstances', but also to 'the Common Market with the problems it creates'. He did not omit to give relevant advice to the wider population too: 'a Greek person should face the state not as a poor person, but as a proud citizen, because, in one way or another, he has become a great warrior..., a diligent farmer, a bold seaman, a progressive immigrant, but he never fully became...a Western-type citizen. [In] his relations with the state...[he always had] the perception of a poor person dealing with a tyrant. We have to dispel such perceptions...'.[138]

Ironic as this latter reference to tyranny may sound, coming from a person who was serving as a Minister of a dictatorial regime, it was indicative of the tone with which the leaders of the dictatorship addressed citizens with regard to their relations to the state. In the same congress,

[135] This institution is now called the Athens University of Economics and Business.

[136] 'There need to be corrections and modifications in the fiscal mechanisms and individual responsibility of the taxpayers; The Minister and the Deputy Minister of Economics spoke in a congress of tax officers', *Makedonia*, 19.08.1967, p. 7.

[137] Ibid.

[138] Ibid.

the Deputy Minister of Economics Spyridon Lizardos stressed that in the 'new Greek state' that the regime was going to establish, problematic 'methods, systems [and] perceptions should be forgotten, remaining only as a memory of a standard that discerns the bad past from a period of…regeneration'; now, the people and the state should develop a spirit of cooperation:

> Excesses and transgressions should and will be eliminated. The state makes peace with citizens through its affection and reaffirms the rigour of the law through its [system of] justice. The state's services should…[treat] citizens properly and with fairness…[e]ach one of you… are the bearers of this duty, and there is no more room for complacency…, in face of the…great moments our country lives, desiring to put an end to misery, utilise its power… and, in the teeth of any [opposition], stand proud and with the head up…'[139]

Referring to what the behaviour of tax officers towards taxpayers should be, Lizardos' patriotic and semi-paternalistic rhetoric gave way to warnings and veiled threats:

> In order to restore the good function of the tax authorities as far as their relations with the taxpayers are concerned, we have to establish…real tax fairness by all means. You know, however, how much we are lagging behind in this area, [in] terms of spirit, organisation, means and method. The spirit of tax fairness….is at a very low level in our country. Such a situation is not acceptable anymore…On this matter, you bear the greatest responsibility…the national government holds you accountable…for handling your responsibilities in the best possible way. Extremism will not be tolerated. We need sound judgment, correct, impartial and fair handling of every case…[T]he latest deplorable incidents of bribes, which, once again, vilified the services and shook society's confidence, must never be repeated. And they will never be repeated, because…, in this case, the law will be [implemented] to the full extent and with exhaustive rigour. The national army rose up in order to establish a state that is moral and just towards all the people…[E]veryone should understand and believe that such aberrations, which will dishonour the state unless…the body of civil servants

[139] Ibid.

> cleanses itself from such worthless and immoral [members], will be treated with ruthless severity.[140]

Such kind of discourse is what probably urged the trade union of tax officers 'in the framework of celebrations for the first anniversary of the Revolution of the 21 April' in 1968 to endorse a resolution through which '[they] declared that 1) The Revolution of the 21st April is the Revolution of the real Democracy, 2) They repudiate[d] any effort to defame as criminal the efforts of the Revolution and that 3) [They] placed their forces at the disposal of the National Revolution'.[141] To such a declaration might have contributed also the regime's announcements of 'new dismissals' of civil servants (some of whom were tax officers) that were considered to be 'disloyal, lacking the required social standing for the exercise of their office, or having a conduct incompatible to their service'.[142]

Generally, it seems that the regime's rhetoric but also the censorship it imposed probably explain why, apart from the points raised by the various Ministers of the regime in their public speeches, in the first years of dictatorship very few critiques appeared in the daily press with regard to the tax officers' behaviour and role. In other words, it seems that, on the one hand, it was in the interest of tax officers to perform their duties in a way that would keep them away from the military courts of the time, while, on the other, it also seems that censorship suppressed the reporting of problems in the relations between taxpayers and tax officers. This would suggest that the dictators' directions were not followed, and this revelation would damage the image of the state.

In broad terms, the situation remained the same throughout the seven-year period of dictatorship. However, the degree of censorship reduced. Specifically, according to Alexandros Argyriou, censorship became less strict from March 1969, when 'foreign radio stations broadcast[ed] the recorded message of the Greek poet and Nobel laureate Georgios Seferis, speaking of "the state of compulsory hibernation" and "anomaly" the Greek people had to live in'.[143] It seems that the lifting of censorship

[140] Ibid.

[141] 'Meeting of Tax Officers Yesterday', *To Vima*, 16.04.1968, p. 8.

[142] 'New Dismissals of officers', *Makedonia*, 02.03.1968, p. 1.

[143] From the introduction of Iakovos Kampannelis' theatrical play 'Our Big Circus'. Alexandros Argyriou was a literature historian and a critic.

contributed also to the fact that the Council of Europe exerted pressure on the junta for the restoration of individual liberties.[144] On 7 October 1969 censorship was officially abolished and,[145] thereupon, the 'perpetual promotion of the regime gave way to hard news coverage, much of it implicitly critical'.[146]

Of course, this change did not mean absolute freedom of press, given that 'the prohibition remained against attacking the present regime or promoting the former'.[147] The situation was 'fraught with pitfalls' for journalists, which, however, indirectly expressed their opposition to the regime, by highlighting, for example, the struggle against dictatorial regimes in other countries.[148] Still, the expression of opinion had its price: 'The colonels retaliated against the press by using covert measures of economic punishment. Circulation was interrupted. Newsprint taxes were applied in proportion to circulation which hit hardest at the popular opposition papers. State advertising was placed selectively and loan facilities which required government authorisation were denied to opposition publishers. The revenue department was used to make harassing inspections and to levy punitive sums of tax'.[149]

In spite of this reality, it seems that official abolition of censorship contributed to the increase in the number of references regarding problematic aspects of the system of taxation from 1970 onwards. For example, in the 29 February 1972 issue of the *Bulletin of the FGI*, industrialists complained about the low level of depreciation rates. Specifically, it was stressed that for the first year of the 'life' of every piece of mechanical equipment, the maximum depreciation rate in Greece was '8%,[150] in comparison to 40% in France, 20% in Germany, 35% in Italy, 30% in Sweden [and] 60% in Britain...'.[151] Low depreciation rates delayed the renewal of mechanical equipment, reducing thus the effectiveness of

[144] McDonald, pp. 58–59.

[145] Ibid., p. 65.

[146] Ibid., p. 67.

[147] Ibid.

[148] Ibid., p. 68.

[149] Ibid., p. 70.

[150] This rate applied in the zones A and B, that is in Athens, Piraeus and the wider region of Attica.

[151] *Bulletin of the FGI*, 20, 232, 29.02.1972, p. 2.

various relevant incentives that the state had introduced. For the FGI, the state policies on this matter indicated 'confusion and inconsistency', because, 'on the one hand the State implores industry to modernise its mechanical equipment and on the other prevents it from doing so by limiting depreciation rates to 8%, considering perhaps that in this way it will have more revenue from taxation in the short run, without realising what itself and the whole economy lose in the long run because of the technological backwardness in production...'. 'It is...very dangerous', continued the article, 'to treat industry as a kind of an experimental animal for development, [t]o try to compromise the State's need for revenues with industry's modernisation'.[152]

In the 31 May 1972 issue of the *Bulletin of the FGI* there was also a critique about taxes in favour of third parties. Specifically, it was noted here that 'the state's advice and requests to industry regarding the [reduction] of production costs to competitive levels could have practical value if they were accompanied by...measures that would eliminate a series of...charges that have nothing to do with production', meaning the 'various taxes in favour of third parties', a reality of the past that was 'unacceptable'.[153]

References to the problematic role of the tax authorities also increased in this period, coming mostly from tax experts but also tax officers themselves. There also appeared some references in the press regarding cases of corruption. One such involved the arrest of a tax officer after having been accused of extortion by a taxpayer in June 1972. The regime's representatives commented on the incident using the type of discourse they were familiar with; specifically, the Deputy Prime Minister of the government Stylianos Pattakos declared, among others, that 'delays...cause, on the one hand, the...citizen's dissatisfaction and on the other...force him to form an unworthy transaction with vicious and opportunist intermediaries or with disloyal civil servants, in order to achieve the speeding-up of the procedures...'.[154]

A significant amount of critique during the time had to do with the problem of bureaucracy. For example, in November 1971 the

[152] Ibid., 20, 231, 15.02.1972, pp. 1–2.

[153] Ibid., 20, 238, 31.05.1972, pp. 3–4

[154] 'The Tax Officer Has Been Brought Before the Interrogator', *Ta Nea*, 22.06.1972, p. 12.

Viomichaniki Epitheorissis magazine referred to the 'Herculean task of exterminating the lernaean hydra of bureaucracy', as it characterised 'the new "campaign" of the Government for the lifting of the purposeless, complex...procedures...which make it impossible for the state mechanisms to function properly, undermine the efforts for progress in our country and prevent the improvement of the relations between citizens and the State'.[155]

Similar points were made by the FGI too, which through its Bulletin noted that, among others, bureaucratic incompetence adversely impacted upon economic development: '[T]he mistakes of the public administration', it was noted, 'burden the whole of the national economy, having usually immensely inhibitive effects on economic progress.'[156]

There were also references about the lack of uniform criteria and principles governing the audits, the complexity and frequency of change of the various tax laws, but also the tax officers' training needs. As for their arbitrariness, it was very often associated with the way the tax laws had been constructed.[157] For example, in a speech that was published in the *Tax Review* in December 1972, Stephanos Sellas, a tax official, noted that, although in the past twenty years the tax services had seen important improvements, there were not any specific regulations governing the way tax audits should be conducted. The available laws contained the provisions that should be implemented in the audits, but they did not include any information about how the audits should be carried out. There only existed the Code of the Status of Civil Servants (Law 1811/1951) which referred, in general terms and among others, to the civil servants' responsibilities and rights, containing also general guidelines about the rules and official orders governing the conduct of civil servants belonging to the Ministry of Economics. In spite of its generality, 'it would have been desirable', noted Sellas, 'that every tax auditor had a clearer view of such texts when taking an oath [in order to assume his duties], and that every tax officer had a copy of [the Code]...I urge you all...to study this [Code]'.[158]

[155] Vovolini Archive, *Viomichaniki Epitheorissis*, Vol. 38, November 1971, 445, p. 11.

[156] *Bulletin of the FGI*, 20, 239, 15.06.1972, p. 3.

[157] Stefanos M. Sellas, 'Problems Relating to Social Psychology During Tax Audits', *The Tax Review*, December 1972, 287, pp. 957–958.

[158] Ibid.

In the same year, in a commentary about, among others, the compulsory law 185/1967 against tax law offences analysed above, Theodoros Staikos, a tax expert, noted that the law was 'a sword of Damocles' that 'unexpectedly criminalised the country's economic life, being introduced without the prior...establishment of modern Economic Laws, and being based mostly on the excessive formalism [and] improvisation of the Tax Code'.[159] Criticising the Tax Code and characterising it as an 'experimentation...against [the] [n]ational [e]conomy, being subject to constant modifications', Staikos noted that due to the complexity of the various provisions of the Code, taxpayers' accounting books were usually found to be inaccurate. Owing to this, taxpayers would have to face 'a) the imposition of a fine, b) the arbitrary assessment of gross revenue for multiple fiscal years with the use of the maximum net profit rate and without taking into consideration business expenses, and c) a criminal prosecution'.[160] The phrase 'you will either compromise or I will audit [your books]', continued Staikos, 'should stop being heard and we should, at last...introduce in our country too the modern accounting and audit systems that apply in the healthy economies of the EEC countries'. Staikos noted that in such systems, accounting and auditing principles were based on scientific methods and offered the ability to conduct audits on an individualised but also secure basis.[161]

The law 185/1967 was criticised also in the *Bulletin of the FGI*, again with regard to the lack of uniformity in auditing rules. Here, it was noted that, according to a tax expert, 'having three tax officers separately auditing the accounting books of a large company and making the same assessment for the level of its [taxable] income, would be a random coincidence, under the current tax regime'.[162] It was also recorded that tax experts agreed that the lack of accounting control mechanisms, the lack of any certain criteria that would allow the distinction between tax evasion and tax avoidance but also the arbitrary penalisation of certain acts made the law unacceptable. It was clear, the article continued, 'that the prosecution in penal courts as "offenders against the law" of large numbers of

[159] Theodoros Staikos, 'The Problem of Tax Audits', *The Tax Review*, February 1972, 277, pp. 81–82.

[160] Ibid., p. 82.

[161] Ibid., p. 83.

[162] *Bulletin of the FGI*, 17, 195, 15.08.1970, p. 1.

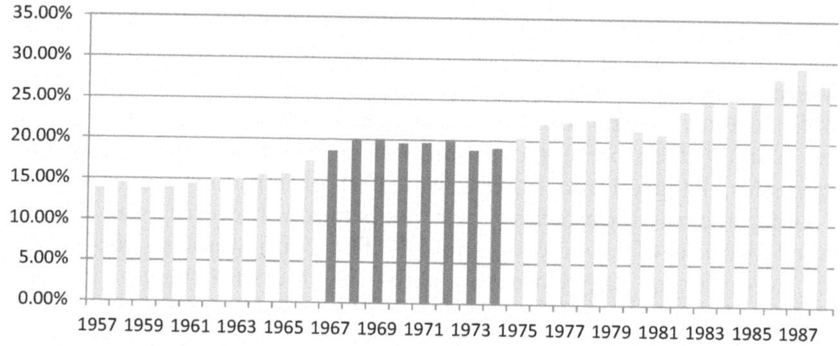

Chart 4.6 Tax revenue, % GDP (1967–1974) (*Source: Long-term Statistical Series of the Greek Economy*, pp. 13; 86–87)

companies that are perfectly reputable and have an excellent tax-paying record' was a result of provisions that were not well-thought-of. Overall, the article stressed that the law needed to change, because some parts of it were 'clear disincentives for private entrepreneurial initiative'.

It should also be noted that in spite of its severity, with the exception of the first years of its implementation, the law did not seem particularly effective in terms of increasing tax revenues. This is indicated by the fact that, as Chart 4.6 shows, after 1969 there was no clear positive trend in the ratio of Tax Revenues/GDP. More broadly, in the Bank of Greece Governor's annual reports for 1972, 1973 and 1974 there were no references on any reduction of tax evasion or improvement of the function of the tax services, as was the case in the reports for previous years, such as 1968, 1969 and 1971.[163]

Indeed, it seems that there was not any improvement in the function of the tax services throughout the seven years of dictatorship. On the contrary, during the coup the problems in the broader public sector grew much larger, something that undoubtedly adversely affected the

[163] As noted previously, in the reports for 1968 and 1969 the increase in tax revenues was attributed to the increase of the national income and the measures against tax evasion that contributed to the better capture of the tax base. Also, in the report for 1971 it was noted that the better capture of the tax base due to the 'further improvement of the function of the tax services' might had contributed to such an increase in tax revenues for that year (Bank of Greece, *Bank of Greece Governor's Annual Report for 1971* (Athens: Bank of Greece, 1972), pp. 83–84).

tax services too. The case of George Langrod indicated some of the issues in the public sector. As noted in the previous chapter, he visited Greece in 1963 in order to offer advice for the reorganisation of the public services (see pp. 68–69). According to Argyriades, certain obstacles existed which prevented promotion of research in administration. Argyriades, Langrod and others, were part of a group that attempted to overcome such obstacles, their cooperation however, was discontinued because of the dictatorship.[164] The coup was also the reason why, according to Argyriades, the 'ambitious' ideas for the creation of a School of Public Administration following 'more or less' the model of the National School of Administration (ENA) in France did not materialise at that point.[165]

Generally, as Zolotas noted in 1975, the dictatorship left public organisations and the broader public administration in a state of 'generalised disruption'.[166] In more detail, in the last pages of the previous chapter, it was noted that, with regard to the system of tax administration, the dictatorship led to the demise of the Central Service of the Ministry of Economics, a structure of the system of taxation that operated relatively satisfactorily up to this point, in comparison to what followed next. According to Charalampos Nikolakopoulos, the former president of the trade union of tax officers, the Central Service 'had the executive role of administration and legislating. That is, it was focused on the administrative issues of the tax services throughout the country (transfers of officers, payroll, etc.) and on creating tax legislation such as the VAT, taxes according to the Code of Accounting Books and Records, etc'.[167] Ioannis Photopoulos, who served as an executive of the Service during the period 1965–1981, noted:

> When I entered the Central Service in 1965, the procedure followed was this one: there was a need of…ten people for permanent posts in

164 Argyriades, 'Ethics and Governance', pp. 3–4.

165 Ibid., p. 2. This school, called The National Centre for Public Administration and Local Government, was finally established in 1983 (Argyriades, p. 3 and 'National Centre for Public Administration and Local Government', *Mission* http://www.ekdd.gr/ekdda/index.php/en/2012-06-29-09-59-33) [accessed 2.11.2014], in Greek).

166 Xenophon Zolotas, *Our Economic Problem – A TV discussion* (Athens: The Bank of Greece – Surveys and Talks Archive, 1975) p. 8.

167 Nikolakopoulos, interview excerpt.

> the Service. First, the responsible inspectors recommended the thirty best employees from the peripheral services of the ministry. They were highly knowledgeable, had executive capacities, spoke foreign languages, etc. Out of those thirty people, who would be seconded to the ministry for two years, the ten best would be chosen. Those ten best would be transferred to the Central Service of the ministry, with increased responsibilities but also higher wages. Within those two years, a thorough evaluation of the candidates' operational capabilities took place. At the end of this strictly supervised procedure, reports of operational capacity were produced. Those of the thirty who were not finally chosen…, went back to the peripheral services they had come from, with absolutely no negative reference or suspicion with regards to their capabilities and competences in their role as employees of the ministry. In other words, this Central Service, in which I was privileged to be chosen to work, functioned perfectly. We had a great library, and generally, we were offered all the necessary means in order to faultlessly implement the decisions of the various governments, without however being subjected to any influences from them.[168]

The Service was essentially dismantled after 1967, as the junta regime 'dismissed a large number of capable employees for political reasons'.[169] From this point onwards, noted Photopoulos, the members of the Service came directly from the peripheral tax offices, lacking the necessary training and executive capabilities. The argument that tax officers did not receive the necessary training was supported also by the retired tax officer mentioned previously, who joined the Ministry of Economics in January 1974, a few months before the fall of the dictatorship: 'We had no training. I was given a post in a department and the director used to tell me what to do. If your manager wanted you to learn, you would learn. If not, he kept the knowledge to himself and you were asked to do all the dull work'.[170]

Adding to this point, in an article originally written in 1995, Photopoulos noted that the dismantling of the Central Service of the Ministry of Economics by the dictatorial government 'was a severe blow to the creation of executives of high scientific standards; its results became obvious several years later, with the decline in the quality of the tax bills

[168] Photopoulos, interview excerpt.

[169] Ibid.

[170] Retired tax officer requesting anonymity, interview data.

that were proposed in the Parliament and of the interpretative statements issued [by the Ministry of Economics] in cases of controversial [tax] matters'.[171] Confirming Photopoulos' point in a more general sense, Kazakos noted that the people the junta appointed as executives in the various ministries were 'distinctively uneducated'.[172]

Indeed, in order to understand how the generalised disruption of the public services (part of which were the tax services too) manifested itself during dictatorship, one has to examine what measures the junta undertook in order to achieve the modernisation of the civil service it had been proclaiming since 1967. In the same manner, one needs to examine whether the dictators' fervent condemnations of corruption had any real impact on the public services. In such terms, it should be noted that the junta indeed dismissed a large number of civil servants, but no reliable information has been found about whether such dismissals were on grounds of corruption or incompetency. On the contrary, there has been a considerable amount of material suggesting that the modernisation the regime had declared failed. This is because, in spite of the regime's rhetoric for the need to eradicate corruption, reorganise and clean up the public sector, the dismissals of civil servants were made not on the basis of their integrity and professional capabilities, but, as Photopoulos noted, on the basis of whether or not they were loyal to the regime.

For example, on 26 April 1967, five days after the imposition of the dictatorship, the junta announced a plan for the 'reorganization of government administration',[173] with Stylianos Pattakos, the Minister of Internal Affairs, declaring that '[n]epotism, corruption and demagoguery must be purged from the government'.[174] In the same manner, on 3 May 'the abolition of bureaucracy' was announced,[175] with the cabinet deciding 'the obligation of all civil servants to defend their actions on application by citizens, within 3 days for simple cases and 7 days for more complicated affairs', and also stressing that '[i]ntervention by [third]

[171] Ioannis Photopoulos, 'The Administration of the Greek Tax System', *Enterprise*, reprint, issue 63, 2010, p. 896.

[172] Kazakos, pp. 269–270.

[173] Peter Schwab and George D. Frangos, *Greece Under the Junta* (New York: Facts on File, 1970), p. 24.

[174] Ibid., pp. 24–25.

[175] Ibid., p. 25.

parties, influence peddlers and contact men in government is prohibited'.[176] Peter Schwab and George Frangos noted that the regime also drafted three decrees '[providing] for the termination of the term in office of 'all special advisers and senior officials of state organizations…as well as for the abolition of certain provisions which are opposed to the common sentiment of justice and morality'.[177]

However, according to the historian Thomas Gallant, '[most of the dictators'] domestic initiatives were aimed at removing anyone whose loyalty to the regime was suspect…'.[178] Indeed, in the text of the three decrees the regime produced it was stated that '[c]ivil servants…are formally dismissed…if their disloyalty is established; the provisions of the constitution concerning irremovability [of civil servants] and all those protecting labor agreements are suspended in the cases referred to'.[179] Those accused of disloyalty would be the ones found to have and/or promote 'Communist or anti-national ideas', or those who had 'any form of contact or relations with the holders of these opinions'.[180] For the verification of loyalty, the decrees stated that 'all…civil servants…must submit to the responsible minister…a written declaration of their loyalty…'.[181]

According to a documentary focusing on the period and characterising the regime's declared principles of meritocracy as 'only imaginary',[182] the dictatorship dismissed hundreds of thousands of civil servants that were not 'approved of',[183] giving their posts to people who were friendly to the regime.[184] For example, a large number of teachers who were considered to be 'dangerous' were fired and replaced by retired teachers. Younger

176 Ibid.

177 Ibid.

178 Gallant, p. 199.

179 Schwab and Frangos, p. 25.

180 Ibid.

181 Ibid., p. 27.

182 'The Time Machine (I Mihani tou Chronou): The Dictatorship's fascism and spoils' (23:20–24:18), in Greek (available here: https://www.youtube.com/watch?v=x0lVB0-Cl8s). The documentary aired in NET, subsequently NERIT, the state-owned public broadcaster in Greece.

183 Ibid.

184 Ibid., 25:00–25:08.

teachers were hired only with a 'certificate of social ideals'.[185] Also, it has been noted that, in order to better control the public sector, the dictators usually appointed retired military officers in key positions in it, giving them the title of the 'Commissioner of the Administration'.[186]

The fact that no actual modernisation of the civil service took place was something even followers of the regime admitted. For example, in November 1967, only seven months after the imposition of the coup, Savvas Konstantopoulos, the publisher of the newspaper *Free World* that supported the dictatorial regime, admitted, in a letter he sent to Konstantinos Karamanlis, that the 'revolution' had failed in achieving its goal to 'resolve some permanent…problems in order to… make a step of progress and normalise public life'.[187] Among the reasons for such failure, wrote Konstantopoulos, was that almost none of those in the government had political skills and none was willing to use the services of competent technocrats: 'Part of the military officers proclaimed that people which [in the past] had some public role should not get involved in the revolution. Thus, they turned to those who were incompetent or inexperienced'.[188] The 'revolution's' failure, continued Konstantopoulos, was also due to the fact that there was often a complete lack of any serious organisation: 'Solemnly taken decisions were recalled. Laws that had been published at the Government's Gazette were withdrawn. Measures that had been already communicated, changed from one moment to the next'. In such a state, continued Konstantopoulos, 'the Government does not move forward; it is like a car stuck in the mud. No progress has been made in the education and the administration, in spite of the fact that it has been seven months since the 21st of April. No revolutionary measures and no profound changes [have been implemented]'.[189]

185 Ibid., 12:25–12:40. Certificates of social ideals were 'public certificates which were issued by a competent authority (the army or the police) and attested that the citizens [who had them] were not, themselves or other members of their family, communists, or even friendly to communist ideals' (Athanasios Karafillis, 'Certificates of social ideals: A case of social justice or injustice in the selection of candidate students for the Pedagogical Academies'. http://eriande.elemedu.upatras.gr/?section=985&language=el&page706=1&itemid706=1113 [accessed 11.1.2016], in Greek.

186 'The Dictatorship's Fascism and Spoils', 44:23–44:42.

187 The 'Konstantinos G. Karamanlis' Foundation, Konstantinos G. Karamanlis Archive Vol. 07, *A Period of Ordeal, 1963–1974* (Period B', 21.4.1967–24.7.1974), pp. 49–50.

188 Ibid., p. 50.

189 Ibid.

In the same vein, Yannopoulos, writing in 1972, noted that even the Greeks who initially tolerated the junta were now 'critical of the regime's inability to cope with the country's basic problems. The lack of any political programme and the low quality of the junta's collaborators are evidence enough that the regime cannot claim to lead the country towards modernization'.[190]

Also, it was proven over time that the regime's anti-corruption rhetoric was mostly a facade. Even its supporters acknowledged that political 'nefariousness' had re-emerged, taking often the form of self-promotion but also personal favours and spoils towards friends and relatives.[191] Indeed, in the documentary mentioned above it was stressed that 'the junta was denouncing clientelism, yet it did spoils all the time. Whatever one needed, e.g. an export license, etc., he had to turn to the military officers'.[192] Moreover, in spite of the fact that the regime proclaimed its willingness to enforce a sound and honest administration system, the wage of the Prime Minister more than doubled and that of Ministers and Deputy Ministers increased from DRS 22,400 to DRS 35,000.[193] Members of the government also took advantage of their position in order to benefit friends or members of their families.[194] For example, relatives or friends of the dictators were given governmental posts;[195] Papadopoulos, the leader of the government up to November 1973, appointed his brothers to high-ranking positions in the public sector[196] and public works of many million drachmas were awarded to relatives of the vice president of the Cabinet and Minister of Internal Affairs Stylianos

[190] Yannopoulos, 'The State of the Opposition Forces', p. 173.

[191] The 'Konstantinos G. Karamanlis' Foundation, Konstantinos G. Karamanlis Archive Vol. 07, *A Period of Ordeal, 1963–1974* (Period B', 21.4.1967–24.7.1974), p. 50.

[192] 'The Dictatorship's Fascism and Spoils', 8:56–9:37.

[193] This was done through compulsory law 5/1967 ('Iospress', *The Forgotten Scandals of the 'Nation-Saving' Revolution* http://www.iospress.gr/ios2010/ios20100725.htm [accessed 2.12.2015], in Greek).

[194] 'The Dictatorship's fascism and spoils', 22:20–22:50.

[195] Ibid., 34:12–34:29.

[196] Ibid., 22:20–22:50.

Pattakos,[197] the same person who, in 1967, declared that corruption and nepotism should be 'purged'.[198]

It has also been argued that those who were close to the regime were able to receive very generous business loans.[199] Indicative of this was the case of Pavlos Totomis, president of the Hellenic Industrial Development Bank (ETVA). He had also served as a Minister of Public Order of the junta, and was accused of illegally providing loans during that period. According to the press of the period, more than DRS 1.5 billion were squandered from ETVA. After the fall of the regime, Totomis was sentenced to more than four years imprisonment.[200]

Because of such developments, as Dimitras notes, the Greek people realised at some point that 'the junta had failed to "purify" political life and was gradually becoming a regime with long term aspirations and of a "corrupted" nature similar to its predecessors'.[201]

In such a framework, and because the situation described above referred to the public sector as a whole, one realises that during the seven-year period of dictatorship there was not any improvement in the function of the tax services. Sources suggest that civil servants were judged not on the basis of their capability to adequately perform their duties but on whether they were friendly to the regime or not. Equally, the lack of any actual modernisation in the system of public administration has indicated that the situation in fact deteriorated during the dictatorship. Moreover, perhaps part of the body of tax officers had become less arbitrary in their decisions out of fear of been accused of breaking the law and having to face the emergency military courts of the time (something that cannot be certain due to the lack of reliable sources during the period). This, however, did not indicate any actual improvement in their professional capabilities. It seems that the policies of the junta guaranteed the deepening of the dismantling of the public services. Therefore, the tax system

[197] Ibid., 38:10–38:53 and 'The General Secretariat of the Government', *Georgios Papadopoulos Government*. http://www.ggk.gov.gr/?p=1261 [accessed 9.12.2015], in Greek.

[198] See p. 28.

[199] 'The Dictatorship's Fascism and Spoils', 40:20–40:40.

[200] Ibid., 40:46–41:44.

[201] Panayote Elias Dimitras, 'Changes in Public Attitudes', in *Political Change in Greece Before and After the Colonels*, eds Kevin Featherstone and Dimitrios K. Katsioudas (London: Croom Helm, 1987), p. 66.

kept on contributing to the degree of uncertainty in the economy. This would become clearer in subsequent years, which saw a slowing down of the rate of economic growth and a reduction in the level of investment in industry.

Conclusion

This chapter focused on the years of dictatorship in Greece, which saw the introduction of particularly important incentives for the promotion of industrial development. It was during the junta that industry's share of the national product reached its highest level; still, the industrial sector was faced with difficulties, one of which, it has been argued here, was the way the tax system functioned. The junta dismantled democracy and inflicted a 'severe [and] long-lasting blow... [to] the democratic procedures which, in the peoples' conscience, legalise political decisions'.[202] During the dictatorship, the administrative burdens of the tax system increased. No serious initiatives for the modernisation of the services were undertaken. Moreover, there were an increasing number of complaints about the bureaucracy and complex procedures followed in the tax services as well as a large number of dismissals of competent officers. Owing to this development, the Central Service of the Ministry of Economics, which, through its administrative and legislative duties supported the function of the tax bureaus, was essentially dismantled. A large number of the Service's executives were dismissed for political reasons by the regime, getting replaced by officers that lacked the necessary training and professional capabilities.

More broadly, in spite of espousing the creation of a 'purer' and more efficient state, the junta actually established a regime in which inefficiency and corruption in the public sector increased. This affected the tax services too. Because of such developments, the tax system became even more illegitimate than before. As the next chapter will show, the very real problems burdening the system would become much more obvious in the following period which saw the restoration of democracy but also the consolidation of the slowdown in the economy. It was during this period of recession that the weaknesses of the tax administration became

[202] Antonis Karkagiannis, 'What Did the Junta of'67 Left Behind', *I Kathimerini*, 22.4.2012. http://www.kathimerini.gr/456126/article/epikairothta/ellada/ti-afhse-pisw-ths-h-xoynta-toy-67 [accessed 28.12.2014], in Greek.

of a particularly explicit impact, making it even clearer that the way the system functioned discouraged industrial investment.

Bibliography

Primary Sources

CHROTEX Archive

Board of Directors Meeting Minutes, various dates.

Professor Michalis Psalidopoulos Personal Archive

Bulletin of the Federation of Greek Industrialists (FGI) (1966–1988).

The Hellenic Literary and Historical Archive (ELIA)

IZOLA Files, Report of the Board of Governors for 1967 (no page number available).

IZOLA Files, Report of the Board of Governors for 1970, p. 6.

The 'Konstantinos G. Karamanlis' Foundation, Konstantinos G. Karamanlis Archive

Vol. 07, *A Period of Ordeal, 1963–1974* (Period B', 21.4.1967–24.7.1974), pp. 49–50.

Vovolini Archive

Viomichaniki Epitheorissis, Vol. 38, November 1971, 445, p. 11.

Newspapers, Magazines and Serial Publications

a) Newspapers

Capital, Dimokratia, Eleftheria, Empros, Imerisia, I Avgi, I Kathimerini, I Naftemporiki, O Economicos Tahydromos, Makedonia, Rizospastis, Ta Nea, To Vima, To Vima tis Kyriakis (in Greek).

b) Magazines and Serial Publications

The Accountant, Tax Review, The Bulletin of Tax Legislation, Bulletin of the Chamber of Commerce and Industry of Athens.

Interviews

Kyriakopoulos, Ulysses.

Nikolakopoulos, Charalambos.

Photopoulos, Ioannis.

Retired Tax Officer Requesting Anonymity.

of the Revolutionary Movement http://istorika-ntokoumenta.blogspot.co.uk/2013/06/21-1967.html, in Greek.
'The General Secretariat of the Government', *Georgios Papadopoulos Government.* http://www.ggk.gov.gr/?p=1261, in Greek.
The Republic of Cyprus, 'Press and Information Office', *The 1974 Turkish Invasion and Its Consequences.* http://www.moi.gov.cy/moi/pio/pio.nsf/All/6F5DD418DD053ED1C2256D6D001E7571?OpenDocument.

Secondary Literature

Dimitras, P. E., 'Changes in Public Attitudes', in *Political Change in Greece Before and After the Colonels*, eds Kevin Featherstone and Dimitrios K. Katsioudas (London: Croom Helm, 1987).
Freris, A. F., *The Greek Economy in the Twentieth Century* (London and Sydney: Croom Helm, 1986).
Gallant, T. G., *Modern Greece* (London: Arnold, 2001).
Kazakos, P., *Between State and Market* (Athens: Patakis, 2001), in Greek.
Markezinis, V., *Greece of Crises, A Personal Essay* (Athens: Livanis, 2011).
McDonald, R., *Pillar & Tinderbox, The Greek Press and the Dictatorship* (New York: Marion Boyars, 1983).
Mitchell, B. R., *International Historical Statistics: Europe 1750–2005* (New York: Palgrave Macmillan, 2007).
Panselina, G. M. and Mavroeidi, M., *The Federation of Greek Industrialists, 1907–2007 – A Century in the Service of the Idea of Entrepreneurship* (Athens: Economia Publishing, 2007).
Photopoulos, I., 'The Administration of the Greek Tax System', *Enterprise*, reprint, issue 63, 2010
Provopoulos, G. A., *The Public Sector of the Greek Economy, Recent Trends and Economic Repercussions* (Athens: Foundation for Economic and Industrial Research, 1985).
Psalidopoulos, M., *History of the Bank of Greece, 1928–2008* (Athens: The Bank of Greece, 2014), in Greek.
Schwab, P. and Frangos, G. D., *Greece Under the Junta* (New York: Facts on File, 1970).
Sellas, S. M., 'Problems Relating to Social Psychology During Tax Audits', *The Tax Review*, December 1972, 287.
Staikos, T., 'The Problem of Tax Audits', *The Tax Review*, February 1972, 277.
Tsakas, C., 'Greek Business Ahead of the European Challenge: State Strategy and Private Interests from the Association with the EEC to Democratic Transition' (unpublished doctoral thesis, University of Crete, 2015), in Greek.

Documentaries

'The Time Machine (I Mihani tou Chronou): The Dictatorship's Fascism and Spoils'. https://www.youtube.com/watch?v=x0lVB0-Cl8s [accessed 11.2.2014] (aired on NET, subsequently NERIT), in Greek.
'The Trial of the Junta' (Aired on NERIT), in Greek.

Official Publications

Bank of Greece Governor's Annual Reports, Various Issues.
Long-term Statistical Series of the Greek Economy.
Statistical Yearbook of Greece, Various Issues.

Web Resources

Argyriades, D., 'Ethics and Governance from a Comprehensive Perspective: How Are We Going to Face the Multiple Challenges of Our Times', Panteion University of Political and Social Sciences, Centre of Governance and Sustainable Development. http://www.dee.gr/mediaupload/publications/20100618_ithiki_kai_diakibernisi.pdf, p. 2, in Greek.
BBC, 'On This Day', *1974: Greek Military Rule Gives into Democracy* http://news.bbc.co.uk/onthisday/hi/dates/stories/july/23/newsid_2515000/2515819.stm.
'Federation of Greek Industrialists'. http://www.sev.org.gr/online/generic.aspx?id=12&mid=600&lang=gr, in Greek.
'Greece: The Junta 5 Years After the Coup', *The Harvard Crimson*, 21.4.1972. http://www.thecrimson.com/article/1972/4/21/greece-the-junta-5-years-after.
'Iospress', *The Forgotten Scandals of the 'Nation-Saving' Revolution*. http://www.iospress.gr/ios2010/ios20100725.htm, in Greek.
Karafillis, A., 'Certificates of Social Ideals: A Case of Social Justice or Injustice in the Selection of Candidate Students for the Pedagogical Academies'. http://eriande.elemedu.upatras.gr/?section=985&language=el&page706=1&itemid706=1113, in Greek.
'National Centre for Public Administration and Local Government', *Mission*. http://www.ekdd.gr/ekdda/index.php/en/2012-06-29-09-59-33), in Greek.
'Our Big Circus' ('Censorship During the Junta', 21.4.2013. http://chatzelenisgeorge.blogspot.co.uk/2013/04/blog-post_21.html, in Greek.
Stebilis, D., '21 April 1967: The Ending of a Chronic Political Crisis and the Beginning of a Dark Period', *History – Theoretical Texts, Documents*

Yannopoulos, G., 'The State of the Opposition Forces Since the Military Coup', in *Greece Under Military Rule*, eds Richard Clogg and George Yannopoulos (London: Secker & Warburg, 1972).

Yanoulopoulos, Y., 'Greece: Political and Constitutional Developments 1924–1974', in *Greece in Transition, Essays in the History of Modern Greece 1821–1974*, ed John T. A. Koumoulides (London: Zeno, 1977).

Zolotas, X., *Our Economic Problem – A TV Discussion* (Athens: The Bank of Greece – Surveys and Talks Archive, 1975).

CHAPTER 5

A 'Tax Surprise' Amidst Economic Recession, 1974–1981

Introduction

The years examined in this chapter saw Greece faced with problems on a variety of different fronts. After the collapse of the coup, a national unity government that had to work towards the restoration of democracy was formed under the leadership of Konstantinos Karamanlis. With the legalisation of the Greek communist party and the holding of a referendum that led to the abolition of the monarchy, this period saw the establishment of a new political and social reality.[1] The new government was also obliged to absorb the shock of the second and last phase of the Turkish attack in Cyprus. It started on 14 August 1974, lasted for two days and, apart from the human losses and the destruction of infrastructure, meant the occupation of 36.4% of the island.[2] According to Xenophon Zolotas, those days were marked by a 'generalised discouragement and disruption… in view of the danger of a conflict with Turkey'.[3]

[1] Kazakos, p. 293. The referendum took place in 8 December 1974 (Petros Papakonstantinou, 'The Restoration of Democracy', in *Greece in the 20th Century, 1970–1980*, I Kathimerini – Epta Imeres [Athens: I Kathimerini, 19.12.1999], pp. 12–13).

[2] 'TVXS', *Attila II: the Last Chapter of the Cyprus Tragedy*, 14.8.2010. tvxs.gr/news/κόσμος/αττίλας-ιι-το-τελευταίο-κεφάλαιο-της-κυπριακής-τραγωδίας [accessed 30.3.2014], in Greek.

[3] 'Drachma for 60 Years', p. 15.

Z. Pittaki, *Exploring the roots of systematic tax avoidance in Greece*, Palgrave Studies in Economic History,
https://doi.org/10.1007/978-3-030-71979-1_5

Such a climate, in the context of the international economic recession of the time, contributed to a deterioration in all the basic macroeconomic indicators of the economy: inflation and unemployment rose, the growth rate of GDP and the level of investment fell and the balance of payments deficit increased. This period also saw an increase in the number of civil servants, a considerable rise of public expenditure through a rise in social transfers and public servants' salaries and pensions and, as a result, a considerable increase in public borrowing.

It was during that time that Greek industry entered a stage of stagnation, which was marked by a reduction in the share of investment of manufacturing in GDP. Apart from the adverse developments in the economy, the industrial sector was also faced with the uncertainty caused by the agreement for full membership in the EEC. It was eventually signed in May 1979; another development sending bad signals to business was the wave of nationalisations of large failing companies that started during that time.

Similar to previous periods, an additional difficulty came from the system of taxation. This was a time when the level of taxes increased, probably as a result of the additional needs for revenues due to the state's fiscal expansion, but also due to the increasing levels of tax evasion from the late 1970s. New taxes were imposed on business, having usually in the form of special contributions, and the corporate income tax rate increased.[4] At the same time, the problems with the functioning of the tax mechanisms worsened. The impact of the dismissals of officers during the period of dictatorship kept burdening the tax administration, which also had to deal with a significant increase in the tax legislation's complexity and frequency of change. This was something indicated by the relevant critiques, coming from tax officers too. Tax officers complained also about their workload and the pressure they were under in order to collect more revenues.

Added to this, mistrust between taxpayers and tax authorities and the arbitrariness of the latter did not diminish. This was in spite of the fact that the government implemented relevant measures, such as the issuing of circulars containing instructions for the behaviour of tax officers during

[4] It has to be noted that an examination of the distribution of the income tax burden among the various occupations indicates that from the mid 1970s onwards it was not the entrepreneurial classes who paid the majority of taxes in this period.

audits, but also the abolition of law regarding certain penal sanctions for tax law offences.

There was also an increasing number of incidences of tax officers who were accused of corruption and blackmailing. In the view of such developments, and in a climate of generalised economic disruption and uncertainty, the tax system was pointed out more regularly as a component of the economic environment that seemed to discourage investment initiatives. The coming pages will first present an overview of the features of the Greek economy during the period; there will also be an analysis of industry's performance and entrepreneurs' concerns due to various developments in the economy. Last, there will be an analysis of the difficulties and the relevant concerns because of the way the tax system functioned.

Economy and Industry

In April 1975, in his first report as the Governor of the Bank of Greece after the restoration of democracy, Xenophon Zolotas wrote that the Greek economy was 'in a particularly precarious state, being characterised by recession, a high rate of inflation and a serious deficit in the balance of payments'.[5] To the deterioration of the balance of payments contributed 'the quadrupling in the price of petroleum products but also the emergency imports of defence material as a result of the Cyprus crisis'.[6] The state budget had also been burdened by the dictatorial regime's 'unplanned increase of public expenditure'.[7] There was also a sharp reduction of investment in housing and a reduction of revenue from tourism, which was again partly a result of the events in Cyprus and the general uncertainty they spurred.[8] Moreover, there was an increase in unemployment because of the reduction in the level of production but also due to the fact that there were fewer opportunities for emigration. This was because of the recession in other European countries during the period, especially West Germany, which, up to that point, had attracted the majority of Greek excess labour.[9]

[5] Psalidopoulos, *History*, p. 274.

[6] Ibid.

[7] Ibid.

[8] Kazakos, pp. 294–295.

[9] Ibid., p. 295.

In view of such developments, the government declared its willingness to curb inflation, promote growth and implement a rationalisation in the way the economy functioned.[10] The proclaimed economic philosophy which underpinned the policies of the government was that of a 'radical liberalism' that adhered to the principles of the free market economy, while at the same time accepting that the state should have 'enhanced regulatory capacities' and work towards the establishment of 'social solidarity'.[11]

In such a framework, among the first measures undertaken by the government in August 1974 were the increase in the level of social transfers,[12] the increase of the minimum wage, the increase in the salaries and allowances of civil servants as well as the increase of retired civil servants' pensions and benefits.[13] In terms of the government's fiscal policies, spending cuts of DRS 2.5 billion in the regular budget were announced, but also, the imposition of a special contribution of DRS 10 billion[14] that had to be paid by both natural persons and indigenous corporations or foreign companies whose income was taxed according to legislative orders 3323/1955 and 3843/1958.[15] According to the government, this contribution would cover the increased national defence expenditures because of the events in Cyprus and the troubled relations with Turkey.[16]

Generally, from 1974 onwards, the state started implementing policies that might be considered interventionist, at least in comparison to the pre-1974 era.[17] Actually, throughout the period 1975–1981 and in

[10] Ibid., p. 296.

[11] Ibid., pp. 296–297.

[12] Ibid., p. 310.

[13] 'The Minister of Coordination Mr Zolotas Analyses the New Economic Measures', *To Vima tis Kyriakis*, 18.8.1974, p. 11.

[14] Papakonstantinou, p. 14.

[15] 'Mr Zolotas Analyses the New Economic Measures', p. 11. The legislative orders mentioned here are the pieces of legislation with which the tax reforms of the 1950s were implemented. Legislative order 3323/1955 concerned taxation of individual income and legislative order 3843/1958 corporate income taxation. More information about the specifics of the two laws can be found in Chapter 3.

[16] Ibid., and Papakonstantinou, p. 14.

[17] Psalidopoulos, *History*, p. 45.

spite of its declarations, the government followed expansionary fiscal policies, increasing public borrowing from 8.5% of GDP in 1977 to 12% in 1980 and 17.2% in 1981. As for credit policies, they were expansionary towards the public sector, but not towards the private one.[18] This was so in spite of the fact that, in the five-year development plan 1976–1980, the government proclaimed that private initiative was of great importance for the development of the economy and that, for this reason, would face no kind of competition from state initiative.[19]

Overall, there was an increase of state expenditure as a share of GDP (from 24.8% in 1973 to 38% in 1981). Also, as will be analysed in more detail later, a large number of companies were nationalised and new public organisations were established.[20] Such developments led to an increase in the magnitude of the public sector mainly from the mid-1970s onwards.

In such a context, during the period 1975–1981 the number of civil servants (and therefore also the state's expenditure for civil servants' wages) started increasing rapidly. More specifically, the number of civil servants—without taking into account those working in nationalised companies—was growing at a rate of 5% per year; as a result, during the period they came to make up 25% of the total working force in the country.[21] Indeed, despite coming from a political party supporting the principles of free market, Karamanlis' government 'showed a strange tendency towards nationalising banks and other companies, increasing the already very large numbers of people employed, directly or indirectly, by the state'.[22]

Karamanlis' policies were met with criticism also by the representatives of business. The following point he raised during a meeting between members of the Government and members of the FGI in 1975 was characteristic: 'I want Greece to enter the EEC and for this what I need above all is the country to have social peace, because Europeans must see how mature we are. For this reason you must give money to your employees to satisfy them'. When one of the FGI's representatives replied that such tactics might be misunderstood, leading the managers of the various

[18] Kazakos, p. 300.

[19] Ibid., p. 299.

[20] Ibid., pp. 308–310.

[21] Ibid., p. 310.

[22] Richard Clogg, in Kazakos, p. 314.

public organisations to 'wastefulness and deficits', one of the members of the government retorted that the industrialists were trying to 'teach [the government] lessons'.[23]

Of course, it is a fact that the increase of state expenditure was an international tendency at the time, and also that the Greek public sector's share over GDP was smaller than the EU average.[24] In the same vein, Kazakos notes that from 1974 to 1979 the country's macroeconomic performance was, on a comparative level, satisfactory, as the annual growth rate was higher than that of the OECD or the EEC, on average.[25]

Still, it has been argued that the reason why the ratio of public expenditure to GDP was smaller in Greece was that, in comparison to other countries, Greek GDP was growing faster up until the late 1970s.[26] As Kazakos notes, through such an increase, 'populist expectations towards the state and politicians were established, as well as behaviours coming from political bodies and vested interests that became uncontrollable when circumstances changed…'.[27] The increase of public expenditure along with the rising tax evasion contributed to the great rise of public deficit from the 1980s onwards. As a matter of fact, the repercussions of such developments would become clear already from the late 1970s, when the economic downturn came.[28]

It should be noted here that there was a mild recovery in the economy after 1976. This recovery, however, was not to last, as it coincided with the second oil crisis and the international recession it caused,[29] leading to a gradual reduction in the growth rate of the GDP from 6.41% in 1978 to 3.61, 2.06 and 0.18% in 1979, 1980 and 1981, respectively (Table 5.1).

[23] From the newspaper *To Vima*, in Kazakos, pp. 314–315.

[24] Source: Vasillios G. Manesiotis and Robert D. Reischauer, 'Greek Fiscal and Budget Policy and EMU', in *Greece's Economic Performance and Prospects*, eds Ralph C. Bryant, Nikolaos H. Garganas and Georgios S. Tavlas (Bank of Greece and The Brookings Institution, 2002), p. 144.

[25] Kazakos, pp. 304–305.

[26] Ibid., p. 310.

[27] Ibid.

[28] Ibid., pp. 304–305.

[29] Psalidopoulos, *History*, pp. 45–46.

Table 5.1 GDP growth rate (%), 1974–1981

1974	*1975*	*1976*	*1977*	*1978*	*1979*	*1980*	*1981*
−1.81	5.11	6.05	2.95	6.41	3.61	2.06	0.18

Source: Long-term Statistical Series of the Greek Economy, p. 10

There was also a further surge of inflation spurred by oil, the price of which increased by 150% between late 1978 and late 1980.[30]

In this context, 1980 marked the beginning of a period characterised by low growth rates and deterioration in all the indicators of the degree of dynamism in the economy, and especially that of the percentage of investment to GDP.[31] 'We are going through one of the most difficult times of our modern history', noted the president of the Union of Corporations and Limited Liability Companies in late April 1980. This view was typical of the general climate regarding the situation of the economy at the time.[32]

Of course, there were concerns about a series of other negative developments in the economy even before 1980. Psalidopoulos notes that since 1978 certain features of the economy 'threatened [the country's] fiscal stability', such as 'an increase of consumption expenses and particularly an interest in imported durable goods and luxury goods, a reduction of savings, an increased demand for real estate and a considerable rise in the price of flats in the centre of Athens and the wealthy suburbs…'.[33] During the period 1970–1977, 'the number of cars tripled', 'the number of telephone appliances doubled' and 'the number of boutiques more than tripled'. There was also an 'excessive increase in the number of nightclubs, taverns, etc'.[34] Such an increase in consumption was not matched by a respective increase in production—for example, and as will be analysed further later, investment in manufacturing was reduced.[35]

[30] Ibid., p. 277.

[31] Yiannis Milios, 'The Greek Economy', p. 18.

[32] Union of Corporations and Limited Liability Companies, Board Meeting Minutes 24.4.1980, p. 138.

[33] Psalidopoulos, *History*, p. 289.

[34] Xenophon Zolotas, ibid.

[35] Psalidopoulos, *History*, p. 290.

The turn to consumption became more intense after 1981. This was for the most part due to reasons relating to the income policies which were implemented by the government in this period and to the new source of funding provided to Greece after its membership in the European Community.[36] In fact, the agreement for the accession was signed in May 1979, but the starting date was that of the 1st of January 1981.[37] Among others, the agreement provided that Greek legislation would conform to that of the Community and that a number of structural changes would take place, such as the country's adaptation to the Common Customs Tariff within a transitional period of five years and the introduction of the Value Added Tax after a transitional period of three years.[38]

It has been argued that the economic policies implemented during the period denoted that Greece was not suitably preparing for its accession to the EEC.[39] The main factor that was considered to have prevented the country from smoothly adapting to the European reality was the state mechanism: the way that the public sector had been expanded up to that point indicated that a certain 'politico-economic front' had been created that would oppose reforms. For this reason, it would function problematically within the new competitive environment of the European Community.[40] Psalidopoulos stressed that Greek politicians failed—or refused—to understand that accession to the EEC meant that the political system's behaviour should change in order to successfully adapt to the new European environment.[41] After the accession, the Greek state did not avoid expansionary tactics and implemented policies that increased public debt. In spite of the occasional reforms, the state used EEC funding not to modernise, but in order to keep on sustaining a 'counterproductive model of development'.[42]

Added to these were the entrepreneurs' concerns of what full membership in the European Community would mean. According to the Union

[36] Ibid., p. 289.

[37] Ibid., pp. 47–48.

[38] Ibid.

[39] Kazakos, p. 301.

[40] Ibid., p. 303.

[41] Psalidopoulos, *History*, p. 298.

[42] Ibid., p. 299.

of Corporations and Limited Liability Companies, in 1976 most of the Greek firms were adversely affected by their ignorance of what the impact of the country's accession to the EEC would be. In such a state, it was stressed that 'every…effort to further develop…the business…is made in view of unknown dangers and possibilities, because of the lack of any adequate information'.[43] This sense of uneasiness was reflected also in CHROTEX's Board meeting minutes. The notes from the meeting of the 14th April 1975 showed that in view of the country's accession to the EEC, import duties had been reduced and would be almost non-existent in five years' time. It was stressed that this fact, along with the one that the products of 'developed European industries will enter the Greek market almost freely', would inevitably create a state of 'turmoil' and 'agitation'. Indeed, it was summed up that: 'within the narrow boundaries of the Greek market of nine million population, the struggle [of competition] is going to be hard'.[44]

Such assessments, however, overlooked the fact that from 1968 and as a result of the Athens Agreement in 1961 the European Community imposed zero tariffs on all manufacturing products imported from Greece. This, according to Zolotas, contributed to an increase in the share of Greek manufacturing products exported to the EEC as a share of total Greek exports, from 10.5% in 1962 to 39.5% in 1977.[45] On the contrary, in 1978 Greece still imposed reduced tariffs on one-third of the products it imported from the EEC.[46] The association agreement provided for an abolition of all tariffs by 31 October 1984.[47] Of course, there was uncertainty, which did not always have to do with the fact that entrepreneurs were not given enough information by the state. Membership in the EEC was a venture the various implications of which could not be easily estimated. For example, as mentioned in a 1980 study, Greece would have to adopt the common external tariff (CET), according to which tariff rates imposed upon imported goods from third countries would have to

[43] Union of Corporations and Limited Liability Companies, Board Meeting Minutes 4.4.1976, p. 146.

[44] CHROTEX Archive, Board of Directors Meeting Minutes, 23/12/1963–2/05/1977 p. 245.

[45] Xenophon Zolotas, *Greece's Contribution in the European Community* (Bank of Greece: Athens, 1978), pp. 22–23.

[46] Ibid., p. 24.

[47] Ibid.

be reduced. It was noted that this would affect labour-intensive industries, however, whether CET would lead to an increase of imports would depend 'to a large extent on the relevant price elasticities of demand and supply and the ability of third country exporters to market their products in Greece'.[48]

Actually, accession to the EEC was not the only reason for nervousness among entrepreneurs. A source of further concerns was also the wave of nationalisations of large private companies that started in this period. The years analysed in this chapter saw the nationalisation of companies such as the Olympic Airways, the Aspropyrgos Oil Refineries and the Emporiki Bank Group, and the establishment of public companies such as the Hellenic Aerospace Industry. For the Federation of Greek Industrialists such developments indicated that the government was in a state of a certain 'social-mania' that is, it had an excessive eagerness towards implementing pro-socialist policies.[49] Still, it seemed that the government's decision to nationalise these companies was triggered also by the stance of the companies themselves. For example, in the case of the Aspropyrgos Oil Refineries, as noted previously (p. 103), the state bought back the refinery after the Niarchos Group excessively delayed fulfilling its contractual obligations.

These developments impacted the investment climate in the country. More broadly, and apart from nationalised companies, it has been generally accepted that in the mid-1970s Greek industry started losing whatever dynamism it had gained up to that point, with the reduction in the rate of increase of production. In 1979 it entered a phase of 'protracted stagnation'.[50] In these years the serious structural weaknesses of the industrial sector started coming to the surface.[51] Such weaknesses would become more prevalent in the next period, which saw an array of failing companies, the so-called 'problematic' ones.[52]

[48] G. Yannopoulos, 'Sensitivity of Industrial Sectors to Common Market Competition', in *The Mediterranean Challenge: IV, The Tenth Member – Economic Aspects* (Sussex: Sussex European Research Centre, 1980), p. 84.

[49] Panselina and Mavroeidi, pp. 430–432.

[50] Kazakos, p. 402.

[51] Ibid., p. 305.

[52] Psalidopoulos, *History*, p. 49.

In more detail, Manolis Xanthakis noted that in the second half of the 1970s, the basic needs of the population had been covered. Indeed, he argued that there could be no further expansion in constructions, a significant industrial sector of the country. The increase in the cost of raw materials squeezed the profit margins for the broader secondary sector of the economy; also, a severe blow to the manufacturing sector, which covered 80% of its funding needs through borrowing, came through the increase in the cost of credit.[53] Especially since 1977 onwards, the adverse international and domestic circumstances 'greatly upset the financial balance of many large Greek firms and made them unable to pay back the debts they had assumed'.[54] Specifically, between 1978 and 1981 the number of loss-making companies increased by 20%, whereas the losses increased by 143%, amounting to DRS 23.8 billion.

Return on Equity in manufacturing also reduced after 1975; to be specific, it was 6.2% during the period 1975–1981 in comparison to 8% during 1958–1968 and 14% during 1969–1974.[55] Moreover, the fact that, especially from 1980 onwards, the cost of labour started increasing because of the government's income policies, combined with the decline in investment, harmed the viability of the Greek industry. This point was especially important in view of the new competitive environment it was faced with after association with the EEC.[56] In such a framework, as Chart 5.1 shows, for the majority of the years covered in this chapter the rate of increase of investment in manufacturing was negative.

Also, as Chart 5.2 shows, with the exception of 1978–1980, there was a decreasing trend, throughout the period, in the share of investment in manufacturing over GDP.

A further indication of the situation in the industrial sector comes from an examination of the number of enterprises' extended factories and workshops. As Chart 5.3 shows, this number remained, in general terms, stagnant throughout the 1974–1981 period.

[53] Manolis Xanthakis, *The Crisis of Greek Manufacturing and State Intervention* (Athens: Papazisis 1989), p. 21.

[54] Ibid., p. 26.

[55] Ibid., p. 34.

[56] Kazakos, p. 301.

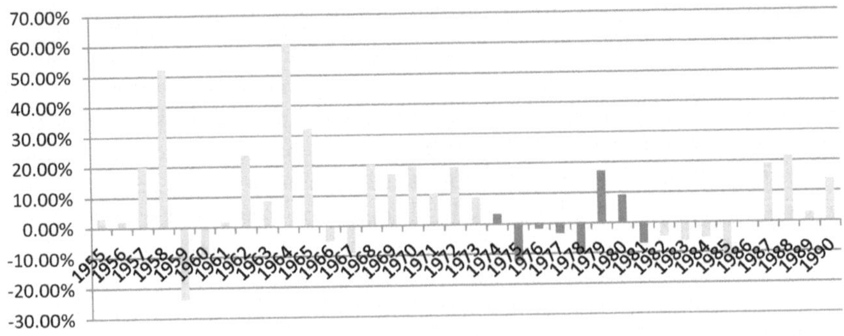

Chart 5.1 Annual rate of increase, gross private investment in fixed capital in manufacturing, 1974–1981 (*Source: Long-term Statistical Series of the Greek Economy*, p. 27)

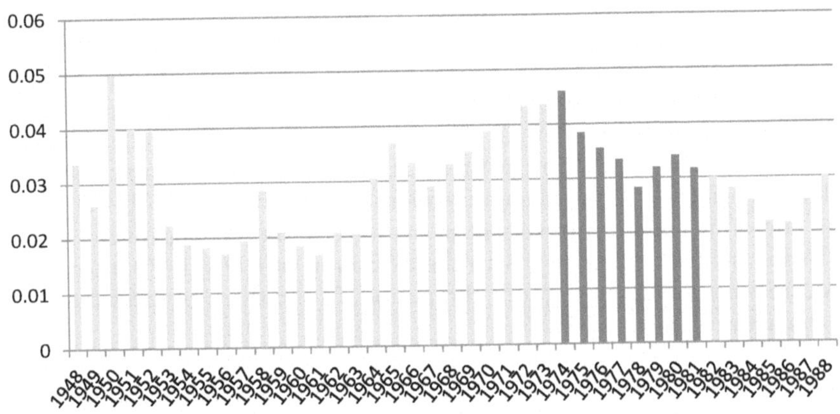

Chart 5.2 Manufacturing, gross private investment in fixed capital, % GDP (1974–1981) (*Source: Long-term Statistical Series of the Greek Economy*, pp. 10; 27)

The same stagnation is indicated through an examination of the number of new factories and workshops established annually, as Chart 5.4 shows.

The fact that Greek industry lost its dynamism during the years examined in this chapter reflects a series of adverse developments in the economy during this period, some of which were examined in the

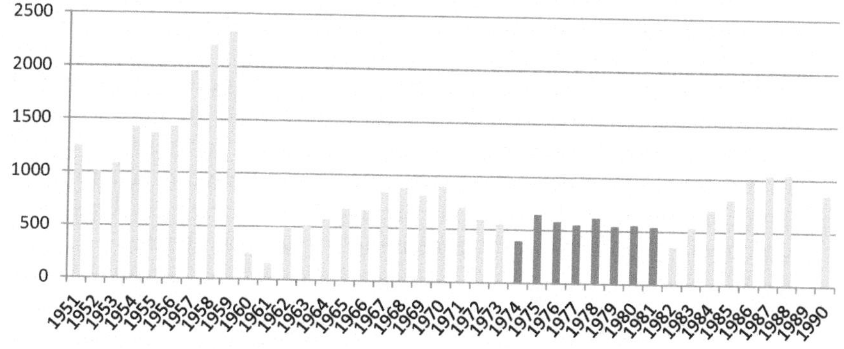

Chart 5.3 Number of extended factories and workshops of industrial and handicraft enterprises, 1974–1981 (*Source: Statistical Yearbook of Greece*, various issues[57])

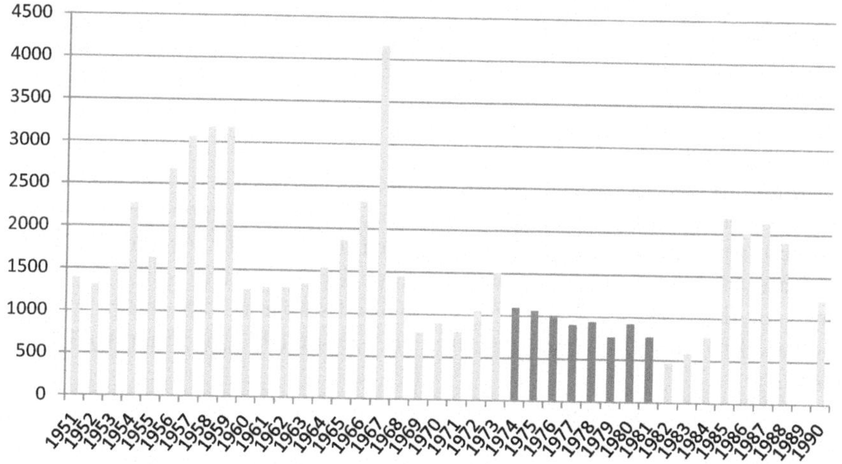

Chart 5.4 Number of new factories and workshops of industrial and handicraft enterprises, 1974–1981 (*Source: Statistical Yearbook of Greece*, various issues[58])

[57] See Chapter 3, p. 42, footnote no. 26.

[58] See Chapter 3, p. 42, footnote no. 26.

previous pages. There were also a number of weaknesses in the broader economic environment. One of such weaknesses was the way the tax system functioned. As various critiques but also relevant studies during the period indicated, the system of taxation seemed to be a component of the economy that was causing difficulties to business, again confirming Baumol's model about the interaction between taxation and entrepreneurship. More detail about the difficulties caused by the system of taxation will be offered in the remaining part of this chapter.

The System of Taxation

As relevant studies have indicated, there was an increase in the tax burden after the fall of the coup regime.[59] Indeed, a few months after the DRS 10 billion special contributions imposed on individuals and firms because of the Cyprus crisis, in a campaign speech in southern Greece Karamanlis stressed that there was a need 'to support the exercise of [state] intervention through taxation, so as to drastically reduce the unequal distribution of national income in order for a part of it to be transferred from the wealthier to the poorer social classes'.[60]

Greece had also to overcome a series of problems that the incoherent economic policies of the junta had created; to cover the increased expenditures of the budget, stressed Karamanlis, the government had to impose 'some taxes too'.[61] The first period after the fall of dictatorship saw a 5% increase in the corporate income tax rate for the first time for 25 years, since for the period 1950–1973 it remained stable at 35% and in 1974 it increased to 40%. This rate increased to 45% in 1981 and then to 49% in 1985.[62]

[59] Agapitos, p. 47.

[60] The 'Konstantinos G. Karamanlis' Foundation, Konstantinos G. Karamanlis Archive Vol. 08, *The Restoration of Democracy, 1974–1977* (Period A', 24.7.1974–3.9.1975), p. 210.

[61] Ibid.

[62] Source: for the period 1950–1980: Vasilios Manesiotis, 'Tax Structure Change During Economic Development: The Case of Greece' (PhD thesis, Northwestern University, 1985), p. 50; for the period 1981–2008: Yanis Varoufakis and Tasos Patokos, 'Business Taxation Amid the Crisis', Centre of Research – Athens Chamber of Commerce and Industry, p. 30 [in Greek].

The increase of the tax burden that such developments signified certainly did not please business, especially firms that were not making profits. For example, in IZOLA's 1976 Board of Directors' report it was noted that during 1975 new taxes burdening the company (such as real estate taxes and special levies) amounted to DRS 14.7 million.[63] IZOLA was making losses at the time and deemed such taxation 'unfair': 'we call it unfair because the State, in view of its national needs, has the right to impose even 100% taxation on any gains stemming even from inflation – [but] in our case there are no profits! There is only an increase of losses'.[64]

It is also worth noting here that, according to the opening article of the November 1975 issue of the *Bulletin of the FGI* entitled 'Tolerance Limit', while Greek industry showed an understanding of the government's needs and accepted assuming the biggest part of the burden from the increased national defence expenses, it could not give anything more: '...after the successive...charges that it had to sustain, with this new lump sum contribution of the DRS 10 billion, [i]ndustry reaches the ultimate limit of its taxpaying capacity...any new burden imposed upon it will induce the fatal outcome of the weakening of productive activities and ... employment and will put social harmony in jeopardy'.[65]

The spirit of such complaints becomes better understood when taking into consideration the differential treatment that Greek governments traditionally conferred to certain types of business. The most salient example is that of the Greek shipping industry. Indeed, Greece has been described as a tax exempt or a 'zero-tax jurisdiction' for shipping. As Thomas Mayr and Raymond McGrath stress, '[i]n positively discriminating in favour of shipping, Greece stands out among all other countries and represents a benchmark for comparing other regimes. Greek law 378/68 exempts from taxation all shipping companies and dividends

[63] The Hellenic Literary and Historical Archive, IZOLA Files, Report of the Board of Governors for 1976, p. 18.

[64] Ibid., p. 20.

[65] *Bulletin of the FGI*, 'Tolerance Limit', 30.11.1975, p. 1.

distributed by them to shareholders'.[66] It should also be noted that back in the 1950s, the Greek government had introduced law 2687/1953 entitled 'On investment and the protection of foreign capital', for the promotion of foreign direct investment. This legislation offered incentives for investment projects that were approved by the government on an individual basis. One of the most important incentives was that for a certain number of years the tax rate for profits stemming from such projects would remain stable. This piece of legislation had superior status relative to ordinary laws, that is, it could change only when the Constitution itself changed.[67] Laws of a similar kind did not exist for the indigenous industrial sector.[68]

In the same vein, it was noted in a 1977 newspaper article that, instead of an effort for radical reform, what happened in the tax system since the restoration of democracy was a continuous increase of the tax burden. Specifically, it was noted that, apart from the special contribution of DRS 10 billion, since the fall of the junta the government had introduced several other pieces of legislation resulting in the imposition of new taxes or the increase of the burden of the already existing ones. These were

[66] Thomas P. Mayr and Raymond H. McGrath, 'Tramp Shipping: The Role of Taxation in International Resource Allocation', *Maritime Policy & Management*, 24:3 (1997), pp. 266; 269. Of course, it should also be noted that it is not easy for the Greek state to waive the 'tax amnesty' of the shipping sector, as it seems that ship owners could easily respond to an increase of taxation by simply 'migrating' to other countries (see 'Ship-Owners: If You Tax Us, We Will Leave', *To Vima*, 12.6.2012. http://www.tovima.gr/finance/article/?aid=461954 [accessed 28.4.2015], in Greek). For information about the pre-1950s tax treatment of the shipping industry in Greece see Gelina Harlaftis, *A History of Greek-Owned Shipping – The Making of an International Tramp Fleet, 1830 to the Present Day* (London: Routledge, 1996), pp. 231–233; 237–240.

[67] See Athanasios Tsiouras, 'Return to Development with Direct Foreign Investment', in *Niches of Freedom and Development – Proposal for the Functioning of a Special Economic Zone in Greece* (Brussels: Friedrich Naumann Stiftung Für die Freiheit, 2016), p. 4, Vasilis Karamitsopoulos, Antonis Koumpias, Orestis Pastellas and Mariela Tiliakou, 'Proposal for the Establishment and Functioning of a Special Economic Zone in Greece', in *Niches of Freedom*, p. 7, Psalidopoulos, *History*, p. 212 and Panos Kazakos, 'The Devaluation of the Drachma', *I Kathimerini*, 23.6.2013. http://www.kathimerini.gr/491454/article/epikairothta/ellada/h-ypotimhsh-ths-draxmhs [accessed 21.4.2016], in Greek.

[68] Similar laws for the protection of foreign capital investment had been introduced during the period of dictatorship too (1967–1974), some of which remained effective in the post-dictatorship era. The same holds for the preferential treatment of shipping companies.

legislative order 84/1974 as well as laws 231/1975 and 254/1976 introducing new taxes, law 12/1975 regarding the increase of already existing taxes, and law 11/1975 regarding property taxation.[69]

Special taxes were introduced again when new emergencies occurred in subsequent years. For example, in summer 1978 another special contribution was imposed, on the occasion of an earthquake in Macedonia that, according to the government, had caused material damages and a loss of revenue amounting to DRS 10 billion.[70] The press, while recognising the new national emergency, noted that the tax policies implemented were inconsistent, given that, immediately after the earthquake, the government itself had declared that the damages would be covered through special budget reserves.[71] Apart from this, it was also mentioned in a newspaper report that the state's tax revenues for the fiscal year were 15–20 billion more than the amount that had been anticipated in the budget for 1978, something, that, again, raised questions about whether the government really needed to impose a special contribution in order to cover the repair expenses.

Such tactics, the report noted, made Greek taxpayers mistrustful towards the tax system. On the occasion of this specific contribution, it was stressed that the taxpayers had 'every right to seek evidence that their sacrifice...will not fund the over-expenses of the state mechanism'.[72] The opposition parties raised relevant critiques. For example, Andreas Papandreou, the leader of the PASOK[73] party, characterised the government's measures as counterproductive and destabilising, noting that they would result in a further discouragement of investment initiatives.[74]

The increase of the tax burden was reflected in the increase of the tax revenue too. Specifically, with the exception of 1980 and 1981, there was an increase of tax revenues' share to GDP in comparison to previous periods (see Chart 5.5). Such an increase however, was considered 'slow',

[69] P. Mpakoyiannis, "Vassal' Taxpayers and the 'Sultan-like' System of the Tax Services', *To Vima*, 2.2.1977, p. 6.

[70] 'Honest Tax Returns but also Honest Deals', *To Vima*, 26.8.1978, p. 1.

[71] 'Another One-Sided Policy of Austerity at the Expense of the People', *Rizospastis*, 26.8.1978, p. 1.

[72] 'Honest Tax Returns'.

[73] PASOK stands for Panhellenic Socialistic Movement.

[74] 'Honest Tax Returns'.

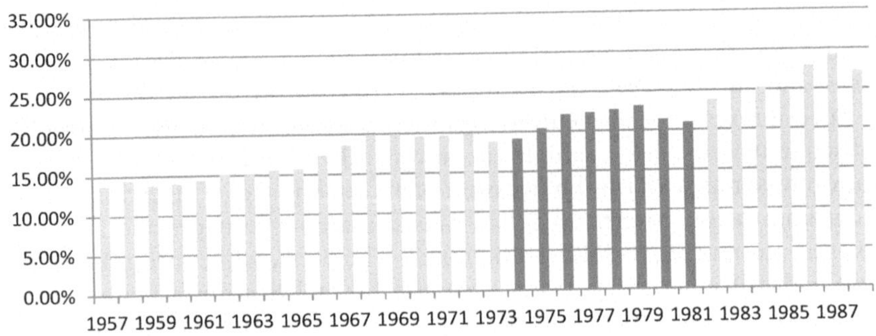

Chart 5.5 Tax revenue, % GDP, 1974–1981 (*Source: Long-term Statistical Series of the Greek Economy*, pp. 13; 86–87)

and this was attributed to the narrow tax base of the country as well as to the rising levels of tax evasion.[75]

For Kazakos, the increase of tax evasion positively related to the fact that the number of self-employed people was also increasing during the period[76]; in the same vein, in late 1979 Zolotas argued that the income policies followed in the immediately previous period resulted in a 'redistribution of income in favour of… the self-employed and small business owners, who made money outside the official economy'.[77] This increased the illegitimacy of the tax system and therefore also exacerbated tax evasion.

Of course, the tax system was also burdened by a series of shortcomings that related to administrative malfunctions and affected the measures that had been introduced in order to further the economic development of the country and reduce the tax burden. Measures like these were, for example, tax incentives, which although being less generous than those offered by the state during the dictatorship, kept on being introduced for the promotion of industry. One such category of incentives appeared in late September 1975, when the Deputy Minister of Coordination Ioannis Mpoutos declared the provision of a series of measures aiming to support economic development in the border areas of Greece. One

[75] Kazakos, pp. 311–313.

[76] Ibid.

[77] Psalidopoulos, *History*, p. 293.

of these measures was aimed at the newly established or the expanding 'industrial, manufacturing, tourist, mining, transport, construction, live-stock, agricultural and fishing enterprises', offering important incentives, such as a reduction of the turnover tax by 75% and a 50% reduction to the real estate transfer tax, for the first five years from the beginning of such enterprises' production.[78]

In general, the type of tax incentives introduced at the time indicates that the state's interest in the years following the restoration of democracy was focused on the regional areas of Greece. Legislation regarding new tax incentives at the time was introduced only with laws 289/1976 and 849/1978, both aimed at the promotion of regional industry. Other laws of the period that have been identified and that belonged to the general category of tax incentives legislation merely introduced amendments to already existing provisions. Specifically, law 159/1975 concerned amendments in the incentives law 4171/1961 and law 316/1976 concerned amendments in law 148/1967 regarding incentives for the promotion and improvement of the function of the capital market.[79]

However, it seems that the problem with tax incentives rested not in their quantity, but rather their quality, effectiveness and also in the way the state-monitored their implementation. It was also mentioned in a newspaper report that such incentives were not differentiated by sector, as there had been no in-depth study of the special needs of each specific sector. For this reason, the incentives would not be as effective as they could potentially be. As for the concessional terms offered for the establishment of industrial units in the border areas of the country, it was mentioned that they had attracted, among others, 'shrewd people who, aiming mainly to snatch a loan, wanted to solve their economic problems at the expense of society'.[80]

With regards to the broader body of legislation introducing tax incentives, the *Bulletin of the Chamber of Commerce and Industry of Athens* noted that it was complex and difficult to implement. For this reason, it argued that tax incentives legislation had to get simplified, in order

[78] The 'Konstantinos G. Karamanlis' Foundation, Konstantinos G. Karamanlis Archive Vol. 09, *The Restoration of Democracy, 1974–1977* (Period B', 4.9.1975–21.10.1977), pp. 39–40.

[79] Private information supplied, see also the issues of the *Code of the Greek Law Journal* (*Kodikas Nomikou Vimatos*).

[80] 'The Reality Without Embellishment', *I Kathimerini*, 21.1.1979, p. 9.

to accommodate the country's developmental needs and encourage new productive investment plans.[81]

More generally, that the tax system was causing difficulties was acknowledged not only by representatives of business, but those of the state too. For example, in the report of the Governor of the Bank of Greece for 1980, Governor Zolotas noted that the domestic and international conditions that would allow the country to quickly return to long-term growth were 'still absent'.[82] He stressed that for the reduction of inflation, the improvement of the balance of payments and the support of domestic economic development, it was necessary for the state to promote policies favouring productive investment, especially in industry.[83] Among others, these policies related to the establishment of a more stable and friendly tax system that would serve the 'developmental pursuits' of the country.[84]

In the same report, it was mentioned that for the promotion of investment there should also be a re-examination of a series of disincentives that had the form of state regulations and 'interventions in the economic life'. Such disincentives, stressed Zolotas, created obstacles 'to the smooth function of the market [and] the rational allocation of resources', but also 'neutralis[ed] and render[ed] ineffective any developmental incentives and inhibit[ed] the assumption of business initiative…'.[85] In 1979 the Bank of Greece produced a study that analysed such disincentives, that burdened predominantly the industrial sector.[86] The study was conducted by the so-called Disincentives Committee, presided by Zolotas, with the participation of the 'productive classes', which had been called upon to 'point out…the circumstances or law provisions that created obstacles or confusion and had halting effects on entrepreneurial activities'.[87] One hundred and three professional bodies and individual companies participated in the

[81] Dim. Tsigris, 'Tax Incentives in Developing Countries', *Bulletin of the Chamber of Commerce and Industry of Athens*, January 1975,1, pp. 13–24.

[82] Bank of Greece, *Bank of Greece Governor's Annual Report for 1980* (Athens: Bank of Greece, 1981), p. 17.

[83] Ibid., p.18.

[84] Ibid.

[85] Ibid.

[86] Bank of Greece, *Proposals of the Disincentives Committee* (Athens: Bank of Greece, 1979), p. 3.

[87] Ibid.

initiative, among which were the Federation of Greek Industrialists, the Athens Chamber of Commerce and Industry and various other Chambers of the country, as well as the Union of Corporations and Limited Liability Companies.[88] According to the study, there were disincentives relating to exports, disincentives relating to production and investment, financial disincentives, but also tax and fiscal disincentives. There were 13 different types of disincentives belonging to this last category, seven of which related to issues such as the lack of clarity and frequency of change of the tax legislation, the problems in the function of the tax justice but also the way tax officers conducted audits and implemented tax legislation.[89] The next pages will offer an analysis of such problematic aspects of the system of taxation. The character and number of complaints and critiques that will be examined seem to suggest that complexity of the legislation increased during the period and that, in spite of the efforts of the state, the problem of mistrust between tax authorities and taxpayers did not diminish.

To begin with, almost two months after the fall of the junta regime the government announced that there would be changes in the administration of the tax services. A relevant newspaper article noted that hierarchy within the services needed to be restored, because heads of tax offices that were the junta's protégés had been appointed as directors, whereas, at the same time, directors of tax services were obliged to receive orders from subordinates who happened to have the support of the regime.[90] To remedy the situation, it was decided that the public servants who had been fired by the junta would be reinstated. However, it was still recognised that it would be particularly difficult to restore hierarchy within the services.[91] In a memorandum addressed to Karamanlis in December 1974, the Governor of the Bank of Greece pointed out that 'during dictatorship the more capable civil servants…were removed from their posts…as a result there is a lack of competent executives. [The] services should be staffed again by competent and experienced personnel;

[88] Ibid., pp. 227–232

[89] Ibid., pp. 163–224.

[90] 'Hierarchy Within the Tax Services Gets Restored', *Makedonia*, 3.9.1974, p. 1.

[91] Psalidopoulos, *History*, p. 279.

on this matter the State should spare no expense'.[92] Yet, the government's reflexes were not particularly quick. The 14 January 1975 issue of *Rizospastis*, the Greek communist party's newspaper, highlighted that almost six months after the restoration of democracy, among the leaders of the trade union of tax officers there were still people who, not only supported the junta, but had also participated in the sacking of colleagues who were not approved by the dictatorial regime.[93]

Also, in February 1976, in a speech in the Chamber of Commerce and Industry of Athens, the Minister of Economics announced that a series of measures for the modernisation of the tax system would be introduced. The aim of measures would be, among others, to reduce tax avoidance[94] and improve relations between the state and the taxpayers.[95] According to the announcement, the Ministry of Economics believed that the large majority of citizens had high levels of tax conscience. Therefore, the reduction of tax avoidance could not be achieved with policing measures; instead, it could only be realised through adjustments that would improve relations between taxpayers and the state and would cover gaps in legislation that 'maintain[ed] the tendency towards tax avoidance'.[96] The Minister also announced the reform of the Tax Code through measures such as the abolition of certain complex accounting records and their replacement by simpler ones, as well as the reduction and simplification of the accounting records that should be submitted in the tax authorities. Further promises included the provision of rights for 'fast resolution of the tax differences' to the authorities.[97] However, there were voices which stressed that such fast-track procedures in the Tax Code led to arbitrariness, something that, indirectly and directly, encouraged tax evasion and tax avoidance. The way the tax system functioned, according to those voices, 'sabotaged' business planning.[98]

92 Ibid.

93 'Protest of the Elected Tax Officers', *Rizospastis*, 14.1.1975, p. 8.

94 For the precise meaning of the term tax avoidance, see footnote 3, Chapter 1.

95 *Bulletin of the Chamber of Commerce and Industry of Athens*, February 1976, 2, p. 12.

96 Ibid., p. 12.

97 Ibid., pp. 12–13.

98 *Bulletin of the Chamber of Commerce and Industry of Athens*, September 1976, 9, p. 60.

Another impediment to business planning was the tax legislation's complexity and frequency of change. These were permanent characteristics of the tax legislation, however, it seems that the number of critiques regarding them grew larger in this period, as opposed to the 1950s and the 1960s. For example, in the annual general meeting of the shareholders of the National Bank of Greece in summer 1977, its Governor Angelos Angelopoulos asked for the reformation and simplification of the tax system, 'for the fair and rational allocation of the tax burden'.[99] In the same period, in the sixth Congress of the Chamber of Commerce and Industry of Greece the leader of the main opposition party in the Parliament, Georgios Mavros, noted that in order to take advantage of its association with the EEC, Greece needed an environment conducive to development. For this, the state needed to implement 'clear policies', as what long-term business planning needed was 'a climate of trust and stability'. Yet, 'the frequent changes of the tax legislation and other surprise alterations and contradictory policies' were serious disincentives for the country's economic development.[100] Entrepreneurs that were interviewed for this research and who have been active in the Greek industry since the late 1970s supported precisely the same view. One of them, Stelios Argyros,[101] noted the following:

> I do not think that it could be argued that companies in Greece were ever overtaxed, because there has been a series of measures that reduced the tax burden, such as tax incentives...on the other hand, companies in Greece were never taxed in a stable manner. They never had even a five years horizon so as to know on the basis of which tax policies they should program their commercial and industrial plans. This is an obstacle for good entrepreneurship. For bad entrepreneurship, it is not an obstacle,

[99] Ibid., July–August 1977, 7–8, p. 12.

[100] Ibid., pp. 49–50.

[101] Apart from being involved in business, Argyros has also served as a member of the European Parliament, the vice-president of UNICE, a member of the Executive Committee of the Trilateral Commission, the President of the World Textile Institute and the President of the Board of Directors of the Federation of Greek Industrialists (see 'Stockwatch' *Stelios Argyros* http://www.stockwatch.com.cy/nqcontent.cfm?a_name=bod_view&bodn_id=5747&lang=en and http://mba.aegean.gr/attachments/article/87/ArgyrosSteliosCV.pdf [accessed 7/12/2015]).

> because people involved in it consider the non-payment of taxes to be an obligation, even in a low-tax environment.[102]

Apart from showing that the constant changes in the tax law framework were unsettling for business, this view elucidates Baumol's idea about forms of 'unproductive entrepreneurship'[103]—in this case, entrepreneurship that focuses mainly on evading taxation—that arise in environments in which institutions such as the system of taxation do not function properly.

Another entrepreneur stressed that the instability analysed at this point characterised not only the tax, but also the broader body of Greek legislation:

> My view is that it is not the level of tax rates that was an obstacle to the country's developmental efforts, or that it contributed to the failure of such developmental efforts. Of course tax rates have been high, which was a disincentive… but this was a problem of a secondary, or thirdly importance. The number one problem was the total absence of stability in the legislative framework … every government, since the decade of the 1950s onwards, claims that what was done previously was wrong, and promises that it would establish a sound system with regards to taxes, investment [rules], etc. However, many of the governments change this system even 3 or 4 times within 4 years, adding or removing details, making the Greek entrepreneur feel that he was to walk a tightrope. A project starts in one way, it gets completed in a different way, and also functions in a different way…[104]

In the same vein, the annual activity report for 1979 of the Union of Corporations and Limited Liability Companies mentioned that for the advancement of private investment, political, economic and financial stability, but also tax stability and consistency were needed. However, it stressed that such conditions were not met in the case of Greece and that the tax system was anything but stable: there were only 'continuous changes' in it, which, combined with the various special contributions

[102] Stelios Argyros, interview excerpt.

[103] See Baumol, 'Entrepreneurship'.

[104] Entrepreneur no. 3 requesting anonymity, interview data.

and other taxes, created a picture of 'striking tax instability, prohibitive of investment activities'.[105]

Indeed, the frequent changes of the tax system usually led to increases of the tax burden. For example, the change of the Tax Code at the beginning of 1977 introduced an increase of fines for the cases of tax law offences. Here, the fine for the most serious offences would increase to DRS 125,000 from DRS 25,000, whereas, in cases of repetition of the offence, the fine could reach DRS 600,000 from previously DRS 75,000.[106] Due to the fact that there was little consistency in the naming of the various kinds of fines appearing in the annual budget reports, it is not easy to explore how the various categories of fines that the state-imposed changed from period to period. However, it seems that there was indeed an increase of fines in the 1970s. For example, the share of fines that were imposed by the directors of tax bureaus in the total revenues of the budget was increasing throughout the 1970s, whereas it decreased from 1980 up to 1990. The share of the same kind of fines in the total amount of fines saw also a very rapid increase from 1970 up to 1980.[107] With regards to the fines imposed specifically in 1977, it seems that they were aimed, on a first level, at the reduction of tax evasion. Yet, from a wider perspective they were part of the government's efforts to sustain the increased expenditure of the 1977 budget, as they were accompanied by policies that clearly aimed to increase tax revenues such as the increase in the taxation of dividends, the imposition of capital gains taxation upon real estate owned by firms, the increase of turnover tax and the acceleration of the procedures governing the assessment and collection of excise duties.[108]

In August 1978 a new tax law introduced measures against tax evasion, being accompanied by the introduction of irrefutable presumptions of wealth. These presumptions would be the ownership of private cars, rent payments, recreational craft maintenance costs as well as costs for the

[105] Union of Corporations and Limited Liability Companies, Board Meeting Minutes 24.4.1980, pp. 135–136.

[106] *Bulletin of the Chamber of Commerce and Industry of Athens*, January 1977, 1, p. 13.

[107] Ministry of Finance, *Annual Reports for the Execution of the Budget*, various issues.

[108] *Bulletin of the Chamber of Commerce and Industry of Athens*, February 1977, 2, p. 10.

remuneration of domestic staff, drivers, etc.[109] In the first discussion in the parliament there were MPs asking for the bill to get withdrawn, characterising it 'a sword coming against honest and dishonest taxpayers'.[110] For the state however, irrefutable presumptions were necessary for combating tax evasion; it was also noted that this was a tactic followed in other European countries too.[111] Apart from such measures, it was indicated in the text of the bill that another bill would soon follow, introducing measures such as the reform of the tax scale through the reduction of the tax rate for the lower income brackets and the increase of it for the higher ones.[112]

When he commented on the new tax bill, the president of the Union of Corporations and Limited Liability Companies Stratis Andreadis stressed that the most serious obstacle hindering private investment was the uncertainty stemming from the tax system. He added that '[t]he [former] director of the International Monetary Fund [Johan] Witteveen considered the existence of a stable tax and monetary framework as the first prerequisite for [the promotion of] private productive investment. Yet nowadays we are in a state of, not simply tax uncertainty, but tax surprise'.[113]

It was also noted that within four years, four special taxes had been imposed upon firms, whereas what was needed was not the imposition of new taxes but the better organisation of the system for the more efficient collection of the already existing ones. In a relevant memorandum sent by the Union to the Ministry of Economics it was noted that the surprise caused by the barrage of tax laws and the burdens it incurred on companies 'weakened and upset the planning [of such companies]'.[114] It was also mentioned in the press that in a period of 'desperate efforts' for the

[109] 'A Few Employees Will Be Exempt from Presumptions of Wealth', *To Vima*, 24.8.1978, p. 1.

[110] 'The First Discussion About the Bill on Tax Evasion', *I Kathimerini*, 21.9.1978, p. 6.

[111] Ibid.

[112] 'The Main Provisions of the Tax Bill', *To Vima*, 24.8.1978, p. 2.

[113] Union of Corporations and Limited Liability Companies, Board Meeting Minutes 31.8.1978, pp. 230–232.

[114] Ibid., p. 232.

promotion of investment, the new, 'sudden' tax measures, increased the uncertainty of the 'business owner–investor'.[115]

Of course, a further persistent problem which existed was that of bureaucracy, 'the greatest scourge of the public administration', according to the Chamber of Commerce and Industry of Athens.[116] The president of the FGI believed that 250–320 days were needed on average for the state to authorise and give permission for the establishment of an investment project.[117] On this matter, the March 1978 issue of the *Bulletin of the FGI* considered that the way tax services functioned as an obstacle to business initiative and the advancement of productive activities. This was so because, either due to lack of willingness to undertake responsibilities or because of an excessive formalism, they usually ended up hampering the realisation of investment projects. As an example, the issue of corporate dividends was mentioned. More specifically, it was noted that the tax and administrative courts but also the Legal Council of the State accepted that if 100% of the shareholders of a corporation agreed, no dividend had to be paid in a given fiscal year. In this way, the profits could be used to fund the extension of an investment project. The tax authorities, however, did not recognise the courts' decisions, nor the Legal Council's consultation. According to the FGI, this was because they anticipated that, instead of financing investment projects, corporations would just save such profits, turning them into non-taxed reserves, something that would mean revenue loss for the State.[118]

On top of all these issues was one of the problematic relations between tax officers and taxpayers; it has to be noted that, on one level, the state undertook some measures with which it attempted to improve such relations and reduce tax officers' arbitrariness. For example, almost a month after the restoration of democracy, legislative order 248/1973 which was based on compulsory law 185/1967 (see p. 121) regarding the imposition of penal sanctions in cases of tax law infringements was abolished. The justification for the abolition was that the provisions of this legislative

[115] 'The Reality Without Embellishment', *I Kathimerini*, 21.1.1979, p. 9.

[116] *Bulletin of the Chamber of Commerce and Industry of Athens*, February 1978, 2, p. 59.

[117] *Bulletin of the FGI*, 15.9.1977, 365, p. 2.

[118] Ibid., 15.3.1978, 377, p. 2

order 'led to the oppression…of the taxpayers, especially those of a lower income, and worsened their relations with the tax authorities'.[119]

Also, in late August 1975 the Minister of Economics issued a circular containing 'strict instructions for impeccable behaviour and objective judgment' to the tax officers, on the basis of the 'legitimate complaints' of citizens proving the 'unforgivable obsession of, thankfully, a few tax officers in following clearly…inappropriate behaviour'.[120] This initiative of the ministry was applauded by the press. A newspaper article suggested that, through this circular, but also a series of similar ones that had been issued in the past, the state recognised tax officers' arbitrariness and lack of professionalism during audits. The article also mentioned that the state should monitor the tax officers' behaviour and impose strict and exemplary sanctions on those acting 'as if they were the citizens' petty-satraps and rulers'.[121]

However, despite such initiatives, the problem did not seem to diminish. Indeed, there were cases in which the arbitrariness of the tax system stemmed not from the behaviour of individual officers, but from the general philosophy with which the tax legislation, the tax services, but also the Ministry of Economics functioned. For example, the 8 October 1975 Board meeting minutes of the Union of Corporations and Limited Liability Companies mentioned that according to paragraph 4 of the article 52 of law 3323/1955 and article 5 of legislative order 328/1974, if a firm disagreed with the tax authorities' decision about the tax that had to be paid and appealed to the courts, it was obliged to pay the full amount of tax due in a single payment. On the contrary, if it compromised with the tax authorities, it could pay it in eight instalments. For the Union, such legislation indirectly forced firms to accept an 'onerous compromise'.[122]

In the same meeting, the vice president of the Union noted that the tax services ranked firms in various classes and 'decided in advance how

[119] 'The Minister of Coordination Mr Zolotas Analyses the New Economic Measures', *To Vima tis Kyriakis*, 18.8.1974, p. 11.

[120] 'The Behaviour of Some Tax Officers Is Inappropriate', *I Kathimerini*, 20.8.1975, p. 9.

[121] 'Daily Matters', *I Kathimerini*, 18.8.1976, p. 5.

[122] Union of Corporations and Limited Liability Companies, Board Meeting Minutes 8.10.1975, p. 130.

much more tax each one should be paying'.[123] What he meant with such a comment was that, regardless of the information contained in companies' accounting books, tax audits would always result in such companies paying more taxes than those that would normally correspond to the economic results they declared.

Some years later, in the 26 September 1979 meeting of the Board of the Union it was unanimously agreed to send a complaint to the Minister of Economics in order to ask for his intervention in a case that, according to the Union, affected the credibility of the ministry and of the system of public administration in general. In this document, the Union referred to a past meeting with the Minister. In this meeting, the Union had asked that there be an explicit provision obliging the Ministry of Economics and various others services of the public administration to comply with the decisions taken by the Council of State and the Supreme Court of Greece. In reply, the Minister of Economics was 'surprised', and stressed that such compliance was one of the basic rules of good administration. When, however, the members of the Union referred to specific cases showing that such a rule was not followed, the Minister 'was astonished' and promised that a relevant provision would be added to a bill on measures against tax evasion drafted during that period (see p. 175). However, almost twelve months later, no relative provision obliging public servants to comply by the decisions of the Council of State and the Supreme Court of Greece had been legislated, and no relative communication had been issued by the Ministry of Economics.

The Union received, in September 1979, a document from the ministry, which referred, to their disappointment, to a different matter than the one at stake. In the Union's Board meeting minutes, it was stressed that the Ministry of Economics had sent this irrelevant document either because of a misunderstanding or in a deliberate attempt to cloud the issue. The Union asked again the Minister to intervene and provide a solution to the matter.[124]

Furthermore, as was the case in previous periods, there was again an important amount of criticism regarding the way tax officers themselves implemented tax laws. For example, in April 1981 the Chamber

[123] Ibid., pp. 130–131.

[124] Ibid., 26.9.1979, pp. 70–72.

of Commerce and Industry of Athens addressed a request for an 'in-depth reformation of the Tax Code and the tax auditing procedures' to the Ministry of Economics. It was stressed that the way the Code was enforced caused the entrepreneurs' distress and that what was needed was a simplification of the complex and costly procedures of keeping accounting books. Also, it was noted that policing tactics on the part of the tax authorities needed to stop, that formalities should be abandoned and 'a climate of better cooperation between taxpayers and tax officers should be established'.[125]

The Chamber was equally critical when, in May 1981, the Ministry of Economics announced that the tax audits concerning the fiscal year 1980 led to the collection of 47.2% more tax revenue than the one declared by corporations in their tax returns. The announcement stressed that such a result was achieved through the increase in the effectiveness of the tax services and the tax officers' efforts to curb tax evasion. However, according to the Chamber, there was also the possibility that such increased revenues were the result of the tax authorities' overzealousness. This should be the object of an examination, it was noted, because there had often been instances of inaccurate tax assessments 'that led firms to great troubles, or even to extinction'.[126] In fact, there were indeed measures that indirectly promoted such overzealousness, by relating, for example, the compensation of directors of tax offices with the level of tax revenues that they would achieve (see p. 175).

It should be noted at this point that tax officers had their own perspective to offer when being the objects of such criticism. For example, in relation to the issue of overzealousness, they stressed that the directors of the tax offices were not only pressed by the state for the quick collection of revenues, but also had to deliver facing 'a sea of tax legislation'.[127] Referring to the broader problems of the system of taxation in August 1976, the trade union of tax officers also argued that there were not enough personnel in the tax services, and that the number of tax officers

[125] *Bulletin of the Chamber of Commerce and Industry of Athens*, April 1981, 4, pp. 31–32.

[126] Ibid., May 1981, 5, p. 3.

[127] 'Tax Directors, Wronged and Misunderstood', *Tax Review*, July 1980, 378, p. 498.

should increase from 5,500 to 8,000 employees.[128] Some stressed nevertheless that the number of tax officers was not small. This was argued also by a tax expert, who wondered, in a newspaper commentary: 'There are 7,000 tax officers in West Germany, aren't 5,500 officers enough for Greece?'[129] Of course, such kind of counter-argument did not take into consideration the difference in the degree of tax compliance between Greece and Germany.

In relation to the criticism that their work was counterproductive, tax officers argued that this was because of their excessive workload and the multitude of tasks they had to perform. For example, the retired tax officer that participated in this research, noted: 'tax offices had the audit, tax and judicial sections, but there were also a lot of chores… it was like working in a construction site. We did all the small tasks, sometimes we even processed issues relating to postal services'.[130] In the same vein, the August–September 1980 issue of the *Tax Review*, commented that 'the labourer, the pensioner, the small trader, for every piece of documentation they receive from the state, go directly to the tax office in order, usually, to start a fight, even in cases in which they are receiving money back'. It was also noted that more than 50% of the tax returns submitted were without 'tax interest', that is, they generated zero-tax revenues for the state. However, the same time-consuming procedures followed in all other returns had to be followed for those returns too.[131]

Apart from this, it seems that, as in previous periods, tax officers received insufficient training. For example, in April 1980 the Ministry of Economics decided to offer tax officers accelerated training seminars on auditing business accounting books. However, such seminars lasted only for 15 days and were aimed only at newly recruited employees.[132]

It is also important to note that tax officers themselves recognised that some of their colleagues did not fulfil their roles. For example, in the December 1980 issue of the *Tax Review* it was highlighted that there was

[128] 'Tax Officers Ask for Legal, Economic and Moral Guarantees', *Makedonia*, 6.8.1976, p. 3.

[129] Th. Staikos, 'The Cost of the Civil Services', *I Kathimerini*, 24.12.1976, p. 5.

[130] Retired tax officer requesting anonymity, interview data.

[131] 'Unproductive Work in the Tax Services', *Tax Review*, August–September 1980, 379–380, p. 578.

[132] 'Micro-Economics', *I Kathimerini*, 15.4.1980, p. 9.

a large number of directors of tax offices who were interested 'only in chatting to the phone', and who, instead of being committed in solving the problems arising in the service, preferred to 'wait peacefully in their posts till the time of retirement comes, never caring about a thing'.[133]

However, a problem that was probably greater than the indifference of the tax officials, was that of corruption. There were many references in the press of the period about incidents where tax officers were arrested for blackmailing and bribery. In most of the cases, tax officers were accused of asking owners of companies for a bribe in order to not examine the company's accounting books, or to reduce (or not impose at all) the fines that had to be paid because of mistakes found in such books.[134] It was common in the cases referred to here that they came to light after the owners of the blackmailed companies filed reports to the police. Of course, it should certainly be expected that, in general, there would also be business owners—or taxpayers, more broadly—who would prefer to pay bribes, encouraging thus corruption and contributing to the problem of tax evasion. Still, that there were also people who preferred to complain to the police indicates that tax officers' corruption was a real issue that harmed business; if this was not so, every owner of a blackmailed company would simply pay the bribe, without making any kind of complaint to the authorities. This was not the case, however. On the contrary, the situation with corrupt tax officers created an adverse climate, indicative of which is the following point made by the pre-mentioned entrepreneur Stelios Argyros:

> It would help if the tax system was stable and structured in such a way that the taxpayer did not come into contact with the tax officers. For example, in the US, tax audits take place on a random basis, and therefore the entrepreneur does not work thinking that 'tax officers will be coming every month and blackmail me'. He also knows however that if he is found

[133] 'Directors of Tax Officers and Bureaucracy', *Tax Review*, December 1980, 383, p. 834

[134] The following are examples of such cases: 'Two Tax Officers Were Arrested for Bribe Taking', *I Kathimerini*, 17.9.1976, p. 8; 'Two Tax Officers Were Arrested for Bribe Taking – They Asked for 10,000 to Cover Infringements', *I Kathimerini*, 6.10.1979, p. 4; '14 Months Incarceration for a Tax Officer Because of Bribing', *I Kathimerini*, 28.8.1980, p. 3; 'A Tax Officer Was Arrested While Receiving Marked Bills- He was Blackmailing a Trader', *Ta Nea*, 27.2.1978, p. 16; '3 Years Incarceration for Two Tax Officers for Bribery', *Ta Nea*, 13.12.1978, p. 16.

to have gone against the law in one of these random checks, he will end up in prison. Because of this, he complies with tax legislation.[135]

A case of corruption that attracted a lot of publicity considered the blackmailing of the Shell Oil subsidiary in Greece, in May 1977.[136] According to newspaper reports, the tax officers arrested had asked the company for a bribe of DRS 6 million in order to not reject its accounting books[137] and determine its taxable income on an *ad hoc* basis,[138] something that would incur a fine of DRS 200 million.[139] It was noted that the fact that officers with monthly salaries of DRS 10,000–15,000 had been given the authority to impose such heavy fines indicated that the whole system of audits had to be re-examined.[140] This was because it was very difficult for people who had to carefully calculate their expenses in order to pay for their daily basic needs 'to resist the temptation of hundreds of millions [drachmas]'.[141]

This seemed to be a valid point, as tax officers often complained about issues relating to their salary and the prospects of getting a promotion within their services.[142] For example, in view of an incidence of bribery of tax officers in early August 1976, the president of the National Union of Tax Officers noted in a press conference that for the reduction of tax evasion and the implementation of fairer tax policies, a restructuring of the tax system was needed. He also argued for a restructuring of the tax services and an increase in the wages of tax officers, wages that were often 'lower than those of the service staff working in the companies they

135 Stelios Argyros, interview excerpt.

136 'Daily Matters', *I Kathimerini*, 14.5.1977, p. 5.

137 'Criminal Proceedings Were Initiated Because of Bribery from Tax Officers', *I Kathimerini*, 14.5.1977, p. 1.

138 'Tax Officers Attempted to Blackmail Shell for DRS 6 Million', *To Vima*, 13.5.1977, p. 1. By 'ad-hoc' it was meant that the determination of taxable income would be done without taking into consideration any information about revenue and expenditure contained in the firm's accounting books.

139 'Daily Matters', *I Kathimerini*, 14.5.1977, p. 5.

140 Ibid.

141 Ibid.

142 'The Construction of a New Payroll is of National Importance', *I Kathimerini*, 20.4.1977, p. 1.

audit'.[143] What was also necessary was an improvement in tax officers' working conditions, stressed the president, as well as 'legal protection from external interventions and pressures', the latter probably referring to cases in which tax officers were approached by taxpayers offering them bribes.[144]

Apart from the challenges that they were faced with when performing their duties, it has to be noted that the salaries that tax officers received were not lower than those of civil servants belonging to other Ministries. For one thing, they were, at times, the recipients of special allowances; in May 1979 for example they received a special allowance for the fast processing of 1.5 million tax returns concerning previous fiscal years. The government expected the allowance to function as an incentive that would 'assist in the fight against tax evasion and increase the revenue collected by the tax officers'.[145] This confirms what has been noted by the retired tax officer that participated in this research: 'We worked also in the evenings, and on Saturdays. And we always got an extra pay in comparison to the other civil servants. There was always something extra, a slight differentiation, in the form of either an overtime or an allowance'.[146] As a matter of fact, it seems that the only ones who were paid better than the tax officers were customs officers; it is probable therefore that when complaining about their salaries, tax officers had in mind the salaries customs officers received:

> The only ones who had higher salaries and were therefore privileged were the customs officers, who were receiving a Customs Services Aid (DETE) ... because of this aid, the difference between their salaries and the salaries of all other civil servants in the Ministry was large. So, the equalisation of our salaries with that of the customs officers was one of our ongoing demands.[147]

143 'Tax Officers Ask for Legal, Economic and Moral Guarantees', *Makedonia*, 6.8.1976, p. 3.

144 'Tax Officers Ask for Legal Guarantees', *I Kathimerini*, 6.8.1976, p. 7.

145 'Special Allowance to the Tax Officers for the Processing of 1.5 Million Cases', *I Kathimerini*, 18.5.1979, p. 2.

146 Retired tax officer requesting anonymity, interview data.

147 Nikolakopoulos, interview excerpt.

Such an equalisation and, more broadly, the increase of tax officers' wages started in 1989, noted Nikolakopoulos, when the Ministry of Economics established audit groups for the enforcement of the VAT and the Code of Accounting Books and Records. Officers participating in such audit groups would receive overtime remuneration which gradually became a permanent component of their monthly salaries.[148]

However, it seems that an increase in the wages of tax officers would not be enough to reverse the bad climate surrounding relations between tax authorities and taxpayers and erase the latters' general disappointment with the tax system. This was so in spite of the fact that, during this period, the state made efforts to combat corruption. For example, in early January 1979 the Ministry of Economics announced measures against bribery in tax services and customs. In the relevant circular issued, entitled 'Protection of the social standing of the employees of the Ministry of Economics', the officers of the Ministry were called upon to become 'the bearers of a new strict ethic characterised by the faithful…performance of duty, the…impartial serving of the citizens, the ruthless combating of bribe-giving or bribe-taking [and] the safeguarding of the people's money…'.[149] Specifically with regard to the tax services, the orders of the Ministry of Economics were that 'no tax officer would stay at the same tax service for more than three years'. In the circular it was also mentioned that there would be re-assessments of tax cases by officers different than those carrying out the initial audits and transfers of a large number of tax officers to different tax bureaus. The circular also introduced the option of periodically repositioning the directors of tax services, the establishment of random check teams staffed by tax officers chosen by the deputy general director of the Inspection Service of the Ministry of Economics, as well as the establishment of new criteria with regard to the promotion

[148] Ibid., interview data. According to Nikolakopoulos, when the government changed, tax officers demanded that such overtime payments become permanent, that is, that they would be receiving them regardless of whether they participated in audit groups or not. This was accomplished in the beginning of the 1990s, and the aid was named Aid for the Assessment and Collection of Third Party Taxes (DIVEET). In the course of time, the amount of DIVEET that each tax officer received on a monthly basis increased very much. That is, whereas, in the beginning of the 1990s, it amounted to approximately the 10% of tax officers' wage, it ended up, in the 2000s, being greater than their basic salary.

[149] 'Measures Against Bribe-Taking and Bribe-Giving Were Announced', *I Kathimerini*, 13.1.1979, p. 8.

of tax officers. It was then that it was decided that 15–20% of promotions would take place on the basis of merit, and not on the basis of years in service. It was also suggested that the staff capacity reports produced periodically by the services should not characterise from the outset all tax officers as 'excellent', but, on the contrary, should be 'more strict and objective' in order to reward the most capable and 'moral' officers.[150] Still, along with all such measures containing tax officers' arbitrariness, this same circular provided that 'enterprises' expenses should be checked with absolute rigour and get rejected if not accompanied by the relevant documentation'.[151]

More generally, the culture of mutual mistrust that had been cultivated between taxpayers and the tax authorities was expressed also by the fact that, as noted in a newspaper article, tax authorities tended to consider every taxpayer as an à priori tax evader. With regards to high-income earners who honestly declared it to the tax authorities 'because they wanted to sleep at night', it was stressed that they were faced with the tax officials' suspicions. It was said that: 'the fact that you are declaring this amount of income means that you actually earn much more'.[152] As for the option of making an appeal to the courts in order to challenge a decision made by the tax authorities, this was not something to be recommended, continued the article, given the bureaucratic and troublesome procedures that had to be followed in such cases. The result of all this was that taxpayers considered that they were faced with a despotic tax system.[153]

Additionally, while, on the one hand, the state introduced measures against tax officers' arbitrariness, on the other, it gave them more incentives to be overzealous when collecting tax revenues. An example of this is the fact that almost nine months after the circular giving instructions for 'impeccable behaviour and objective judgment' to the tax officers (see p. 166), the state issued a new circular through which the compensation of directors of tax offices would depend on the level of tax revenues they would achieve. For the government, this was an extra incentive for

[150] 'From Now On, Giving Bribes to Tax Officers Will be Impossible', *Ta Nea*, 13.1.1979, p. 1.

[151] 'Measures for the Proper Function of the Tax Services', *Bulletin of the Chamber of Commerce and Industry of Athens*, April 1977, 4, pp. 11–12.

[152] P. Mpakoyiannis, 'Vassal' Taxpayers', p. 6.

[153] Ibid.

the processing of tax cases. For some voices even from within the ruling party though, such a policy rewarded those tax officials who, through their actions 'increased the tax burden throughout Greece'.[154]

In the same vein, there were laws that had been introduced in order to curb tax evasion and tax officers' corruption, which, however, most of the time, also increased tax officers' authority and thus, their potential arbitrariness. For example, in January 1978, the formation of special tax inspection teams was announced, in order to contribute to the fight against tax evasion. These teams of tax officers were characterised by the front pages of the press of the period as 'commando-like' groups[155] that would have the authority to act as the police, carrying out surprise inspections on professionals' and companies' accounting books and records, on a 24-hour basis. Amongst the groups' responsibilities would be to daily inform the Ministry of Economics about their findings. The Ministry could then publicise the names of tax law offenders in cases of severe offences. More importantly, the inspection teams would have the authority to reject accounting books on a 'fast-track' basis and then determine taxable income ad-hoc, that is, disregarding any information about revenue and expenditure contained in the accounting books.[156] In this context, some noted that tax evasion was used as a pretext by the government, which formed such inspection groups in order to start 'hunting for taxes'.[157]

The relevant draft bill containing such measures was entitled 'On the assumption of measures against tax evasion and other relevant provisions' and got publicised by the government on 23 August 1978. Amongst its other provisions, the bill also announced the formation of the body of Sworn-in Valuers, having as its main purpose the valuation of property for taxation-related matters. In a parliamentary discussion, the MP of the

[154] 'The Remuneration of the Directors of Tax Services', *I Kathimerini*, 29.5.1976, p. 11.

[155] In later periods, instead of 'commando' the equally unfortunate 'rambo' nickname was used to describe such groups: (see for example Pr. Hatzinikolaou, 'Firm Audits: Equipped with Laptops, the Tax Services' Rambos Storm Businesses', *I Kathimerini*, 8.11.2006. http://www.kathimerini.gr/267986/article/oikonomia/ellhnikh-oikonomia/elegxoi-se-epixeirhseis-me-laptop-eformoyn-oi-rampo-ths-eforias [accessed 3.5.2014], in Greek.

[156] 'Commando-Tax Officers Against Tax Evaders', *Ta Nea*, 26.1.1978, p. 1.

[157] 'A Wild Hunting for Taxes Begins', *Rizospastis*, 26.1.1978, p. 1.

ruling party Athanasios Krikos noted that the Body would protect the taxpayers from the tax officers' arbitrariness, who, 'in order to ingratiate themselves with their superiors, very often impose[d] higher taxes than they should'.[158] Still, the general appreciation of the press was that the bill provided tax officers with 'excessive powers'[159] and aimed to intimidate taxpayers introducing 'unprecedented penalties and fines'.[160] More specifically, and apart from the measures mentioned above, the establishment of services for the control of the movement of goods was decided, in which tax officers would have the authority to undertake investigating tasks even without a relevant order from a Prosecutor. The inspectors of the tax services would also have the right to perform investigations in order to retrieve the taxpayers' books and records, again even without a Prosecutor's order, but also the authority to order the re-examination of any tax case.[161]

For the Chamber of Commerce and Industry of Athens, the bill provided Inspectors of tax offices with increased powers, introduced 'crippling penalties' and 'handed the taxpayer over to the uncontrollable judgment of the directors of tax offices'.[162] It is characteristic that at the time, the state itself openly acknowledged how rampant the problem of corruption was. Indicatively, even the Secretary of State Konstantinos Stephanopoulos admitted, in a relevant Parliamentary discussion, that apart from bureaucracy, one of the main problems of the public sector was that there were many services in which bribing was a standard practice.[163] Referring to the end of the period this chapter examines, the retired tax officer that participated in this research noted:

> At around 1980 the director of my department was talking about an officer who, with the things he did, earned a second salary. For example, he issued certificates; if you bribed him, he issued them faster. Or, in the department

158 'Special Allowance to the Tax Officers for the Processing of 1.5 million Cases', *I Kathimerini*, 18.5.1979, p. 2.

159 'A Few Employees Will Be Exempt from Presumptions of Wealth', *To Vima*, 24.8.1978, p. 1.

160 Ibid.

161 'The Main Provisions of the Tax Bill', *To Vima*, 24.8.1978, p. 2.

162 'The Chamber's Objections for the Tax Issue', *Bulletin of the Chamber of Commerce and Industry of Athens,* September 1978, 9, p. 27.

163 *Bulletin of the Chamber of Commerce and Industry of Athens,* May 1981, 4, p. 3

> where they stamped (for authentication purposes) the accounting books and records, he wouldn't stamp, say, 10 invoice books, but only one, in order for you to have to come again [and bribe him]. This officer gave to the trade unionist of the ruling party his vote. And to this trade unionist he turned if he needed something, giving him of course, in return, some kind of 'gift'.[164]

As has been shown in the previous chapters, similar events, and, more broadly, problems in the relations between taxpayers and tax officers were present in previous periods too. What was different in this case was that this situation co-existed with a clear deterioration in the country's general economic performance. In combination with the state's increased needs for tax revenues, this reality increased the tension between the two parties. The fact that the press used the word 'commando' to refer to the groups of tax officers performing audits during the end of the period, indicates the exacerbation of the situation.

Conclusion

During the years that are examined in this chapter Greece was exiting from a tumultuous seven-year period of dictatorship and had to prepare for its full membership in the EEC, while at the same time absorbing the Cyprus shock and the impact of an international economic recession. From a macroeconomic perspective, the distinguishing factor in this period in comparison to the previous ones is the gradual increase of public expenditure and the weakening of the economy, expressed through a worsening in all its basic indicators.

Industry also started losing its dynamism, entering a stage of stagnation that was marked, among others, by a reduction in the rate of increase of production and investment. Amongst the difficulties that industry was faced with was a worsening of the problems caused by the tax system. Specifically, fiscal expansion but also the increase of tax evasion led to the introduction of special contributions, the increase of fines for tax law offences as well as the increase of corporate income tax rate. At the same time, the administrative burdens of the tax system increased substantially. This was because of the rise in the frequency with which new tax laws

[164] Retired tax officer requesting anonymity, interview data.

were introduced and the resulting increased complexity of the legislation. Complaints regarding such problems, coming also from tax officers themselves, increased, whereas the measures that the state undertook to contain the tax officers' arbitrariness during audits and ease the problem of mistrust between them and the taxpayers did not seem to pay off. Moreover, as in previous periods, tax officers received insufficient training.

Equally, the state's efforts to tame corruption did not seem to bear substantial fruit and there were numerous incidences of tax officers being accused and arrested for blackmailing and asking for bribes. These developments indicated that, in combination with the deterioration in the economy and the rising of public expenditure, the impact of the problems burdening the way the tax system functioned became more explicit. In other words, the evidence presented in the previous pages suggests that it was now clearer that such problems seemed to discourage industrial investment. This would become even clearer in the next period during which the recession deepened to such an extent that Greece came very close to bankruptcy, and industry found itself well on the road of de-industrialisation. Not only that, but, as will be shown in the following chapter, during these years the dysfunctionalities burdening the system of taxation would become a matter of open conflict between tax officers, taxpayers (and thus also entrepreneurs) and the state.

Bibliography

Primary Sources

CHROTEX Archive

Board of Directors Meeting Minutes, various dates.

Professor Michalis Psalidopoulos personal archive

Bulletin of the Federation of Greek Industrialists (FGI) (1966–1988).

The Hellenic Literary and Historical Archive (ELIA)

IZOLA Files, Report of the Board of Governors for 1976, p. 18.

The 'Konstantinos G. Karamanlis' Foundation, Konstantinos G. Karamanlis Archive

Vol. 08, *The Restoration of Democracy, 1974–1977* (Period A', 24.7.1974–3.9.1975), p. 210.

Vol. 09, *The Restoration of Democracy, 1974–1977* (Period B', 4.9.1975–21.10.1977), pp. 39–40.

Union of Corporations and Limited Liability Companies Archive

Board of Directors Meeting Minutes (1957–1989).

Newspapers, Magazines and Serial Publications

a) Newspapers

Capital, Dimokratia, Eleftheria, Empros, Imerisia, I Avgi, I Kathimerini, I Naftemporiki, O Economicos Tahydromos, Makedonia, Rizospastis, Ta Nea, To Vima, To Vima tis Kyriakis (in Greek).

b) Magazines and Serial Publications

The Accountant, Tax Review, The Bulletin of Tax Legislation, Bulletin of the Chamber of Commerce and Industry of Athens.

Interviews

Argyros, Stelios.

Entrepreneur no. 3 requesting anonymity.

Nikolakopoulos, Charalambos.

Retired tax officer requesting anonymity.

Official Publications

Bank of Greece Governor's Annual Reports, various issues.

Bank of Greece, *Proposals of the Disincentives Committee* (Athens: Bank of Greece, 1979), p. 3.

Long-term Statistical Series of the Greek Economy.

Ministry of Finance, *Annual Reports for the Execution of the Budget*, various issues.

Statistical Yearbook of Greece, various issues.

Web Resources

Milios, Y., 'The Greek Economy in the 20th Century'. http://users.ntua.gr/jmilios/Oikonomia_Eikostos1ab.pdf [accessed 20.12.2014], pp. 1–24, in Greek.

'Stockwatch' *Stelios Argyros*. http://www.stockwatch.com.cy/nqcontent.cfm?a_name=bod_view&bodn_id=5747&lang=en and http://mba.aegean.gr/attachments/article/87/ArgyrosSteliosCV.pdf.

'TVXS', *Attila II: The Last Chapter of the Cyprus Tragedy*, 14.8.2010. tvxs.gr/news/κόσμος/αττίλας-ιι-το-τελευταίο-κεφάλαιο-της-κυπριακής-τραγωδίας, in Greek.

Secondary Literature

Agapitos, G. I., *Income Taxation in Greece* (Athens: Centre of Planning and Economic Research, 1986), in Greek.

Baumol, William J., 'Entrepreneurship: Productive, Unproductive, and Destructive', *Journal of Political Economy*, Vol. 98, 5, 1 (Oct., 1990), 893–921.

'Drachma for 60 years', in *Four Interviews of Xenophon Zolotas in Economicos Tahidromos* (Athens: Economicos Tahidromos,1988), pp. 3–18, in Greek

Harlaftis, G., *A History of Greek-owned Shipping – The Making of an International Tramp Fleet, 1830 to the Present Day* (London: Routledge, 1996).

Karamitsopoulos, V., Koumpias, A., Pastellas, O., Tiliakou, M., 'Proposal for the Establishment and Functioning of a Special Economic Zone in Greece', in *Niches of Freedom and Development – Proposal for the Functioning of a Special Economic Zone in Greece* (Brussels: Friedrich Naumann Stiftung Für die Freiheit, 2016).

Kazakos, P., *Between State and Market* (Athens: Patakis, 2001), in Greek.

Manesiotis, V., 'Tax Structure Change During Economic Development: The Case of Greece' (unpublished doctoral thesis, Northwestern University, 1985).

Manesiotis, V. G. and Reischauer, R. D., 'Greek Fiscal and Budget Policy and EMU'. in *Greece's Economic Performance and Prospects*, eds Ralph C. Bryant, Nikolaos H. Garganas and Georgios S. Tavlas (Bank of Greece and The Brookings Institution, 2002).

Mayr, T. P. and McGrath, R. H., 'Tramp Shipping: The Role of Taxation in International Resource Allocation', *Maritime Policy & Management*, 24:3 (1997).

Panselina, G. M. and Mavroeidi, M., *The Federation of Greek Industrialists, 1907–2007 – A Century in the Service of the Idea of Entrepreneurship* (Athens: Economia Publishing, 2007).

Psalidopoulos, M., *History of the Bank of Greece, 1928–2008* (Athens: The Bank of Greece, 2014), in Greek.

Tsiouras, A., 'Return to Development with Direct Foreign Investment', in *Niches of Freedom and Development – Proposal for the Functioning of a Special Economic Zone in Greece* (Brussels: Friedrich Naumann Stiftung Für die Freiheit, 2016).

Varoufakis, Y. and Patokos, T., 'Business Taxation Amid the Crisis', Centre of Research – Athens Chamber of Commerce and Industry.

Xanthakis, M., *The Crisis of Greek Manufacturing and State Intervention* (Athens: Papazisis, 1989).

Yannopoulos, G., 'Sensitivity of Industrial Sectors to Common Market Competition', in *The Mediterranean Challenge: IV, The Tenth Member – Economic Aspects* (Sussex: Sussex European Research Centre, 1980).

Zolotas, X., *Greece's Contribution in the European Community* (Bank of Greece: Athens, 1978).

CHAPTER 6

A 'Wild Tax Hunt' in the Era of Rapid De-Industrialisation: 1981–1989

Introduction

The period 1981–1989 was characterised by stagflation, increasing deficits and deteriorating competitiveness.[1] During those years the downturn that had initiated in the 1970s intensified and in 1981 the Greek economy was in the 'worst possible state'[2] with a sharp decline in GDP and a reduction in real wages. By comparison, the magnitude of the public sector and the public deficit kept rising. This period was merely a projection of a problematic past to a new environment, one that exposed the structural weaknesses of the Greek economy.[3] Due to the fiscal expansion and policies implemented by a state that was continuously intervening in the market process,[4] public expenditure as a percentage of GDP rose particularly fast.[5] Most notably, during 1980–1985, it grew faster than any

[1] Kazakos, p. 396.

[2] Ibid., p. 307

[3] Zacharias Demathas, 'Greek Economy and European Community', in *Greece in the 20th Century, 1980–1990*, I Kathimerini – Epta Imeres (Athens: *I Kathimerini*, 25–26.12.1999), p. 23.

[4] Kazakos, pp. 354–355.

[5] See Table 6.2, p. 5.

Z. Pittaki, *Exploring the roots of systematic tax avoidance in Greece*, Palgrave Studies in Economic History,
https://doi.org/10.1007/978-3-030-71979-1_6

other OECD country.[6] As a matter of fact, the country narrowly escaped bankruptcy in 1985.

Such a deterioration in the economy affected the industry. Investment in manufacturing decreased, but also production: according to the president of the FGI, 1982 was 'the worst year for Greek industry', one during which the reduction of production reached 5%, 'an unprecedented percentage'.[7] As a result of such developments, imports increased, the number of large companies fell, the wave of nationalisations intensified and the stagnation of the 1970s was followed by de-industrialisation, which now became a familiar term. The magnitude of the crisis was manifested by the fact that, at its culmination, at around 1983, '11 out of the 19 industrial sectors of Greece, the pride of post-war industrialisation, suffered great losses'.[8]

Apart from the deterioration in the economy, the industrial sector was facing difficulties also probably due to the impact of the increased competition with other European countries since full membership to the EEC was achieved. There were other reasons too. For example, it is possible that industry's competitiveness got reduced due to the appreciation of the drachma because of the influx of European funds since the late 1970s.[9]

However, additional difficulties were caused by the system of taxation. As in previous periods, it was not the number one problem of the economy. However, it had now become a much greater issue in comparison to earlier years. During the 1980s, there was a further increase in the corporate income tax rate and new special contributions were imposed upon both firms and individuals.[10] These developments probably reflected the fact that the state was in great need of revenue due to the pressing budget deficits but also the rising levels of tax evasion.[11] Yet again, the system of taxation was still plagued by bureaucracy and insufficient organisation. The frequency of relevant critiques also indicates that taxpayers' frustration due to complex procedures and confusing and

[6] *Bulletin of the FGI*, March 1988, 499, pp. 2–3.

[7] Ibid., June 1983, pp. 7–8.

[8] Kazakos, p. 359.

[9] Ibid., p. 410.

[10] As previously noted, from the mid-1970s onwards it was not the entrepreneurial classes who paid the majority of taxes in this period.

[11] Kalyvianakis et al., pp. 275–279.

frequently changing legislation increased during this period. On top of all this, and in spite of the fact that the state undertook relevant measures, the problem of inadequately trained, arbitrary and potentially corrupt tax officers, and also the mistrust between them and taxpayers, did not seem to diminish. More importantly, in a context of generalised disruption in the economy, such problems had become much more serious in comparison to previous periods, taking the form of a matter of open conflict between the state, taxpayers/entrepreneurs but also tax officers. Among others, the latter also complained about transfers of civil servants from various ministries to that of Economics that took place at the time. Such transfers exacerbated the deterioration in the quality and professional capabilities of the tax authorities that had initiated during dictatorship.

Such an adverse climate, which even witnessed incidents of violence between tax officers and taxpayers during audits, was anything but favourable to business. In fact, the evidence presented in the coming pages suggests that during this time it became clearer than ever before not only that the way the tax system functioned discouraged business initiative and thus also an industrial investment, but also that it sparked severe tensions and conflict among large parts of society. The chapter will proceed as follows: there is first an analysis of the new political reality that emerged with the elections of October 1981; then the characteristics of the economy and the industrial sector during the period are examined. The remaining part of the chapter is focused on an analysis of various developments in the tax system.

Politics, Economy and Industry

After the electoral battle of 18 October 1981, Papandreou's Panhellenic Socialist Movement (PASOK) was brought to power and Greece acquired 'a one-party socialist government for the first time in [its] history'.[12] The new government introduced changes of a progressive nature. For example, it lowered the minimum age of voting to 18, passed a law that brought elements of democratisation to the system of public higher education and recognised the contribution of those who fought in the resistance during the Second World War. This extended to support for the regional administrative bodies and also allowing civil marriage. With such

[12] Psalidopoulos, *History*, pp. 299; 302.

changes 'a climate of freedom and trust to the democratic institutions was established'.[13]

Also, the assumption of government by PASOK brought about a 'renewal' of the personnel of the various ministries and public bodies, a 'redistribution of power which gave access to…it to social groups that for decades were or felt excluded…After decades of right wing-conservative governments, ascension of PASOK [to the government] offered a symbolic but also substantial satisfaction to a large part of the population that felt sidelined and barred from the benefits of power'.[14] However, such a change gave rise to the expression of new attitudes in peoples' relations with the powers of state too. In this sense, the social policies of the new government contributed to the consolidation of a new 'mindset' of claiming and maintaining vested rights, especially from the part of the trade unions. A type of 'protectionist statism' arose, which, combined with the economic policies the government implemented, led to the increase of public deficit and debt, and to the creation of a state of 'artificial…prosperity'.[15] More generally, the government's policies during the period had a negative impact on the economy.[16]

Of course, the economy Papandreou inherited was already weak, burdened with stagflation and a soaring public deficit.[17] The difficult situation the new government was faced with was recognised also by the Bank of Greece, as two days after the elections, a note sent by its Governor Xenophon Zolotas to Apostolos Lazaris, the person who would become the new Minister of Coordination, characterised the state of the economy as 'critical' (Table 6.1).[18]

However, the realisation of the problems did not also mean the assumption of measures in order to overcome them. It seems that with the exception of some aspects of monetary policy, there were not any important structural improvements in the economy throughout the 1980s.[19]

[13] Kazakos, p. 365.

[14] Christos Lyrintzis, 'Change and Demystification', in *Greece in the 20th Century, 1980–1990*, I Kathimerini – Epta Imeres (Athens: *I Kathimerini*, 25–26.12.1999), p. 9.

[15] Ibid.

[16] Ibid., p. 10.

[17] Kazakos, p. 351.

[18] Psalidopoulos, *History*, p. 302.

[19] Demathas, p. 23.

Table 6.1 GDP growth rate (%), 1980–1990

1980	*1981*	*1982*	*1983*	*1984*	*1985*	*1986*	*1987*	*1988*	*1989**	*1990***
2.06	0.18	0.57	0.41	2.92	3.39	1.73	−0.72	4.46	3.66	−0.35

*Provisional data
**Estimation
Source: Long-term Statistical Series of the Greek Economy, p. 10

Table 6.2 Public expenditure, % GDP (1955–1986)

1955	*1960*	*1965*	*1970*	*1975*	*1980*	*1985*	*1986*
19.7	23.9	26.7	29.4	32.8	36.8	51.5	49.1

In 1986 market prices, *Source: Bulletin of the FGI*, March 1988, 499, p. 2

The level of prosperity had probably increased, but, in the course of time, as the basic characteristics of the mechanisms of the economy remained the same, its structural problems actually grew larger.[20]

In more detail, in spite of the fact that, at the time, there was a consensus in the rest of Europe that there should be efforts in order to achieve monetary stability and implement restrictive macroeconomic policies, Greece followed a different path, with the exception of the years 1985–1987.[21] Apart from this brief differentiation, more details of which will be offered below, the 1980s[22] saw 'excessively expansionist' macroeconomic policies.[23] According to Demathas, the increase of public expenditure (see Table 6.2) was also a result of the government's efforts to establish a certain level of 'social justice'. These attempts were without, however, the necessary funds to achieve this goal.[24] In such a context, there was a great increase in the level of public deficit and debt. Specifically, the share of public deficit over GDP was −16.1% in 1990 as

[20] Ibid.

[21] Kazakos, pp. 353–354.

[22] This was so for the first years of the 1990s too.

[23] Kazakos, pp. 354–355.

[24] Demathas, p. 22.

opposed to −2.6% in 1980 and the share of debt over GDP was 80.7% in 1990 as opposed to 28.6% in 1980.

Greece was on the verge of bankruptcy in 1985, when the current account deficit had surged to $3.3 billion. The assumption of a $1.75 billion loan from the European Solidarity Mechanism and the introduction, in October 1985,[25] of a programme of stabilisation were important measures. Their influence, according to the then Governor of the Bank of Greece, Dimitris Halikias, averted bankruptcy 'at the very last moment'.[26] The stabilisation programme, which was accompanied by a 15% devaluation of the drachma[27] has been characterised as an 'austerity break'.[28] The programme provided, among others, for an automatic wage indexation every fourth month as well as a reduction in the prices of agricultural products to a level lower than the one of the forecasted inflation. The reduction in the prices of oil on an international level at the time increased the effectiveness of the programme, indicative of which was the considerable reduction in the budget deficit between 1985 and 1987, as Table 5.4 shows.

The programme, however, was abandoned after 1987 and the deficit started increasing again from 1988 onwards. According to the annual report of the Governor of the Bank of Greece for 1991, the result of such developments was that the performance of the Greek economy, instead of converging, diverged from that of Greece's 'European partners'.[29] Commenting on the effectiveness of the programme, Kazakos noted that the stabilisation efforts it involved focused predominantly on income policies. More specifically, those who bore the main burden of austerity were wage earners,[30] as real wages fell by approximately 13.4% within two years.[31] Public investment was also drastically reduced, however, 'the sources of increase of the public deficit remained intact…no effort was

[25] Psalidopoulos, *History*, p. 49.

[26] Kazakos, pp. 374–376.

[27] Takis Katsimardos, 'The Chronicle of the Drachma, Full of Crises, Devaluations and Some…Bankruptcies', *Imerisia*, 02.01.2002. http://www.imerisia.gr/article.asp?catid=26516&subid=2&pubid=53928 [accessed 14.12.2014], in Greek.

[28] Kazakos, pp. 374–376.

[29] Psalidopoulos, *History*, p. 341.

[30] Kazakos, pp. 380–381.

[31] Ibid., pp. 386–387.

made for an effective management of resources'.[32] In such a context, in 1989, two years after the end of the programme, the deficit and debt had increased to 14.4 and 69.9% of GDP, respectively.

It is important to note that the continuously growing public deficit contributed to the increase in the level of demand. This demand, however, was channelled into consumption. Thus, as Konstantinos Drakatos notes, the economy was deprived of necessary infrastructure that could have been obtained, if the deficit had been used to fund public investment.[33] For example, from 15.5% in 1981, the rate of public investment over total public expenditure reduced to 9.0% in 1990.[34]

At this point, one could wonder how full EEC membership affected the Greek economy during the period. On the one hand, the revenue stream from the European Community after the 1981 accession was 'extremely high' and covered, on average, 2.7% of the country's GDP per year.[35] This very significant support, however, did not prove enough to turn around the 'developmental stagnation'[36] that affected the country during the period. Maybe this was because, as it has been argued, the Greek authorities had seen the procedure of the country's accession to the EEC as a predominantly political matter. That is, they did not pay sufficient attention to the economic repercussions of it and did not place the economy at the centre of the negotiations preceding the accession, something that would have probably led to the beginning of an effort of restructuring it.[37] According to Zacharias Demathas, when Greece entered the European Union, it was accompanied by the problems of the 1970s, and specifically, high inflation, an economy controlled by the state, but also 'deficient infrastructure, mechanisms and institutions'.[38]

[32] Ibid., p. 387.

[33] Drakatos, p. 95. Drakatos was an Emeritus Professor of Statistics in the University of Athens.

[34] Ibid.

[35] This holds for the period from 1981 to 2010. See Bitros, p. 11.

[36] Bitros, p. 11.

[37] Demathas, p. 22.

[38] Ibid.

Apart from the deterioration of the economy, the end of the decade was also marked by a series of scandals that had to do with the mismanagement of public funds.[39] The elections of summer 1989[40] were held under the shadow of such scandals and ended up with the formation of a caretaker government. It comprised of a coalition between the right-wing New Democracy and a union of left-wing parties, among which was also the Greek Communist Party. The primary aim of the new leadership was to prosecute those considered responsible for the politico-economic scandals of the previous period, overlooking the serious problems that were burdening the economy.[41] New elections took place in November 1989, which resulted in a new caretaker government, supported by all the parties of the Parliament, this time under the leadership of Xenophon Zolotas, the former governor of the Bank of Greece.[42] The new government undertook some measures for the containment of the crisis, which, however, did not bring any improvements to the structure of the economy.[43]

The deterioration of the economy during the 1980s was reflected also in the industrial sector, in spite of the fact that the new government had declared its willingness to support it. To this end, Papandreou noted the following in the first cabinet meeting of his government: 'All of us, in every corner of this country, should understand that there is a pressing need for productive investment and increase of productivity…'.[44] However, the developments of the decade were adverse on this front. As Chart 6.1 shows, the annual rate of increase of investment in the private manufacturing sector was either very small or negative for the majority of the 1980s.

As mentioned in the previous chapter, the crisis in manufacturing industry had already started in the late 1970s. It is characteristic that

[39] Kazakos, pp. 418–419.

[40] 'The General Secretariat of the Government', *Tzanis Tzanetakis Government*. http://www.ggk.gov.gr/?p=1294 [accessed 4.2.2015], in Greek.

[41] Kazakos, p. 426.

[42] Ibid., p. 427.

[43] Ibid., p. 428.

[44] *Bulletin of the Chamber of Commerce and Industry of Athens*, September 1982, 9, p. 3.

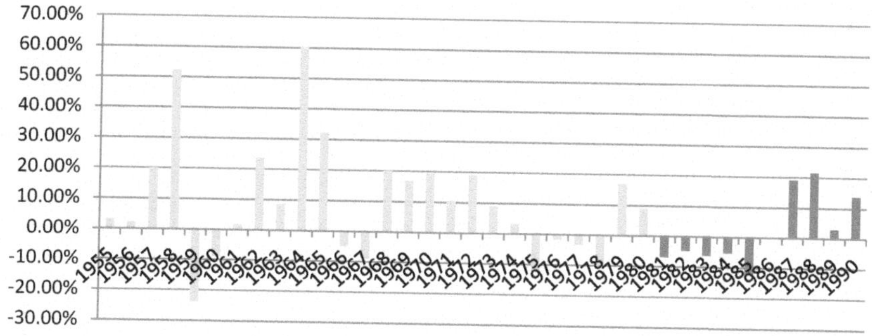

Chart 6.1 Annual rate of increase, gross private investment in fixed capital in manufacturing, 1981–1990 (*Source: Long-term Statistical Series of the Greek Economy*, p. 27. The rate of increase for 1986 is very small (0.11%) so it is not visible in the chart. The figures for 1989 and 1990 are provisional and an estimation, respectively)

according to the Minister of Economics,[45] in 1981, Return on Equity for the 100 largest commercial enterprises was 24.2% whereas for the 100 largest industrial ones only 1.7%.[46] Out of the total 39 'problematic' companies in early 1985, 36 were industrial ones.[47] Between 1975 and 1985 the three sectors with the greatest reduction of their product over GDP were the ones of wood processing and furniture, clothing and footwear and textiles.[48]

According to the president of the FGI, 1982 was 'the first year in [Greece's] post-war history in which losses in industry as a whole exceeded profits'.[49] Characteristic of the situation is that, as Chart 6.2 shows, within the broader period 1951–1990, 1982 was the year that saw the smallest number of new industrial units established annually.

As Chart 6.3 shows, with the exception of 1960 and 1961, 1982 was also the year with the smallest number of extended industrial units.

[45] In his speech in the annual congress of the FGI in May 1983.

[46] *Bulletin of the FGI*, June 1983, pp. 7–8.

[47] Provopoulos, p. 25

[48] *Long-Term Statistical Series of the Greek Economy*, pp. 10–11.

[49] *Bulletin of the FGI*, October 1983, 454, pp. 4–5.

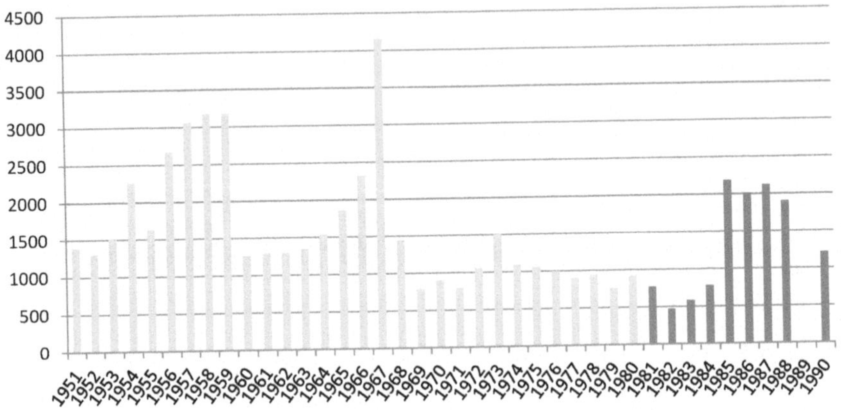

Chart 6.2 Number of new factories and workshops of industrial and handicraft enterprises, 1981–1990 (*Source: Statistical Yearbook of Greece*, various issues[50])

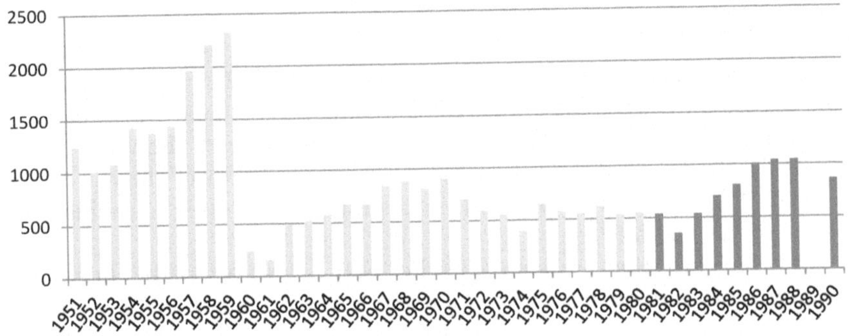

Chart 6.3 Number of extended factories and workshops of industrial and handicraft enterprises, 1981–1990 (*Source: Statistical Yearbook of Greece*, various issues[51])

[50] See Chapter 3, p. 42, footnote no. 26.

[51] See Chapter 3, p. 42, footnote no. 26.

On the whole, the performance of the industrial sector in the 1980s was much poorer than in previous periods, and this was the appreciation of the entrepreneurial classes too. Industry's negative performance, stressed the president of the FGI Theodoros Papalexopoulos in the annual congress of the Federation in 1983, reflected the adverse international economic climate, but was mostly a result of the economic, exchange rate and tax policies followed by the Greek governments over the last years.[52]

In the same vein, in the minutes of the Board meeting of the Union of Corporations and Limited Liability Companies held on 26 April 1983 it was noted that in 1982 the index of industrial production in manufacturing had decreased, for the second year in a row. The reduction amounted to −6.2% and was much greater than the one in 1981 (−0.7%). Such disappointing results were attributed to the recessionary circumstances in the economy, to the reduction in the exports of industrial products, but also, 'to the intensity of the problems and disincentives [facing] industrial enterprises'.[53]

The situation would become worse in the following years; as Kazakos notes, up to 1984 the majority of industrial sectors had negative average annual rates of growth.[54] According to data from the Ministry of Economics, until March 1991 230 companies with 208,000 employees had come under the control of the state,[55] and specifically under the control of the Organisation for the Restructuring of Companies that was established in 1983.[56] This organisation, as Kazakos notes, merely helped failing and non-viable companies to continue functioning 'artificially', at a great cost for the state. Eventually, it ended up symbolising 'the failure of state interventionism in Greece'.[57]

It should be noted that in the period 1985–1989 a relative recovery emerged in industry, probably reflecting the assumption of the stabilisation programme of 1985–1987 by the government.[58] Such a recovery

[52] *Bulletin of the FGI*, October 1983, 454, pp. 4–5.

[53] Union of Corporations and Limited Liability Companies, Board Meeting Minutes 26.4.1983, p. 235.

[54] Kazakos, p. 404.

[55] Ibid., pp. 361–362.

[56] Ibid., pp. 358–359.

[57] Ibid., pp. 363–364.

[58] See p. 5.

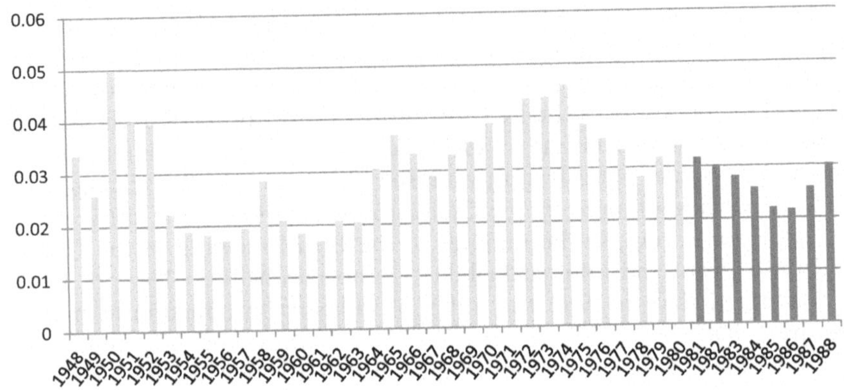

Chart 6.4 Manufacturing, gross private investment in fixed capital, % GDP (1981–1988) (*Source: Long-term Statistical Series of the Greek Economy*, pp. 27, 10)

was indicated by the increase in the rate of investment in manufacturing over GDP, as Chart 6.4 indicates.

There was also a surge in the number of new industrial units in 1985–1987, as Chart 6.2 shows. Similarly, as Chart 6.3 shows, the years 1983–1988 saw an increase in the number of enterprises' extended factories.

However, as stressed before in this study, the various short-term differentiations indicated through charts like the previous three ones should not be taken too literally. For example, the recovery in the mid to late 1980s was followed by a new downturn in 1989–1992. What actually matters the most is the broader picture: on the whole, industry's participation in GDP fell from 17.36% in 1980 to 14.32% in 1990. There was also a continuous reduction in the productivity rate of the manufacturing sector, throughout the 1980s, with the difference between the Greek and the average OECD rate growing larger. In addition to these trends, investment started focusing in 'light' industrial sectors instead of the 'heavy' ones, as was the case before the 1960s.[59] It was in this period that the term 'de-industrialisation' became commonly used in discussions about the economic situation.[60] Kazakos notes that up to that

[59] Kazakos, p. 404.

[60] Ibid., pp. 402–403.

point, Greece's developmental priorities and 'europeanisation' aspirations were centred around industrialisation and, for this reason, the crisis that emerged was 'dramatic', even more so in regional Greece, where 'whole areas saw their industries disappearing'.[61]

In such a context, the number of large companies fell and the share of imports in real consumption increased from 25.8% in 1978–1980 to 43.1% in 1989.[62] Similarly, in a meeting of the Board of the Union of Corporations and Limited Liability Companies the secretary general of the Union noted that, according to European Commission studies, investment in manufacturing was at a very low level in Greece, with no signs of improvement over recent years.[63] It is also a fact that in 1990, the value added of the Greek manufacturing sector was the lowest one among all European countries.[64]

A factor that possibly contributed to the weakness of the Greek industry, as Kazakos notes, was the fact that the influx of European funds from the late 1970s onwards increased the exchange rate of the drachma. It, therefore, created a type of 'Dutch disease' that affected the Greek economy and reduced the competitiveness of its manufacturing sector.[65] Another factor could have probably been the small size of industrial enterprises that prevented them from having easy access to sources of funding.[66] Moreover, according to one of the entrepreneurs that participated in this research, the state's foreign currency controls also proved problematic: 'In 1986 we had to travel abroad in order to participate in various fairs and exhibitions, meet with our clients, etc. The state, considering that our aim was to take our money outside Greece, did not allow us to carry more than $150 in foreign currency every day, something that caused many problems in our activities'. Referring more broadly to the state's stance towards business, this specific entrepreneur, owner of an exporting industrial firm that declared bankruptcy in the early 1990s,

[61] Ibid., pp. 405–406.

[62] Ibid, pp. 399–400.

[63] Union of Corporations and Limited Liability Companies, Board Meeting Minutes 7.3.1989, p. 197.

[64] Kazakos, p. 405.

[65] Ibid, p. 410.

[66] Ibid., p. 406.

also argued that the state was not particularly interested in supporting export-oriented companies:

> No representative of the state had accompanied us in the various international exhibitions we participated. I had asked, for example, the commercial attaché of the Greek embassy in Paris to come to the opening of the [international] exhibition there, in order to represent the Greek state....this was a time when Greece had only recently become a member of the European Union and, because of this, we were treated with a degree of suspicion, even hostility, due to competition reasons. Because of this, we had been allocated the least privileged part of the exhibition. However, the state gave us no kind of help, it showed absolutely no interest.[67]

The January 1982 issue of the *Bulletin of the FGI*, discussed the 'weakness' in investment initiatives and argued that it should be attributed to the business uncertainty. The factors which created this uncertainty, it claimed, were the indigenous and international economic circumstances as well as a series of other issues such as the low return on capital, the high inflation and the high-interest rates, the disincentives created by the bureaucracy of the public sector, but also a number of 'outdated' institutions. There was no further reference to such institutions, however, it was mentioned that among the factors hampering investment was the uncertainty concerning a series of crucial issues. Such issues were the exchange rate policies, the measures regarding the revaluation of companies' fixed assets, the regulation concerning labour relations, the environment, the long-term economic policies enforced by the state, but also property tax and the 'taxation of distributed and undistributed profits'. It was stressed that the uncertainty surrounding those issues obscured the 'rules of the game' and this was something that the state should take care of, in order to promote private investment initiatives.[68] The remaining part of this chapter will analyse the uncertainty stemming from the way the tax system functioned.

[67] Entrepreneur no. 1 requesting anonymity, interview data.

[68] *Bulletin of the FGI*, January 1982, 436, p. 1.

The System of Taxation

When complaining about the lack of clear rules of the game in the tax system, entrepreneurs referred, on one level, to the increased taxation and the special contributions upon firms' profits that the state imposed unexpectedly during the period. For example, in 1982 law 1249 entitled 'On adjustments on direct and indirect taxation, salary issues and other provisions' was introduced, according to which the tax rates on dividends were increased for both listed and non-listed companies. The tax rate of indigenous corporations' and foreign firms' undistributed profits also increased from 40 to 45% in 1981 to 49% in 1985 (see Table 4.5, p. 153). The law also provided for the revaluation of land and buildings owned by companies whose accounting books belonged to the 4th category.[69] The rates with which the increased values of such assets would be taxed were 8% for land and 12% for buildings. A real estate flat tax of 1.5% was also introduced, however buildings and other construction that were owned and used for the productive activities of industrial, commercial and hotel enterprises were exempt from this tax.[70]

In a relevant announcement, the Union of Chambers of Commerce and Industry of Greece expressed its concerns and disappointment for the new law, stressing that it created an adverse economic climate.[71] The introduction of the law had also preoccupied the Union of Corporations and Limited Liability Companies. When it was still at the stage of a draft bill, according to the Union's Board meeting minutes, a delegation comprised of members of the Board of the Union had visited the Prime Minister at his home. In this meeting, according to the president of the Union Stratis Andreadis, the entrepreneurs had expressed their 'deep concerns' about the tax bill, and they stressed that if introduced without any improvement, it would cause inflation, unemployment and 'serious problems to private companies'.[72] In a related discussion among the members of the Board however, the conclusion was that

[69] 4th category accounting books were those following the double-entry system. In 1982, such books should be kept by companies with annual gross revenue exceeding DRS 50 million (Sellas, p. 143).

[70] *Bulletin of the FGI*, December 1982, p. 445, p. 8.

[71] *Bulletin of the Chamber of Commerce and Industry of Athens*, May 1982, 5, p. 27.

[72] Union of Corporations and Limited Liability Companies, Board Meeting Minutes 2.4.1982, p. 125.

'the Administration listens to the representatives of the productive classes merely to keep up pretences, merely to appear as having a dialogue (with them), while it has already decided what to do, except on a few and unimportant...concessions'.[73]

Apart from new laws, and as was the case in the 1974–1981 period too, special contributions were imposed. Specifically, in 1985 a special contribution of 10% upon firms' profits was imposed.[74] A further special contribution of 10% was imposed in 1987, regarding the profits of firms for the fiscal year 1986. It seems that business viewed the introduction of such contributions as tax changes that increased uncertainty. For example, in 1987 the Union of Corporations and Limited Liability Companies sent a memorandum to the Prime Minister, the Ministers of Economics and National Economy as well as various economic newspapers noting that 'the surprise imposition of a new special contribution on business profits...totally overturns any efforts for improvement of the business climate. It restores the climate of uncertainty and abstention from new productive initiatives...the damage it causes to the economy is many times bigger than the postulated fiscal gain'.[75]

In the same vein, it was noted in the *Bulletin of the FGI* that special contributions harmed the business climate because they prevented companies from effectively forecasting their costs and thus planning their activities. It was stressed that there was now a certainty that the government could change, ex post, the terms with which firms planned their activities.[76] The Federation expressed its 'grave concerns' about such developments, which, combined with the increase in the public sector deficit, put in jeopardy, as it was noted, the progress that had been achieved through the introduction of the stabilisation programme two years ago. They also weakened the prospects for a quick recovery of the Greek economy and increased the likelihood that it would go again down the road of 'high inflation, increasing deficits, policing of the market, investment recession and swelling of unemployment'. Such prospects, it was noted, led to a severe deterioration of the business climate, given

[73] Ibid., p. 126.

[74] *Bulletin of the FGI*, October–November 1987, 495–496, pp. 4–5.

[75] Union of Corporations and Limited Liability Companies, Board Meeting Minutes 1.12.1987, p. 11.

[76] *Bulletin of the FGI*, October–November 1987, 495–496, pp. 1–2.

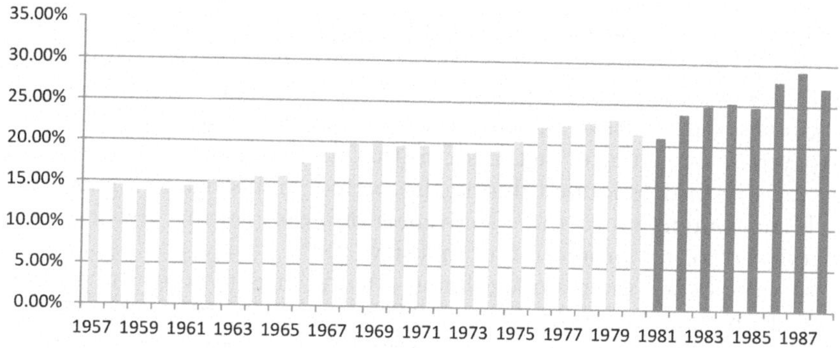

Chart 6.5 Tax revenue, % GDP (1981–1988) (*Source: Long-term Statistical Series of the Greek Economy*, pp. 13; 86–87)

that, as one should reasonably assume, there was no stable framework within which the economic policies would develop: '…the long-term goals of stabilisation and growth give way to short-term political needs, agendas and pressures…the recent developments disrupt continuity, the main element upon which the recovery of the climate during the last two years was sustained'.[77]

All such developments probably contributed to the further increase of the tax burden as a share of GDP during this period (Chart 6.5, p. 196). According to a relevant study, 2,176,204 people filed tax returns in 1987, paying total taxes of DRS 229,526.8 mil, in comparison to 601,677 people in 1970, who paid taxes amounting to DRS 4,052.8 mil. Also, the average tax burden on declared income had increased to 11.2% in 1987 compared to 7% in 1970.[78] However, it should also be noted that the end of the 1980s saw a reduction in the maximum income tax rates for individuals belonging to the higher income brackets. In other words, the tax system became more regressive.[79]

[77] Ibid.

[78] Kalyvianakis et al., pp. 48–49.

[79] Specifically, according to the tax scale for the fiscal year 1955, the individual income tax rate ranged from 5 to 60% for annual incomes ranging from DRS 4 thousand and up to 1 million. Above that, there would be a proportional tax of 60%. There were not any significant changes in 1965, when tax rates ranged from 3 to 55% for incomes ranging from DRS 5 thousand and up to 1 million, whereas the proportional rate above that

Apart from the various new taxes, the tax system was, as in earlier years, burdened by problems such as the excessive bureaucracy, complexity and frequent changes of legislation, lack of sufficient organisation, and of course, lack of trust affecting the relations between tax officers and taxpayers. As a matter of fact, it seems that the problem of complexity of the legislation deteriorated during this period. Industrialists argued that such issues undermined the effectiveness of incentives that the state had introduced for the promotion of industry.

In more detail, the main legislation offering incentives for the promotion of investment during the period was law 1262/1982 entitled 'On incentives for the promotion of economic and regional development of the country and amendments of relevant provisions'. Law 1262/1982 replaced a previous one, 1116/1981, which introduced for the first time the measure of subsidies for the support of investment. In the June 1987 issue of the *Bulletin of the FGI* it was noted that law 1262/1982 was of limited effectiveness, as it was used to support predominantly regional and small-scale investment projects, disregarding, to a large extent, the core industrial areas, wherein the majority of industries were established.[80] It is interesting to note however that shortly after its introduction, business organisations' attitudes towards this law were varied. For example, in an article that was published in the *Bulletin of the Chamber of Commerce and Industry of Athens*, the new law was described as a positive measure, that provided clear information about the scope and extent of subsidies.[81] On the other hand, in the Board meeting minutes of the Union of Corporations and Limited Liability Companies it was noted that the new legislation was not expected to create any significant upturn in business

was 55%. Ten years later, in 1975, tax rates ranged from 3 to 60% for annual income from DRS 20 thousand to DRS 3 million (with the provision that incomes up to DRS 1 million would be taxed with rates ranging from 3 to 5%). Income exceeding the 3 million limit would be taxed with a proportional rate of 60%. In 1985 tax rates ranged from 0 to 63% for incomes from DRS 80 thousand to 4,880 thousand. Income exceeding this amount would be taxed with a rate of 63%. Yet, the maximum rate for incomes of up to DRS 1 million was reduced to 48%. Also, from 1989 onwards the maximum income tax rate would be capped to 50% whereas the maximum rate for income of up to DRS 1 million would be reduced significantly, amounting to 24% (Sellas, pp. 433–434).

[80] *Bulletin of the FGI*, June 1987, 492, p. 4.

[81] B. Dimitriou, 'Important Incentives for Investment', *Bulletin of the Chamber of Commerce and Industry of Athens*, September 1982, 9, pp. 10–11.

activities.[82] Of course, one should take into consideration that the views expressed by the various business organisations reflected the position and role each one of those had in the broader socio-economic environment of Greece of the time. This point was raised in a meeting between the director of the Union of Corporations and Limited Liability Companies, Isidoros Tzallas, and the president of the FGI Theodoros Papalexopoulos, where the latter noted that it would not be to the productive classes' interests if the various bodies of entrepreneurs appeared publicly as having common beliefs and goals. As Papalexopoulos stressed, the Chamber of Commerce and Industry of Athens and all other Chambers of the country were legal entities governed by public law therefore, cooperation between them and other business bodies should be 'very discreet'.[83] Papalexopoulos' point also suggests that perhaps the Chamber's positive appreciation of the law related to the fact that it was governed by public law and therefore influenced, up to a certain extent, by the state.

Further measures for the promotion of investment and exports were undertaken in later years, such as, for example, the provision of exemption from taxation of the 50% of the undistributed profits of 1987 that would be used to finance productive investments and the reduction by 50% of the rates with which the net revenues of companies—apart from those accruing from the sale of their products within the country—would be taxed.[84] There would also be a revaluation of land and buildings of companies; the increase in the value of land would be tax exempt, and the one of the value of buildings would be taxed with a rate of 5%. Further measures would also be adopted for the improvement of law 1262/1982, as well as measures for the promotion of high-technology investments. A special organisation would also be created, in order to identify, study and promote the various investment opportunities emerging in both the public and private sectors of the economy.[85]

As was the case in previous periods, the various views about the effectiveness of such incentives expressed, at best, scepticism. For example, the May 1982 issue of the *Bulletin of the Chamber of Commerce and Industry*

[82] Union of Corporations and Limited Liability Companies, Board Meeting Minutes 29.4.1982, p. 141.

[83] Ibid., 21.3.1984, p. 302.

[84] This measure could be used alternatively to law 1262/1982.

[85] Union of Corporations and Limited Liability Companies, Board Meeting Minutes 2.2.1988, pp. 37–39.

of Athens hosted an article written by an economist, and examining the incentives laws that the state had introduced since the 1950s. Such laws involved, in their majority, credit support and tax reliefs. It was argued that these laws not only did not support the country's efforts for industrial development, but also 'created a series of problematic companies'. The author believed that, apart from the lack of control on the part of the state and the lack of effective credit policies, one of the main reasons that incentives laws did not have the expected results was that the support they provided was not targeted on high-quality investments. For example, the state-funded investments focused on products that were not competitive in the international markets, or supported sectors that suffered from growing 'investment congestion'.[86]

From a quite different perspective, it was argued that what mattered most for the increase of the level of investment were not the incentives, but a favourable macroeconomic context that would promote business initiative. For example, in the *Bulletin of the FGI* a report of the OECD regarding investment in Greece was mentioned, which indicated that general macroeconomic stability was a prerequisite for the increase of the level of investment. It was also noted that the government needed to abandon its tactic of centrally programming investments in the various industrial sectors, but also that firms had to seek alternative sources of raising capital for their investment plans, such as for example through the stock exchange market. There were also some 'complementary' measures, which, however, it was stressed, were of limited scope. These related to investment incentives, the reduction of taxation and the attraction of foreign investment funds. It is important to note that, apart from stressing that such measures were of limited scope, the report also mentioned that investment incentives would be ineffective unless 'progress on a more general level' was achieved.[87]

In their public speeches, the representatives of industrialists expressed similar views. In a talk in the Foreign Press Association in September 1987 for example, the president of the FGI Theodoros Papalexopoulos noted that for the promotion of industrial development what was needed was not the assumption of measures such as investment incentives. In

[86] P. Vakalis, 'Developmental Incentives and Government's Goals', *Bulletin of the Chamber of Commerce and Industry of Athens*, May 1982, 5, pp. 22–23.

[87] *Bulletin of the FGI*, August–September 1987, 493–494, p. 4.

fact, Papalexopoulos stressed, European integration and the new competitive environment emerging indicated that the 'era of incentives' was over. What was needed was the 'purposeful, systematic and planned overcoming of disincentives and obstacles hindering…the function of the economy'. There were four categories of such disincentives, relating to market regulations, the banking system, the 'unequal treatment of private companies in comparison to the public ones', but also, the system of taxation, which should be transformed 'from a revenue-collecting mechanism to a developmental tool'. Papalexopoulos stressed that for this to be achieved, the tax authorities' 'mindset' should change,[88] probably implying, among others, that tax officers' overzealousness in the process of collecting tax revenues should be reduced.

From a fairly similar perspective, in an article published at around the same period in the *Bulletin of the Chamber of Commerce and Industry of Athens*, Themistocles Sarakos, who had served as a councillor of the Athens Traders Association, noted that the biggest part of the various incentives that the state offered for the promotion of productive activities, among which were tax incentives, did not prove particularly effective.[89] This was due to the lack of control on the part of the state, to the unscrupulousness of people who took advantage of such measures in order to serve their own interests, but also, to the existence of various disincentives. What was needed, he stressed, was a simplification of bureaucratic procedures, a specification of the boundaries between state and private initiative, but also stable economic policies and a stable labour and tax legislation: '…if we keep changing the rules of the game…there will be no investments and we will be struggling in vain to achieve the progress of our Economy'.[90]

Actually, the bureaucracy burdening the tax system affected also the Value Added Tax. Its introduction in 1987 had been heralded as a major reform, not only by representatives of the tax authorities, but even entrepreneurs themselves. For example, in the January–February 1984 issue of the *Bulletin of the Chamber of Commerce and Industry of Athens* it was noted that the VAT was expected to considerably simplify the way

[88] Ibid., pp. 5–6.

[89] Th. Sarakos, 'Incentives and Disincentives', *Bulletin of the Chamber of Commerce and Industry of Athens*, January 1986, 1, p. 30.

[90] Ibid., pp. 30–31.

the tax system functioned, by replacing the existing indirect taxes.[91] In the same spirit, in an article that appeared in 1986 in the *Tax Review*, the then president of the trade union of tax officers Apostolos Kostopoulos characterised VAT as 'the biggest post-war tax reform that aspires to turn the whole system of our indirect taxation from a small source of funding…to a …highway of development…With the proper tax policy, the VAT can contribute to a fairer distribution of the tax burden, protect the purchasing power of wage earners, pass on an important part of the tax burden to higher income classes, … and effectively tackle social and economic crises'.[92]

However, when the VAT was finally introduced, it became clear that it suffered from some of the typical malaises of the tax system, involving bureaucratic and complex procedures and being yet another expression of the lack of organisation characterising the broader system of public administration. Indicatively, in a speech in the Foreign Press Association in September 1987, the president of the FGI Theodoros Papalexopoulos noted that not only had the tax replaced only a small proportion of the indirect taxation, but also that the procedures followed for the submission of VAT returns were 'time-consuming and bureaucratic'. These procedures, he thought, placed an 'unsustainable burden' on a large number of companies. Such problems were examples of dysfunctionalities that, according to Papalexopoulos, hindered business activities and the country's economic development more generally.[93] In the same vein, it was mentioned in the *Bulletin of the FGI* at around the same period that the time-consuming procedures required for the return of VAT in exporting companies and companies making investments, deprived them of important funds for long periods of time. In this way, both investment and

[91] *Bulletin of the Chamber of Commerce and Industry of Athens*, January–February 1984, 1–2, p. 10.

[92] Apostolos Kostopoulos 'Is VAT a Contractual Obligation, or a 'Magical Solution'?', *Tax Review*, September 1986, 452, pp. 818–822. Therefore, it seems that the initial reaction of business and tax experts in Greece towards the prospect of the imposition of VAT was different than elsewhere. For example, Neil Rollings notes that in the case of Britain, prior to the imposition of the tax, industry remained, to a large extent, doubtful about its potential implications (see Neil Rollings, *British Business in the Formative Years of European Integration, 1945–1973* (Cambridge: Cambridge University Press, 2007), pp. 238–240.

[93] *Bulletin of the FGI*, August–September 1987, 493–494, pp. 5–6.

exports were inhibited, in spite of the fact that the government stressed that these were 'primary goals'.[94]

Also, in the 7 January 1987 Board meeting minutes of the Union of Corporations and Limited Liability Companies, it was noted that the VAT was introduced 'in a completely overhasty and unorganised manner'. Indeed, it was added, the lack of necessary information, preparation and instructions for the implementation of the law 'led the market to utter confusion'. It was also stressed that the fact that the Ministry of Economics had declared that any mistakes during the initial period of the introduction of the tax would be treated with lenience, meant that it indirectly recognised that it was responsible for the problems. Apart from this, it was also mentioned that the situation created a sense of mistrust towards the tax that resulted in 'a tendency towards avoiding paying it, from the outset'.[95]

The critique did not come only from business. A newspaper article in early March 1988 noted that there were various complaints regarding the VAT return for the fiscal year 1987. The relevant form that had to be submitted was characterised as a 'labyrinth'. This complexity became worse due to the fact that the circular that the Ministry of Economics had sent to the tax offices, offering instructions for the form's completion, contained as many as 79 pages. 'One should imagine', noted the article, 'the trouble and the…time that owners of business…will take in order to study the instructions and complete the return…while the Ministry speaks of simplification of procedures'. Another issue that raised complaints was that whereas in 1987, that was the first year of the implementation of the VAT, taxpayers could submit the final return via post, by 1988 this option was no longer available and every taxpayer had to submit the return either in person or through an authorised representative.[96]

In fact, bureaucracy, complexity and lack of sufficient organisation were characteristics that burdened the tax system as a whole, and not only the procedures concerning VAT, and which, according to the entrepreneurs' complaints, were significant obstacles to business activities. For example,

[94] Ibid., June 1987, 492, p. 3.

[95] Union of Corporations and Limited Liability Companies, Board Meeting Minutes 7.1.1987, pp. 256–257.

[96] 'In the Labyrinth of the VAT Return', *I Kathimerini*, 3.3.1988, p. 9.

it was noted in the Board meeting minutes of the Union of Corporations and Limited Liability Companies that a series of administrative and bureaucratic obstacles were opposing entrepreneurial action. Specifically, it was stressed that the way in which firms were obliged to keep their accounting books and records was 'bureaucratic' and 'beyond any reasonable need'. As a result, firms had to spend 'more time on this bureaucracy rather than their own economic activities'. This reality, it was stressed, along with a series of other problems, contributed to the discouragement of investment.[97]

The same argument was repeated in the *Bulletin of the FGI*. The everyday problems that enterprises were faced with were noted, such as the 'exhausting' bureaucratic obstacles that they had to overcome when waiting to receive VAT refunds or for an investment project to get approved by the administration. Such kinds of problems not only harmed competitiveness and discouraged investment, but also indicated that there were was an inherent issue of inconsistency characterising the governments' most basic pursuits and economic policies.[98] One of the entrepreneurs that participated in this research shared a personal experience on how exhausting the bureaucratic obstacles that faced firms were:

> The lack of organisation in public administration was a huge problem. For example, exporting firms were entitled to tax and duty drawbacks. For this to happen however, customs departments had to check the documents that accompanied each export. This was a very time-consuming procedure and there were huge delays. Only up to 10 exports were processed every day. The response I got when I asked about the delays was that there was not enough staff for the timely processing of each export. At one point, the manager of the customs office suggested that I bring 3-4 employees from my company in order to assist with the checking of documents. He had probably made the same suggestion to other entrepreneurs. This was the only way to speed up the process. In this way, instead of 10 cases, every day 20 or even 30 cases were processed. When our company closed down, it had a total debt of DRS 10 billion, out of which 5.5 billion were owed to us by the customs![99]

[97] Union of Corporations and Limited Liability Companies, Board Meeting Minutes 24.4.1985, pp. 13–14.

[98] *Bulletin of the FGI*, August–September 1987, 493–494, pp. 1–2.

[99] Entrepreneur no. 3 requesting anonymity, interview excerpt.

In the Bulletin of the Chamber of Commerce and Industry of Athens, it was mentioned that the Chamber had sent a memorandum to all political parties which contained its proposals with regard to the various problems of the Greek economy. The most important problems, it was noted, were the continuously widening public deficit and the rising inflation.[100] Among other points, it was stressed that the overregulation and continuous amendments of the legislation discouraged investment. It went on to say that the procedures governing exports, financing, investment incentives, as well as the establishment, extension and merging of companies should be simplified, but also that the tax system should be modernised in order to encourage the increase of productivity. Specifically with regard to the tax code, it was mentioned that it was 'anachronistic and full of pitfalls', and also having such an ambiguity that allowed tax officers to be subjective when interpreting and implementing its provisions.[101]

As in previous periods, such problems were recognised also by tax officers themselves. For example, in an article that appeared in 1989 in the *Tax Review*, written by a tax officer, the following were mentioned about the frequency of change and complexity of tax legislation:

> It is impossible –no matter how good knowledge of the law one has- to make any sense out of the tax [legislation]. Complex provisions, difficult to understand,..., shoddily written...[t]he forms that citizens have to complete are utterly incomprehensible...[e]very piece of legislation in income taxation usually has an average life of approximately one year. Within one year, it changes again. And it is possible to change again with its interpretative circular.[102]

Specifically with regard to the income taxation law 3323/1955 it was noted that it had a record number of amendments, with some of its paragraphs having changed 'dozens of times'. As for the tax officers, they needed to spend an important amount of their time studying about the continuous changes of the tax laws in order to stay informed and be able

[100] *Bulletin of the Chamber of Commerce and Industry of Athens*, May 1989, 5, p. 4.

[101] Ibid., p. 5.

[102] Aris Stamatakis, 'Overregulation in Taxation', *Tax Review*, March 1989, 482, pp. 210–211.

to implement the continuously changing legislation. Their efforts were not, as it was noted, compensated with a 'library allowance'.[103]

An additional issue was again the bad relations between taxpayers and tax officers. Of course, as in previous decades, the representatives of the state stressed, when speaking or writing publicly, the importance of good relations between the two parties. For example, in the first public meeting between the Minister of Economics and the representatives of the Chamber of Commerce and Industry of Athens, the Minister Dimitrios Koulourianos invited all business organisations to submit their proposals for the reform of the tax system. '[I]t is high time you started speaking and we listened', said Koulourianos, while also stressing that the government aimed to simplify the tax system so as to foster a sense of trust between taxpayers and the state. Koulourianos also expressed the hope that tensions between the taxpayers and the tax authorities would reduce, by noting that there would be an agreement with the Minister of Justice for the speeding up of the trials concerning tax cases and that the Ministry would favourably consider the idea of the formation of committees comprised by economists, lawyers, civil servants, etc., that would discuss and possibly settle cases of tax disputes before they reached the courts.[104]

More generally, in their public communications, the representatives of the state attempted to combine requests for the reduction of tax evasion along with pleas for a mood of conciliation to prevail among taxpayers and the tax authorities. For example, in a circular issued in July 1982, the Minister of Economics stressed that the Ministry's main aim was to combat tax evasion, with the audits focusing primarily on big firms. Referring specifically to the tax officers, Koulourianos noted that the Ministry recognised that they were burdened with important and difficult tasks, but also, that the way the tax services functioned was problematic, because of 'the personnel shortage, the accumulation of outstanding items, the increase of the tax returns submitted…, the overregulation and the continuous changes in tax legislation'. Koulourianos expressed the hope that such issues would be resolved, while at the same time asking tax officials to intensify their efforts to collect more revenues and fight tax evasion. In a plea addressed to them, Koulourianos continued in the

[103] Ibid.

[104] *Bulletin of the Chamber of Commerce and Industry of Athens*, April 1983, 4, p. 9.

following words: 'Please, be polite with the taxpayers, so that a climate of cooperation and mutual trust between tax authorities and citizens is cultivated...you should pay particular attention to this. Please, show understanding and make every effort to serve the taxpayers. It is necessary for you to be impartial and fair and, when needed, to exhaust your leniency, within the limits of the law, especially for the taxpayers with low taxpaying ability'.[105]

However, and in spite of such pleas, relations between tax officers and taxpayers did not seem to improve during this period. In fact, only seven months before the publication of this circular, in December 1981, the predecessor of Koulourianos revealed a case in which a tax officer had been arrested for asking for a bribe in order to exempt a professional from remittances taxation. According to the Minister, there was a possibility that a number of other tax officers responsible for remittances taxation were involved in cases such as this one.[106]

Throughout the 1980s, many other similar cases of tax officers being arrested for bribery appeared in the press;[107] like previous periods, most of those cases came to light after the taxpayers involved complained to the authorities. According to an article that appeared in the newspaper *Rizospastis* in September 1983, one such case led to the dismissal of two tax officers and the transfer of the director of the tax service to which they belonged. The person who revealed this specific case by complaining to the authorities was the owner of a handicraft industry, who also made the following statement: 'Groups of tax officers that are in charge of performing audits...operate in an organised fashion and blackmail owners of handicraft industries and shop owners'. The same person also argued

[105] 'The Government Aims to Combat Excessive Tax Evasion', *I Kathimerini*, 23.7.1982, p. 7.

[106] 'A New Case of Bribing of a Tax Officer', *Rizospastis*, 29.12.1981, p. 3.

[107] See, indicatively: 'A Tax Officer Was Arrested for Bribery', *Rizospastis*, 7.8.1982, p. 6; 'A Tax Officer Received a Bribe of DRS 200,000', *Ta Nea*, 7.8.1982, p. 12; 'Did the Officer [Accused for] Bribery Have Partners?' *Ta Nea*, 29.12.1981, p. 1; 'A Tax Officer Was Arrested While Receiving a Bribe', *Ta Nea*, 23.12.1981, p. 1; 'A Tax Officer Was Arrested for Blackmailing and Bribery', *Ta Nea*, 24.11.1983, p. 1; 'On Friday the Trial of the Two Tax Officers', *I Kathimerini*, 7.9.1983, p. 3; 'A Tax Officer Is Accused of Bribe-Taking', *I Kathimerini*, 15.6.1986, p. 2; 'A Tax Officer Was Arrested and Accused for Receiving a Bribe', *I Kathimerini*, 21.5.1987, p. 14; 'A Tax Officer Was Arrested for Receiving a Bribe', *I Kathimerini*, 11.9.1987, p. 8; 'A Tax Officer Was Arrested While Receiving a Bribe...', *I Kathimerini*, 7.9.1988, p. 16.

that every time there was an audit of accounting books, tax officers 'created problems' for shopkeepers, blackmailing them in order to gain bribes 'in exchange for them keeping quiet'. According to the article, after such revelations the Ministry of Economics was considering offering incentives to taxpayers (some of which would potentially have the form of reductions to their tax liabilities) in order to encourage them to file complaints to the authorities for relevant cases. There were also thoughts about establishing complaints desks within tax offices for the re-examination of tax cases.[108]

Blackmailing was not the only kind of criticism addressed to the members of the tax services. As was the case in previous periods too, a usual complaint regarded their general behaviour during audits. For example, in a note in the *Bulletin of the FGI* in November 1988, concerns were expressed for the tactic of tax officers to disregard productive expenses and reject accounting books of companies, 'usually for typical and petty transgressions of the Tax Code'. It was stressed that this situation 'reduced to despair' many companies, especially those of medium and small size, which, because of lacking the necessary funds to turn to the courts, were forced to compromise with the tax authorities.[109] Of course, entrepreneurs' approach to this issue was also a matter of temperament, to a large extent. For example, one of the entrepreneurs that participated in this research described his stance on similar occasions using the following words:

> There are some categories of companies in which, for an agreement to be made and a project to materialise, a lot of travels abroad, dinners, accommodation in expensive hotels, etc. have to be done. When there is a tax audit and those expenses are rejected, this creates a problem. There have been cases in which, for example, the tax auditor rejected expenses that took place in the US as being unrelated to the company's productive activity, because there was not any agreement made with any US company. That is, the auditor did not realise that, in such kind of business, a lot of expenses that are done do not always end up in agreements. There might be, for example, four travels abroad, with only one of them ending up to the signing of a contract. In such cases, different people react in different

[108] 'The Owner of the Handicraft Industry Speaks of an 'Organised Group of Tax Officers'', *Rizospastis*, 18.9.1983, p. 2.

[109] *Bulletin of the FGI*, October–November 1988, 504, p. 7.

> ways. I do not want to have to negotiate with tax officers, so I register no such kind of expenses in my company's accounting books.[110]

Apart from the role of the tax authorities during audits, entrepreneurs complained also about policies of a more general character that the Ministry of Economics implemented in order to tackle tax evasion. For example, whereas, in July 1982, the Ministry had declared that the names of tax evaders would be publicised only after the relevant courts issued their final judgements,[111] the opposite tactic was followed in later years.

In October 1988 the Chamber of Commerce and Industry of Athens characterised the Ministry's announcements with regard to transgressions of the tax legislation by banks, oil companies and commercial and industrial enterprises, as 'unacceptable defamations', attempts to influence the judicial authorities and actions that were besetting the business and investment climate. The president of the Chamber Andreas Kyriazis noted that the cases of companies that had been found guilty of tax evasion by the relevant courts were 'socially unacceptable and economically condemnable'. Yet, the cases that had recently come to light, he stressed, involved companies that were merely having differences with the tax authorities, mainly because of different interpretations of the tax laws. The fact that the Ministry publicised the names of such companies, continued Kyriazis, did not contribute to the reduction of tax evasion, but was probably more of an effort to draw the taxpayers' attention away from the fact that the state was unable to collect the budgeted tax revenues. The increase of the tax revenues, Kyriazis stressed, could not be achieved through the interpretation of tax laws at will.[112]

On the same issue, it was noted in the *Bulletin of the FGI* in November 1988, that even before the relative cases were examined in courts, the state publicised the names of companies the taxable income of which was set higher than the one they had declared in their tax returns. This led to those companies' 'public vilification', and harmed both the relations between taxpayers and the authorities and the business climate. The names of companies were publicised even in cases in which they had

[110] Entrepreneur no. 2 requesting anonymity, interview excerpt.

[111] 'The Government Aims to Combat Excessive Tax Evasion', *I Kathimerini*, 23.7.1982, p. 7.

[112] *Bulletin of the Chamber of Commerce and Industry of Athens*, October 1988, 10, pp. 3; 16.

reached a compromise with the tax authorities and agreed to declare a higher taxable income. In such cases, according to the Federation, the authorities aimed to present such compromises as 'admissions of tax evasion'.[113]

Of course, the pressures that the tax system created reflected also the fact that, during this period, the state was indeed in need of more tax revenue. This was not only due to the increase of public expenditure, but also because of tax evasion which, as mentioned previously, had started growing since the late 1970s. Indeed, this was the finding of a study conducted by Konstantinos Kalyvianakis et al., based on data from the National Accounts and from individual income tax returns.[114] The growth of the shadow economy after 1981 led to an increase of tax evasion, as the study of the economist Nikos Tatsos indicates.[115] Actually, the first attempt to measure tax evasion in Greece was made in 1991 by the Foundation for Mediterranean Studies. It was estimated that during the period 1970–1986 the magnitude of tax evasion amounted to $650 billion.[116]

On the whole, this period examined in this chapter witnessed a disappointing performance of the industrial sector. There was rapid de-industrialisation, a substantial increase of the shadow economy and therefore an increase of business tax evasion. These findings are again in line with Baumol's theory. That is, it is confirmed here that in a framework with problematic tax rules, productive entrepreneurship declines (hence the wave of de-industrialisation and 'problematic' companies), whereas unproductive forms of entrepreneurship, such as business tax evasion, thrive.

These developments led to the assumption of measures that aimed to reduce tax evasion. For example, in January 1983 the Minister of Economics Dimitrios Koulourianos ordered tax services to intensify regular and surprise inspections on firms. The aim, as it was noted, was the reduction of tax evasion and the processing of outstanding tax cases.[117]

[113] *Bulletin of the FGI*, October–November 1988, 504, p. 7.

[114] Kalyvianakis et al., pp. 275–279.

[115] Tatsos, *Shadow Economy*, pp. 91–92.

[116] Ibid., p. 76. For a more extensive analysis on tax evasion see also Chapter 2.

[117] 'Tax Officers' Audits in Firms Intensify', *I Kathimerini*, 14.1.1983, p. 7.

The publication of cases of tax disputes that were accompanied by allegations of provocative tax evasion contributed to the government's efforts. In the case of Aristotelis Onassis' daughter Christina, she refused to pay taxes of DRS 3 billion, which, according to the Greek state, were due after she inherited her father's fortune. Onassis' main argument was that the shares she had inherited belonged to non-Greek (mostly Panamanian) corporations. However, according to an investigation performed by the Greek state, such corporations were merely front companies, specifically set up by Aristotelis Onassis in order to avoid paying his due taxes. It seemed however that Christina Onassis, who actually brought the case before the Courts, was 'not willing to pay a penny'.[118]

In such a context, and almost a year after the country had narrowly escaped bankruptcy, a new tax bill was introduced,[119] which contained, among others, measures for the reduction of tax evasion. In the 29 January 1986 meeting of the Board of Directors of the Chamber of Commerce and Industry of Athens, the Vice President Andreas Kyriazis criticised many aspects of the proposed bill, which, on the whole, as he noted, should be withdrawn and reintroduced after a series of amendments had taken place. Among other points, Kyriazis stressed that the already existing penal legislation (specifically law 820/1978) was enough to protect the interests of the state in case of tax law infringements stemming from deceitful intentions. On the contrary, according to Kyriazis, the criminalisation of every kind of tax offence that the new law introduced 'in a definite and rigid manner' and without the possibility of the examination of the tax cases in a second-degree tax court was 'unacceptable'. He believed that it would unsettle business activities, as well as leading to many injustices against the business community. The adverse climate that such developments would create, continued Kyriazis, would cause a decline of business activities. Furthermore, he argued that it would reduce investment initiatives and 'deteriorate relations between tax authorities and the taxpayers. Also, it would cause asphyxiating congestion in the tax courts which would have to issue rulings on petty and very

[118] "I Will not Pay a Penny', Says Onassis Provocatively', *Rizospastis*, 12.3.1983, p. 9.
[119] This probably concerned law 1591/1986.

simple offences, to the detriment of the entrepreneurial and productive activities, but also of justice itself'.[120]

Commenting on the same subject, in the February 1986 issue of the *Bulletin of the Chamber of Commerce and Industry of Athens,* the former councillor of the Athens Traders Association Themistocles Sarakos noted among others, that, in some cases, it was difficult to discern whether a tax offence took place because of the taxpayer's deceitful intentions or because of his negligence or an error of assessment. Sarakos also noted that there were cases in which 'rigid, malicious or fastidious' tax auditors rejected taxpayers' accounting books for two, even three times in a row. As a result, the latter were left with no income for two or three years. It was also noted that in some cases, the various indirect taxes, special contributions and other kinds of levies that taxpayers had to pay within a year exceeded their annual revenues. On the whole, it was stressed, the criminalisation of tax evasion was part of a policy of 'terrorisation' of taxpayers. It was the state that treated citizens unjustly and thus gave them the right to argue that when evading taxes they were on the defensive, and this, concluded Sarakos, was true in some cases.[121]

A similar point was raised by Dimitris Danilatos, the Secretary General of the Chamber of Commerce and Industry of Athens, in an article published in the same issue. Here, he commented that what made taxpayers evade taxation was the fact that they considered that 'the State asks too much' and that they were certain that the State 'did not use their contributions properly'. Such a reality persuaded taxpayers to consider that not abiding by the tax laws was legalised, if not necessary. In this context, Danilatos stressed, there was no kind of transparency or sincerity in the relations between them and the State.[122]

The government's tax policies were criticised also by the tax officers. At around the same period, the trade union of tax officers deplored 'the unacceptable and irrational methods that [the ministry] introduces in the tax services, which bring great distress to tax officers and taxpayers'. The announcement of the trade union focused on the procedures followed for the calculation of companies' and professionals' taxable income which

[120] *Bulletin of the Chamber of Commerce and Industry of Athens,* February 1986, 2, p. 9.

[121] Th. Sarakos, 'Tax Law Infringements and Penalisation', *Bulletin of the Chamber of Commerce and Industry of Athens*, February 1986, 2, pp. 15–16.

[122] D. Danilatos, 'Tax Burden and Tax Evasion', ibid., p. 11.

were, according to the tax officers, 'endless,...bureaucratic, difficult to explain, incomprehensible...and complicated'. It was noted that in order to manage, tax officers had to have special knowledge but do a lot of studying too. What was also required from the tax officers, the announcement continued, was to complete thousands of documents regarding taxpayers' income within a very short period of time. The announcement concluded by pointing out that the working conditions of tax officers were unacceptable, and that it was because of this reality that 'within two years, 25 tax officers died while on duty'.[123]

Also, in late July 1986 the labour union of tax officers characterised the then Minister of Economics Dimitris Tsovolas' statements in the media to be 'inappropriate and unacceptable'. In these statements, Tsovolas had noted that the recent tax measures were aimed at the ending of tax officers' arbitrariness. For the tax officers, instead of modernising the tax system, the government aimed to 'dishonestly revile' tax officers so as to 'disorientate' taxpayers and shift their attention away from the 'onerous tax burdens' they had to bear. The various local committees of tax officers in Thessaloniki, Macedonia's largest city, also issued a relative announcement. In it, they characterised the Minister's statements as 'derogatory', while also arguing that, tax officers, not only were not arbitrary, but were merely implementing the tax laws, 'trying to cover a series of contradictory pieces of legislation and an unprecedented overregulation...'. The announcement continued to state that tax evasion could be reduced only with the assumption of 'serious and scientifically based initiatives, not with spells and aphorisms' and that tax officer paid back the wages they received from the state 'with untimely deaths'.[124]

To identify whether there was indeed any correlation between tax officers' deaths and the working conditions in tax services goes beyond the purposes of this study. It is quite telling though that the number of deaths of their colleagues were part of tax officers' argumentation when complaining about the pressure they were undergoing when performing their duties. More broadly, tax officers' communications revealed the degree of tension in their relations with the Ministry during this period,

[123] 'Tax Officers Complain About Unacceptable Methods', *I Kathimerini*, 9.4.1986, p. 9.

[124] 'The Tax Officers Argue That References on Arbitrariness Are Misleading', *I Kathimerini*, 19.7.1986, p. 7 and 'The Tax Officers Complain About Mr Tsovolas' Statements', *I Kathimerini*, 24.7.1986, p. 9.

which was probably not only a result of the Minister's comments about the tax officers' arbitrariness. Actually, the members of the tax services had a series of complaints about the Ministry's policies. In some of such complaints, they usually had the support of the opposition parties too. For example, in August 1983 the opposition argued that, while, according to the law, every tax officer should remain in a given tax office for a period of at least three years, there were in fact many illegal transfers of officers who were not followers of the governing party. In an announcement made by New Democracy, the then main opposition party, it was stressed that 'tax officers of great experience and scientific background are rendered useless and are given…inferior positions…. Such transfers, which are done with partisan criteria, are aimed at the…obsolescence of all the unwanted and dissident trade unionists and officers'. [125] Similar accusations were made in later periods too. For example, in mid-September 1984 there were complaints about the transfer of a number of tax officers that were followers of New Democracy.[126] In late September 1984, trade unionists also complained that tax officers were being transferred with 'subjective and political' criteria.[127] In February and September 1985 similar complaints appeared in press, regarding again transfers of tax officers following partisan criteria, according to their trade union.[128]

The tension in the relations between the Ministry of Economics and tax officers was also manifested in a protest of the trade union of the latter in June 1984, regarding the Ministry's 'indifference' towards their requests.[129] In a press conference in June 1986, tax officers again accused the Minister of Economics for the hiring of 300 officers with criteria relating to partisanship, despite the relevant legislation but also despite of the Minister's assurances that recruitment of tax officers would be achieved only through relevant competition. It was noted that the fact that the newly hired tax officers were chosen by the Ministry was a provocation for 'the thousands of unemployed graduates'. Tax officers also stressed that there was a large number of civil servants who were

[125] 'Illegal Transfers?', *I Kathimerini*, 26.8.1983, p. 7.

[126] 'Political Movements', *I Kathimerini*, 14.9.1984, p. 3.

[127] 'Transfers of Tax Officers Continue', *I Kathimerini*, 25.9.1984, p. 2.

[128] 'New Adverse Transfers of Tax Officers', *I Kathimerini*, 1.2.1985, p. 2 and 'New Transfers of Tax Officers with Partisan Criteria', *I Kathimerini*, 26.9.1985, p. 2.

[129] 'Tax Officers on…Indifference', *I Kathimerini*, 14.6.1984, p. 11.

transferred into the tax services. Yet these civil servants possessed no knowledge or previous working experience in the Ministry of Economics; some of them, for example, were previously employed in public sport centres, others in the public horse racing organisation, etc.[130] This latter point has also been confirmed by the former president of the trade union of tax officers Charalampos Nikolakopoulos, who stressed that the transfers were due to the severe shortage of staff in the Ministry of Economics.[131] This was also evidenced by the former official of the Ministry of Economics Ioannis Photopoulos. In a relevant article, Photopoulos commented that, since 1958, tax officers were recruited only through competitions in accordance with the procedures set by the Civil Service Code. Yet, in the 1980s, 'several thousands…were appointed as tax officers after being transferred from various other public services (Greek Horse Racing Organisation, Olympic Airways Catering, the Greek Powder and Cartridge Company, and others), without any kind of qualifications or [having passed any] competition'. The result was, as Photopoulos stressed, that the scientific status of the employees was downgraded.[132]

In a similar fashion to the previous period, tax officers also complained about the prospects of advancement within their services and about their wages.[133] These complaints often found support from people who were not related to their profession. For example, the October 1981 issue of the *Tax Review* republished an article of the academic Angelos Angelopoulos in which he noted that for the reduction of the public sector's deficit the tax system should undergo a series of reforms. Among these reforms were the 'quantitative and qualitative support of the tax officers, and particularly the significant improvement of their remuneration'.[134]

It is worth mentioning that even when cases of bribery of tax officers came to light, their representatives defended their profession. Again, these representatives referred, in their argumentation, to issues such as

[130] 'Mass Recruitment in the Tax Services on the Basis of Favours', *I Kathimerini*, 14.6.1986, p. 9.

[131] Nikolakopoulos, interview data.

[132] Photopoulos, pp. 895–896.

[133] 'Transfers of Tax Officers Continue', *I Kathimerini*, 25.9.1984, p. 2.

[134] *Tax Review*, October 1981, 393, pp. 652–653.

the one of the difficulty of advancement within the services and that of insufficient remuneration. This can be seen in the example of a tax officer who was accused of bribery in July 1986. The trade union of tax officers noted in an announcement that such 'unacceptable and condemnable' events were mainly due to the overregulated and anachronistic tax system and to the fact that there did not exist any definite and objective criteria for the hiring of tax officers neither any rules that regulated their protection. Another reason was, according to the announcement, the fact that tax officers had low prospects of advancement within the services or any wage increases. Specifically, with regard to the latter, it was noted in the announcement that the wages of Greek tax offices should be 'equal to those of the tax officers in EEC member states…'.[135]

Tax officers also described the taxpayers' behaviour as aggressive, and attributed poor relations with them to the broader problems of the tax system. For example, after an incidence of violence against tax officers in the prudential controls in the island of Corfu, one of the parties comprising the trade union noted in a press conference that the bickering between them and the taxpayers 'but also the violence against tax officers', had become 'almost a daily occurrence'.[136] It was stressed that such phenomena demonstrated the lack of trust between taxpayers and the tax authorities. Indeed, it was explained that what caused them was not the overzealousness or any other characteristic in the tax officers' behaviour, but 'the system of taxation' itself. Continuing, the representatives of the tax officers stressed: 'there are many taxpayers who are indignant and there are also some which are preventing us from conducting tax audits…there are many occasions in which taxpayers maltreat us, threaten us or even physically attack us'. There were also, according to the trade unionists, 'not few' incidents in which taxpayers attempted to bribe tax officers.[137]

[135] 'Tax Officers' Remuneration Is Extremely Low', *I Kathimerini*, 3.7.1986, p. 15. As noted in the previous chapter, tax officers' salaries started increasing from the late 1980s onwards.

[136] It was not possible to verify whether the frequency of such events was really that high. The evidence presented here though suggests that incidences of violence between taxpayers and tax officers were indeed a reality. They denoted how poor were the relations between the two parties.

[137] 'Continuous Quarrelling Between Tax Officers and Citizens', *I Kathimerini*, 1.8.1986, p. 1.

Tax officers also engaged in strikes,[138] which were a fairly common occurrence during the period. Repeated strikes created, as the opposition parties stressed, a series of problems for companies. For example, they ran the risk of being accused of violating the Tax Code because the tax services were not operating and so they could not authorise the accounting records they used. Of course, again according to the opposition, there were also companies that took advantage of this situation. In doing so, these companies moved goods around the market without the necessary records. In turn, their actions contributed to the increase in tax evasion.[139]

Apart from the problems created because of the strikes, the general climate deteriorated. This was also a result of the measures that the government undertook in order to curb tax evasion. The Ministry of Economics provided directions to the tax services in late September 1987 which suggested that the processing of the tax cases and the collection of revenues should be done at a faster rate. The emphasis here was upon prudential controls; specifically, according to the Ministry, the directors of tax services were required to form audit groups comprised of two tax officers, for the carrying out of such controls, twice every week. The composition of the groups would vary each time. As was noted in the relevant document sent by the Ministry to all the tax services, the directors of the services had the duty to pass on 'the spark of audit' to their colleagues.[140] In the same vein, in late January 1988 the Minister of Economics announced the creation of special departments for the fast processing of the pending cases within every tax service.[141]

In such a context, during the period there were references in the press about the Ministry of Economics' 'wild tax hunt' against firms, which were accompanied by numerous violent incidents between shopkeepers and tax officers. It was emphasised that the Ministry aimed at the increase of tax revenues using 'all means possible'. According to the

[138] 'Transfers of Tax Officers Continue', *I Kathimerini*, 25.9.1984, p. 2.

[139] 'Problems in the Economy Because of the Tax Officers' Strike', *I Kathimerini*, 2.3.1983, p. 7.

[140] 'Tax Audits Should Be Done with a New Impetus, Says Mr Tsovolas', *I Kathimerini*, 19.9.1987, p. 11.

[141] 'Special Departments in the Tax Offices for Pending Cases', *I Kathimerini*, 28.1.1988, p. 11.

orders of the ministry, every Saturday, audit groups comprised by tax officers checked the implementation of the Tax Code. Among others, they investigated whether the owners of shops issued receipts, whether the various goods in transit were accompanied by relevant documentation, and whether the various firms' inventories were covered by the relevant accounting records. The audit groups also focused upon the implementation of various VAT provisions. For example they checked whether regular VAT returns were submitted and whether the VAT due was paid.[142]

In late September 1988, the press revealed that companies which in their VAT returns had declared that their expenses were much greater than their income had been targeted by the tax authorities. Specifically, it was noted that the Ministry of Economics had declared a 'general mobilisation' of tax officers. They had to perform audits even on the weekend, in order to recover all the companies who 'broke the law' by 15 October. In an announcement characterised as 'aggressive', the Minister of Economics called upon the directors of tax offices to lead the audits 'for the correct implementation of the VAT legislation, the safeguarding of public revenues, which are mainly drawn from VAT, but also, the consolidation of tax conscience'.[143]

In the same period, it was realised in the press that the state was planning to create committees comprised of tax officers. These bodies would examine pending tax cases. The trade union of tax officers opposed the idea, noting that for the consolidation of tax fairness, a set of specific criteria for the assessment of tax law infringements should be established. The trade union went further and suggested that the tax measures should be simplified and all the relative procedures a priori determined. It was also considered that the state asked the tax officers 'to make huge sacrifices and [assume great] responsibilities without any special recognition and additional pay'.[144] Criticising the policies of the Ministry of Economics more generally, the trade union of tax officers stressed, in a relevant announcement: 'For six whole years the Minister establishes committees, drafts tax bills, issues on a daily basis tax orders, announces "revolutionary" tax reforms, [measures] which, in reality, resulted only in millions of unaudited tax cases which are translated in billions of revenue

142 'Directions for a Tax-Hunt in the Market', *I Kathimerini*, 22.3.1988, p. 1.

143 'The Tax Services' Dash for the VAT', *I Kathimerini*, 30.9.1988, p. 11.

144 'More People in the Net of the Real Estate Tax', *I Kathimerini*, 30.1.1988, p. 1.

losses, tax revenues only from wage earners, fast track procedures that generate no revenues, contradictory laws regarding the exemption from tax liabilities [and] dysfunctionality of the tax services...'.[145]

Apart from tax officers, the press that supported the major opposition also criticised the Ministry's initiatives: 'Mr Tsovolas' tax officers wander outside shops..., trying to kill two birds with one stone...the ill-disciplined buyer, who does not ask for a receipt, and the tax evading merchant'. It was believed that because of such measures, which were combined with vehicle traffic restrictions, the situation was proved similar to the one during German occupation. The press stated that 'in every corner of every street..., the occupation forces would plaster leaflets with their brief announcements, all of which started with the word "Verboten" and ended with the threat of 'Death' for the offenders'. The current state in the market of Athens was reminiscent of this period, it was noted in the article: there were empty streets and empty stores, and the commercial traffic had plummeted.[146]

Conclusion

The years examined in this chapter witnessed a severe deterioration of the Greek economy. It was marked by a sharp reduction in GDP but also a severe increase in inflation, a drop in competitiveness and a widening of the public deficit, which led the country one step away from bankruptcy in the mid-1980s. During this period Greece entered a stage of de-industrialisation. The relevant critiques suggested that the reduction in industrial investment also reflected a series of adverse developments in the system of taxation. Indeed, its impact became much more direct than previously. Specifically, during the 1980s, new taxes were imposed upon both firms and individuals, but also, the very pressing problems in the tax administration mechanisms did not diminish.

Actually, the tax administration burden increased during this period. The complexity of procedures and the frequency in the change of tax legislation increased substantially; the increased frequency in the change of legislation reflected also the imposition of new tax laws mentioned

[145] 'Tax Officers' Confrontation with the Minister of Economics', *I Kathimerini*, 20.7.1988, p. 11.

[146] 'From Another Perspective – "Verboten", *I Kathimerini*, 22.1.1988, p. 4.

above. These were introduced in order to cover the state's increased needs for tax revenue due to the widening of the public deficit during this period. Also, excessive bureaucracy and lack of sufficient organisation were still burdening the tax system. Moreover, the state's efforts to reduce tax officers' arbitrariness and mistrust in their relations with taxpayers did not seem successful, and reports about cases of corruption kept on making often appearances in the press.

In the midst of an economic crisis, such dysfunctionalities of the tax administration mechanism had now become clearer than ever before as well as a matter of open conflict. The debate took place not only between taxpayers/entrepreneurs and tax officers, but also between the latter and the Ministry of Economics. A factor that exacerbated the problem was that the state's needs for tax revenues had considerably increased. Yet, other than the intensification of the audits and the increase of fines for tax evasion, no significant measures for the reorganisation of the tax administration were undertaken. Even worse, tax evasion increased, and so did the critique about tax officers' competence to perform their duties. In a context of a severe deterioration in the state of the economy, such developments increased tensions between taxpayers, tax officers and the state. By the end of the 1980s, the Greek system of taxation had become a symbol of poor government administration, corruption within the public sector and deep mistrust between citizens and the state mechanisms.

Bibliography

Primary Sources

Professor Michalis Psalidopoulos Personal Archive
Bulletin of the Federation of Greek Industrialists (FGI) (1966–1988).
Union of Corporations and Limited Liability Companies Archive
Board of Directors Meeting Minutes (1957–1989).

Newspapers, Magazines and Serial Publications

a) Newspapers
Capital, Dimokratia, Eleftheria, Empros, Imerisia, I Avgi, I Kathimerini, I Naftemporiki, O Economicos Tahydromos, Makedonia, Rizospastis, Ta Nea, To Vima, To Vima tis Kyriakis (in Greek).

b) Magazines and Serial Publications

The Accountant, Tax Review, The Bulletin of Tax Legislation, Bulletin of the Chamber of Commerce and Industry of Athens.

Interviews

Entrepreneur no. 1 Requesting Anonymity.
Entrepreneur no. 2 Requesting Anonymity.
Entrepreneur no. 3 Requesting Anonymity.
Nikolakopoulos, Charalambos.

Official Publications

Long-term Statistical Series of the Greek Economy.
Statistical Yearbook of Greece, various issues.

Web Resources

'The General Secretariat of the Government', *Tzanis Tzanetakis Government.* http://www.ggk.gov.gr/?p=1294, in Greek.

Secondary Literature

Bitros, G. K., 'Greece: How and Why Things Turned Upside Down', in *Essays in Applied Economics and Finance*, ed Giannis Katsoulakos (Athens: Athens University of Economics and Business, 2013), pp. 1–45, in Greek.

Drakatos, K., *The Big Cycle of the Greek Economy (1945–1995)* (Athens: Papazisis, 1997), in Greek.

Kalyvianakis, K. et al., *Tax regime, Shadow Economy and Tax Evasion in Greece* (Athens: Papazisis, 1993), in Greek.

Kazakos, P., *Between State and Market* (Athens: Patakis, 2001), in Greek.

Photopoulos, I., 'The Administration of the Greek Tax System', *Enterprise*, reprint, issue 63 (2010), pp. 893–907, in Greek.

Provopoulos, G. A., *The Public Sector of the Greek Economy, Recent Trends and Economic Repercussions* (Athens: Foundation for Economic and Industrial Research, 1985), in Greek.

Psalidopoulos, M., *History of the Bank of Greece, 1928–2008* (Athens: The Bank of Greece, 2014), in Greek.

Rollings, N., *British Business in the Formative Years of European Integration, 1945–1973* (Cambridge: Cambridge University Press, 2007).

Sellas, S. M., *The Greek System of Taxation* (Athens: Papazisis, 1989), in Greek.

Tatsos, N., *Shadow Economy and Tax Evasion in Greece* (Athens: Papazisi, 2001), in Greek.

CHAPTER 7

A Tale of Hope, Disillusionment and Crisis: 1989–2008

Introduction

The last period examined in this book witnessed the alternation of power between the right-wing New Democracy and the centre-left-wing Panhellenic Socialistic Union political parties. In economic terms, the picture was that of a mixed performance. From 1989 and up to 1996, the Greek economy was experiencing a period of stagnation accompanied by deterioration in all major economic indicators and slow GDP growth rates. However, the years 1996–2008 witnessed a gradual recovery characterised by an increase in the general level of investments, a progress that promoted convergence with the economically developed European states. According to International Monetary Fund data, in 2008 Greece was ranked 22nd among the 33 advanced economies of the world.[1] Nevertheless, the long-term structural weaknesses of the economy never disappeared. As will be shown here, the complaints concerning the rigidities and dysfunctionalities of the tax system that kept on creating difficulties for the development of business were strikingly similar to those of previous decades.

[1] Milios, p. 18.

Z. Pittaki, *Exploring the roots of systematic tax avoidance in Greece*, Palgrave Studies in Economic History,
https://doi.org/10.1007/978-3-030-71979-1_7

The General Economic Outlook of the Period

In more detail, in late 1990s Greece entered a phase of preparation for its ascension to the European Monetary Union (EMU). The targets that had been set concerned macroeconomic and fiscal stabilisation, accompanied by the reduction of inflation and public deficit and the promotion of economic development. It is important to note that during this period there was substantial progress in terms of improvements in the monetary and fiscal policy, but a dearth of measures when the structural problems of the economy were concerned. The structural transformation of the Greek economy was, according to the Bank of Greece Director's report, 'slow and insufficient'.[2] The adoption of the euro on 1 January 2001 was heralded as the culmination of a long process of economic stabilisation, the Bank of Greece though kept stressing the need for structural reforms that would lead to further convergence with the economically advanced European countries.[3]

The years 2001–2008 have been characterised as the 'honeymoon' phase of the Greek economy, as the adoption of the common European currency led to a reduction of interest rates that made borrowing money more affordable for both the public and private sectors. The Bank of Greece's warnings for the 'overheating' of the economy, were, in effect, ignored. For the director of the Bank of Greece in 2003, the economy experienced high growth rates but low productivity rates, inflation was increasing to levels higher than the Eurozone average and unemployment rates were not decreasing fast enough. What was also stressed were the upward pressures in the general government debt and the need for structural reforms that, among others, would promote fiscal consolidation and the development of entrepreneurship.[4]

Greece entered an era of additional challenges after the international financial crisis erupted in the United States in 2007. The crisis had a negative impact on the financial and banking systems as well as the deficit in the external balance since there was a reduction in lending and a slump in the country's exports. For the Bank of Greece, the crisis highlighted the economy's fundamental weaknesses and the need for structural reforms that would enhance productivity and competitiveness. It was stressed that

[2] Psalidopoulos, *History*, p. 363.

[3] Ibid., p. 382.

[4] Ibid., pp. 393–406.

one of the necessary steps that had to be taken was the reduction of bureaucracy. The deficit in the external balance of goods and services also increased substantially during this period.[5] Such issues, combined with a sharp decrease in the level of private investment and the decline of lending to businesses, were acutely manifested during the eruption of the debt crisis in 2009.

Economy and Industry

It has been argued that the process of development in Greece was effectively halted after 1973 because of several structural weaknesses of the Greek economy, such as the dysfunctionalities of the tax system.[6] The early 1990s witnessed the introduction of a denationalisation programme that was initially presented in spring 1990 and involved measures such as the privatisation or complete liquidation of problematic companies and the promotion of infrastructure works undertaken by private companies. The idea of privatisation of problematic companies considered 111 companies that employed about 130 thousand people and was implemented despite the vehement criticism it was met with. Among others, the criticism was focused on the opaque conditions under which these denationalisations took place. However, instead of being privatised, the majority of such problematic companies simply went out of business.[7]

Undeniably, the Greek economy entered a phase of intense de-industrialisation in the 1990s.[8] In May 1997 and in a fashion similar to previous decades, echoing Xenophon Zolotas's views about the obstacles hindering economic development in the country, the president of the FGI stressed that what the industry sector needed was not the introduction of more incentives but the elimination of already existing disincentives such as the 'complex nexus of bureaucratic procedures and [...] rules' that discouraged investments. The same point was stressed again during the Federation's general assembly in May 2003, accompanied by a plea for a 'state that is entrepreneur-friendly'. In May 2005 and in the same spirit, the president of the Federation noted that what

[5] Ibid., pp. 431–432.

[6] Alogoskoufis, in Kazakos, p. 454.

[7] Kazakos, pp. 463–471.

[8] Panselina and Mavroeidi, p. 467.

Greek entrepreneurs had to do battle with on a daily basis was not a foreign competition but the state itself, the public administration and the unproductive attitude of organisations and structures that caused 'uncertainty and fear' and made entrepreneurs 'non-competitive'. In a formal statement called 'the Charter of Enterprises' Rights and Responsibilities' that the FGI published in the same year, it was stressed among others that Greek firms had the right to a stable, predictable and transparent tax system that would promote business development and investment.[9] As will be shown below, the sporadic changes implemented in the tax system during this period did not meet this goal and this was a realisation confirmed not only by entrepreneurs but the wider public too.

Developments in the System of Taxation and the Effect They Had on Business

Even in the years preceding the international financial crisis of 2007, the Bank of Greece was clear that one of the areas of the public sector that needed urgent reform was the tax system.[10]

An effort towards this direction came with the introduction of Law 2065 in 1992. This was heralded as a piece of legislation that, through enhanced transparency and coherency, would rectify the imbalances caused by Law 3323/1955. Law 3323/1955, more detail on which was presented in Chapter 3, was criticised for imposing an 'excessively progressive tax scale on an excessively narrow tax base', leaving large parts of the population essentially tax exempt. The new law was also presented to be a means to fight against tax evasion and shadow economy and involved the repeal of a number of tax incentives. The main changes of the law were focused on the taxation of corporate income with the introduction of a new tax scale and flat income tax rates.[11]

In spite of the optimistic declarations that accompanied its introduction, the new legislation was widely criticised and it was mentioned during relevant Parliamentary debates that it opposed the basic constitutional principle that everyone should contribute according to their tax-paying capacity. The new law also introduced a reduction of the income tax rates

[9] Ibid., pp. 472–491.

[10] Psalidopoulos, *History*, pp. 377; 400.

[11] Glykou, pp. 153–154.

for both lower and higher income brackets, something that harmed the progressivity of the tax scale.

The various acts and laws that were introduced after 1992 were of minor importance and certainly did not have the character of tax reforms. It should be noted though that throughout the period from 1991 to 2000 the efforts for fiscal stabilisation that would promote Greece's ascension to the EMU also meant the introduction of measures that aimed at the better capturing of the taxable income and the broadening of the tax base. To this end, new tax bodies were founded, most notably the General Directorate for the Prosecution of Economic Crime (SDOE) in 1997. Also, a unique tax registration number was assigned to every taxpayer.[12]

Such developments did indeed lead to a reduction of the budget deficit, however the average tax burden in the country increased substantially when compared to the OECD average. In the early 2000s, there were fears that this development would push tax evasion to even higher levels. The mid-2000s were marked by an increase in the tax rates of income from employment but also a substantial reduction in the tax rate of profits from the business. Specifically, this rate was reduced from 40% in 2000 to 25% in 2008.[13] Such a development put downward pressure on the level of tax revenues and deteriorated even further the unequal distribution of the tax burden, discriminating against income from salaried employment and in favour of income from profits, harming even further the public's levels of tax conscience. In such a context, during the late 2000s and in a fashion worryingly similar to previous decades, the Greek tax system was characterised—not only by domestic analysts but also international organisations such as the IMF—as controversial, burdening excessively the lower income classes but also too complex and non-transparent.[14]

It should be noted that, as far as entrepreneurs were concerned, the Federation of Greek Industrialists never seized to lament the 'over-taxation'[15] of business (in spite of the reductions in the corporate income tax rate) but also to highlight the structural weaknesses of the tax

[12] Ibid., pp. 154–155.

[13] *The Taxation of Income in Greece*, p. 90.

[14] Glykou, pp. 185–186.

[15] *The Suspended Step of the Stork*, p. 1.

system, stressing that there was an urgent need to rationalise its functioning by introducing a series of improvements. Some of the measures that the FGI proposed included the early publication of tax circulars that concerned business income legislation, the better communication between the Ministry of Finance and businesses as far as the interpretation of tax legislation was concerned, but also the implementation of unified rules and the elimination of 'extremities' during tax audits which often led to the imposition of severe tax penalties even in the cases of simple errors.

In a fashion strikingly similar to previous decades, the FGI also stressed the need for continuous training of the tax officers but also close monitoring of their conduct during tax audits. What was also repeated was the need for the elimination of procedural rigidities as well as the simplification of the tax system and the elimination of tax disincentives.[16]

It is also important to note that throughout the 2000s widely circulated newspapers kept deploring the corruption, bureaucracy and overregulation plaguing the public sector, part of which was also tax administration.[17] Such issues, it was noted, rendered Greece one of the most backwards Western countries as far as the organisation and structure of public institutions were concerned and were blocking any actual efforts for the development of entrepreneurship and the promotion of either indigenous or foreign investment. Hence the sense of disillusionment characterising the period. In 2005, it was noted that the state's promises for the simplification of the tax system did not materialise 'for yet another year'. The tax system was again found to be complex, 'full of riddles' and burdened by the constant and numerous changes of the tax laws. What was needed, it was noted, was the establishment of a simpler, fairer and more efficient tax system that would stop being 'vengeful' towards the taxpayers.[18] Moreover, letters of complaint by citizens kept

[16] *The FGI's Positions on Economy, Sustainable Development, Labour, the State and Institutions*, pp. 27–35.

[17] Y. Kotofolos, 'With 4 Open Fronts in 2005', *I Kathimerini*, 31.12.2004. https://www.kathimerini.gr/economy/local/204993/me-4-anoikta-metopa-to-2005/.

[18] 'Controversies', *Ta Nea*, 04.05.2005. https://www.tanea.gr/2005/05/04/opinions/pipes-anakoloythies.

being published in daily newspapers, arguing, for example, that the state was indifferent towards establishing a fair tax system.[19]

As far as the tax officers were concerned, again similarly to previous decades, they did not deny the severity of problems such as that of tax evasion, corrupt tax officers and the complexity of the tax system.[20] Through their trade union branches though, they never stopped stressing the difficult circumstances under which they had to perform their duties. For instance, reacting publicly to an incident of an attack against tax officers by members of the public, the tax officers' trade union asked for the state's protection and legal support and argued that the members of the tax authorities were working under 'conditions of horror and threat', while being regularly targeted by either 'exasperated and overtaxed' citizens or 'ruthless' groups and lobbies with specific economic interests.[21]

It is also characteristic that in a public statement commenting on the tax officers' career development prospects, one of the tax officers' union branches argued that the state itself was guilty of the capricious implementation of laws and that the government's stance towards tax officers was one of mockery and arbitrariness.[22]

Conclusion

In 2014, the president of the FGI Dimitris Daskalopoulos stressed that 'the worst possible thing for economic stability is tax uncertainty'. The present chapter has shown that the late 1980s–late 2000s period offers a very good example of how the uncertainty caused by the way the tax system functions discourages business initiative and thus also an industrial investment.

[19] 'Reader Letters', *I Kathimerini*, 29.11.2008. https://www.kathimerini.gr/opinion/712004/grammata-anagnoston-28/.

[20] G. Fintikakis, 'Trade Unionists Did Not Say a Word About Corruption', *Ta Nea*, 29.12.2011. https://www.tanea.gr/2011/12/29/greece/koybenta-oi-syndikalistes-gia-ti-diafthora/.

[21] 'Press Release- We Condemn the Aggravated Assault in DOY Acharnon Against Our Colleague', National Union of Tax Officers, 13.2.2018.

[22] 'Mockery and Ridicule for the Technical Training Category', Attica and Cyclades Union of Tax Officers, 31.3.2016.

Bibliography

Official Publications

Attica and Cyclades Union of Tax Officers, 'Mockery and Ridicule for the Technical Training Category' (Athens: Attica and Cyclades Union of Tax Officers, 31.3.2016).

Federation of Greek Industries, 'The FGI's Positions on Economy, Sustainable Development, Labour, the State and Institutions' (Athens: FGI, 2017).

Federation of Greek Industries 'The Suspended Step of the Stork' (Athens: FGI, 2015), in Greek.

Foundation for Industrial and Economic Research, *The Taxation of Income in Greece* (Athens: Foundation for Industrial and Economic Research, 2018), in Greek.

National Union of Tax Officers, 'Press Release- We Condemn the Aggravated Assault in DOY Acharnon Against our Colleague' (Athens: National Union of Tax Officers, 13.2.2018).

Secondary Literature

Milios, Yiannis, 'The Greek Economy in the 20th Century'. http://users.ntua.gr/jmilios/Oikonomia_Eikostos1ab.pdf [accessed 20.12.2014], pp. 1–24, in Greek.

Panselina, Georgia M. and Maria Mavroeidi, *The Federation of Greek Industrialists, 1907–2007—A Century in the Service of the Idea of Entrepreneurship* (Athens: Economia Publishing, 2007), in Greek.

Psalidopoulos, Michalis, *History of the Bank of Greece, 1928–2008* (Athens: The Bank of Greece, 2014), in Greek.

Articles in National Newspapers

'Controversies', *Ta Nea*, 04.05.2005. https://www.tanea.gr/2005/05/04/opinions/pipes-anakoloythies.

Fintikakis, G., 'Trade Unionists Did Not Say a Word About Corruption', *Ta Nea*, 29.12.2011. https://www.tanea.gr/2011/12/29/greece/koybenta-oi-syndikalistes-gia-ti-diafthora/.

Kotofolos, Υ., 'With 4 Open Fronts in 2005', *I Kathimerini*, 31.12.2004. https://www.kathimerini.gr/economy/local/204993/me-4-anoikta-metopa-to-2005/.

'Reader Letters', *I Kathimerini*, 29.11.2008. https://www.kathimerini.gr/opinion/712004/grammata-anagnoston-28/.

CHAPTER 8

Conclusion

This book examined the interaction between business and the system of taxation in Greece, from the mid-1950s to the late 2000s. It has been argued that a series of problematic aspects of the tax system such as the complexity and frequent change of legislation, the insufficient organisation of the tax bureaus as well as the lack of adequate training and arbitrariness of the members of tax services, created difficulties for business. The evidence that this study was based on confirms William Baumol's point about how institutions affect entrepreneurship. That is, it was shown that Baumol was right when indicating that problematic tax rules can lead to unproductive forms of entrepreneurship, such as tax evasion.

However, the focus here was on aspects of the system of taxation that Baumol's model, examining solely tax rates and levels of taxation, neglected. This research showed that, as far as Greek entrepreneurship is concerned, the adverse effects of the system of taxation came mostly from a series of issues that increased its perceived unfairness and illegitimacy. The way that the tax system functioned also increased uncertainty, which was anything but beneficial for investing in business. In the eyes of Greek entrepreneurs, the system of taxation was the personification of the

Z. Pittaki, *Exploring the roots of systematic tax avoidance in Greece*, Palgrave Studies in Economic History,
https://doi.org/10.1007/978-3-030-71979-1_8

uncontrollable 'tax-gatherer' that Adam Smith had identified back in the late eighteenth century.[1]

The narrative developed in the study indicated that there were complaints and criticism about the functioning of the tax system throughout the period under examination. However, the impact of such problems was less explicit during the years of rapid economic growth, that is, from the mid-1950s up to about the mid-1970s. From this point onwards, there was a deterioration in the economy and an exacerbation of the problems in the way the tax system functioned, primarily because of the increase in the complexity and the frequency of change of tax legislation. Because of such developments, the problems caused by the tax system gradually became more explicit and led to open disputes and conflicts between the members of tax administration, entrepreneurs and more broadly, taxpayers, and the Ministry of Economics.

In more detail, and with regard to the evolution of the administrative burdens of the tax system, it should be noted that a series of reforms were introduced in the mid to late 1950s. These reforms mainly aimed at the simplification of the process of filing a tax return. The same period saw improvements in the organisation of the tax bureaus with measures such as the division of each tax office into departments. Also, legislation that contained tax officers' arbitrariness was introduced. However, there was a scarcity of similar measures from the late 1950s to the eve of the dictatorship. For example, it seems that no significant measure towards the modernisation of the organisation of the tax services was undertaken. In the period of dictatorship, 1967–1974, there were an increasing number of complaints about the bureaucracy and complex procedures followed in the tax services. During this period the administrative problems in the tax services were exacerbated, due to the dismissal of a large number of competent officers which eventually led to the dismantling of the Central Service of the Ministry of Economics. No serious initiatives for the modernisation of the services were undertaken. During 1974–1981 the administrative burdens of the tax system increased. This was because of the rise in the frequency with which new tax laws were introduced and the resulting increased complexity of the legislation. As in previous periods, tax officers received insufficient training. The complexity of procedures and the frequency in the change of tax legislation increased

[1] See Introduction, p. 15.

substantially during the period 1981–1989. The higher frequency in the change of legislation reflected also the imposition of new tax laws. These were introduced in order to cover the state's increased needs for tax revenue due to the widening of the public deficit during this period. The last period covered in the book, from 1989 up to 2008, did not see any substantial improvements in the tax system, which kept on being burdened by the malaises of the past.

While the main aim here was to show how the poor functioning of the tax system affected business, the sources that were used are of a quite wider perspective. That is, many of the views presented regarded the dysfunctionality of the tax regime as a whole, and came not from entrepreneurs, but from various other parts of society. Such a variety of sources reflects, on the one hand, the issue of availability: as explained also in the Introduction, it was difficult to obtain access to business archives containing information about a subject as thorny as the functioning of the tax system. The way that the tax system affected investment plans or any other aspect of business decision-making was something that was not often discussed by Greek entrepreneurs, nor, rather, recorded in the relevant sources. This could have contributed the fact that, as the bulk of evidence indicates, such discussions would most probably also contain references on tax evasion and/or corruption.

However, apart from the scarcity of material, the variety of sources employed in this study also reflects the need to corroborate the views expressed by the business. For example, the complaints with regard to the arbitrariness of tax officers were expressed not only by entrepreneurs, but by individual taxpayers and politicians too, and the critique about the obscurity of the tax procedures came also from tax professionals and other experts. The consistency of evidence presented suggests that the complaints and criticism were not simply part of an anti-tax rhetoric voiced by entrepreneurs and their representatives, but that they truly reflected the general public's vexation caused due to the way the tax system functioned.

In such a way, apart from establishing the link between taxation and entrepreneurship suggested through Baumol's model, this work also highlights the importance of context. This reflects the use of the historical institutionalist methodology employed here. As explained in the Introduction, the application of this methodology on the present subject suggests that, in order to study the interaction between the tax system and entrepreneurship in Greece, one needs to understand that tax rules were moulded by historical processes but also to take into account Greek entrepreneurs' 'contextualised worldviews' about the tax regime as a whole. This suggests, in other words, that one needs to explore the Greek entrepreneurs' perceptions and mentalities, irrespective of the degree of their subjectivity, about how the tax system affected them.[2]

It was these perceptions and mentalities that mattered in whether entrepreneurs would invest or not, and such perceptions and mentalities also shaped their views about the tax system. Characteristics of it such as taxes in favour of third parties increased the system's perceived unfairness and illegitimacy, whereas the continuously changing and inconsistent legislative framework increased the sense of uncertainty it created. Such problems had nothing to do with tax rates, which in fact were one of the very few features of the tax system that were certain and non-negotiable.

The evidence presented here suggests that Greek entrepreneurs considered that the way the tax system functioned was posing a systemic threat to their activities. It seems that this realisation also affected their investing behaviour, and this was so irrespective of what precisely their entrepreneurial role involved. As a matter of fact, in this study the term entrepreneur is used in a broad sense. It denotes the people who were responsible for decision-making in firms,[3] regardless of their size or legal form, but also, in a few occasions, self-employed professionals. The level of taxes paid and the precise forms that had to be filed with the tax authorities in each specific case differed, however the evidence indicates that the procedures that these people had to go through in order to abide by the tax legislation were, to a very large extent, common.

Apart from entrepreneurs' contextualised worldviews and the issue of historical process, the specific kind of historical institutionalism employed in this study has an additional characteristic: it views institutions as quite static structures. To use Hall and Taylor's words, here the system of taxation is considered to be a 'relatively persistent [feature]' of the Greek 'historical landscape'.[4] This perspective relates to that of the institutional lock-in, that is, the dynamic-process phenomenon of institutional patterns

[2] For a further elaboration of the 'contexualised worldviews' concept see Wadhwani and Bucheli, p. 10.

[3] As noted in the Introduction, here the key characteristic of the entrepreneur is considered to be the exercise of judgement in decision-making, following the definition proposed by Casson (see Casson, pp. 8–9).

[4] Hall and Taylor, p. 9.

that persist and reproduce themselves overtime.[5] This phenomenon can explain, up to a certain extent, why there was so little progress in the Greek tax system throughout the course of the 54 years examined in this study. Apart from the occasional initiatives, from about the late 1960s onwards there were not any real efforts to improve the training of tax officers, and no substantial measures were undertaken in order to reduce the complexity of legislation. On the contrary, especially after the mid-1970s, there was a substantial rise in the frequency in the introduction of new legislation, and, from the late 1970s, a rapid increase in tax evasion. In other words, the path that the tax system had taken had become, to a very large extent, 'locked-in'.[6]

On the whole, the tax system was constantly creating obstacles to business and was stirring public discontent. It was also found to be ineffective, bureaucratic and inadequately organised even by tax officers themselves, and just seemed to be getting worse over time. The Greek ex-Minister of Economics' idea of wiring tourists, students and housekeepers in order to track down tax evaders quoted in the opening of the Introduction was but a resonance of the current but also all the previous fiscal authorities' desperation over their inability to manage the tax system. In other words, the inability reflected in the Minister's words was identical to that of the tax authorities of the past which, being unable to figure out taxpayers' true income, resorted to poor measures such as the one of taxing them on the basis of their consumption patterns, with the use of instruments such as the 'irrefutable presumptions of wealth'.[7]

Moreover, apart from any degree of institutional inertia, it seems that the lack of substantial progress in the tax system should also be attributed to the lack of sufficient political will on the part of the Greek state to improve the functioning of the system. The obstacles burdening the tax regime were undoubtedly many and of a systemic nature. It is however very difficult to accept that the various governments did all that they could in order to remedy the situation. As a matter of fact, it seems that they did very little. Indicative of this is that they were not particularly eager to look elsewhere, to explore, that is, what lessons could be learned from the way other countries managed their tax administration systems.

[5] Thelen, p. 396.

[6] Ibid., p. 385.

[7] See, for example, Chapter 3, p. 16.

The only relatively serious effort to import ideas from abroad seems to have been the inviting of Georges Langrod in the 1960s in order to receive his advice and technical assistance for the reorganisation of the public sector. Still, as has been explained, very little was done in order to implement Langrod's suggestions.[8] Unfortunately, it seems that the lack of political will to resolve the long-standing issues of the Greek tax system persists till today. Indicative of this is the fact that the state showed no interest in an offer made by the German state in 2015 and proposing the dispatch of 500 tax officers 'in order to support the Greek tax and fiscal authorities in combating tax evasion and waste of public money'.[9]

It is also possible that the substantial reforms that need to be done in the tax system have not yet been implemented because of resistance from within the services. It is, in other words, possible that high-ranking tax officials have tried to inhibit the passing of legislation that would introduce reforms and upset the *status quo* within the services. As Rose-Ackerman and Palifka put it, '[s]tatutes are the result of political deals. They not only express the preferences and ideals of voters and elected officials, but also reflect the interests of those who lobby… to influence provisions in their favour'.[10]

Of course, it also seems that if political will for reform ever exists, there are certain things that could be done in order to improve the situation. One of the contributions of this research is that it has shown that a substantial reform of the tax system would require first of all the introduction of measures that prohibit the frequent change of tax legislation. This could be done with the enactment of relevant constitutional laws. Consistency in the legislative framework and rules would reduce the complexity of the tax regime and would therefore create a sense of stability about it. This would reduce entrepreneurial uncertainty. Among others, there should also be a system of continuous training of tax officers from all ranks as well as better monitoring on the part of the state. This would help the Ministry of Economics not only to track down corruption, but

[8] See Chapter 3, p. 32.

[9] Spiros Dimitrelis, 'The 500 Tax Officers Who Are Ready for Greece', *Capital*, 7.2.2015. http://www.capital.gr/tax/2223675 [accessed 20.2.2016], in Greek.

[10] Rose-Ackerman and Palifka, p. 341.

also to identify the needs of tax officers and help them be more effective when performing their duties.[11]

There are also certain steps that could be taken in order to reduce differential tax treatment and the citizens' resulting sense of tax unfairness. For example, all taxes in favour of third parties and special contributions should be abolished. There should also be a re-examination of tax exemptions offered to certain social groups. In the past, tax incentives and exemptions offered by the state for the promotion of investment were one of the features of the tax system that increased its perceived unfairness. As a matter of fact, tax incentives were overall beneficial for the individual enterprises that managed to take advantage of them. However, as the various studies that were mentioned in the main chapters of this monograph indicate, they were much less effective for the development of the total economy. Also, rightly or wrongly, Greek citizens felt that, through such incentives, entrepreneurs were being unfairly privileged by the tax system.

The reduction of various social groups' differential tax treatment would increase the system's perceived legitimacy and therefore also improve the public's 'tax conscience'. As explained also in the Introduction, low tax conscience is a notion that has been traditionally used in Greece in order to denote taxpayers' negative predisposition towards willingly declaring their true income. However, it is also a notion through which the willingness to evade taxation is directly related to perceptions about the tax regime's illegitimacy. That is, through the perspective of 'tax conscience', tax evasion takes the form of citizens' reaction towards a state that they find to be unfair, illegitimate and untrustworthy.

Overall, the evidence that has been presented in this work suggests that the establishment of a socially fairer, less complex, less arbitrary and more stable and consistent tax system would increase its legitimacy and therefore lead to the reduction of tax evasion. This would not only improve Greece's fiscal position in the long run, but would also be a major step towards improving state-civil society relations in the country. As has also been illustrated here, the tax system is in need of specific measures that would modernise the functioning of the tax services. Further research examining the possible steps that should be taken in this regard would be

[11] This could be done, for example, with the development of special software that tax officers could use during audits.

useful. It seems that such research should also take into consideration relevant measures that were implemented in countries with similar problems. On the whole, any step that the Greek administration could undertake in order to establish a more legitimate, stable and effective tax mechanism would lead to a reduction of economic uncertainty. This would benefit entrepreneurship and therefore help Greece to gain the developmental impetus it now needs more than even before in its modern history. Moreover, as shown in the Introduction, the establishment of more effective tax administration mechanisms is a major issue in a number of European states. Therefore, the implications of the analysis here are relevant for other countries too. Indeed, one of the current efforts in a number of European states is to develop investment friendly tax systems also by simplifying the tax procedures and improving the functioning of the tax services. A number of countries have undertaken such measures; for example, France introduced simplified tax returns; Italy set up a simplified tax regime for self-employed people and Poland introduced a simplified accounting system for microbusinesses.[12] The findings of the present research can prove useful for relevant studies, especially those focusing on countries with tax systems similar to that of Greece, such as for example Italy.

This research also contributes to Greek historiography by showing how the poor functioning of the system of taxation affected entrepreneurship and therefore also the broader economy from the mid-1950s to the late 2000s. In a number of important works considering this period[13] there are no or very few references to the role of taxation, let alone the functioning of the tax administration per se. Here however it is argued that tax rules had an impact on Greek entrepreneurship. It is also suggested that what entrepreneurship needed the most was not lower tax rates but a reliable tax administration mechanism and a stable tax regime.

Moreover, this study analyses in detail problems of the Greek tax system that were briefly mentioned in relevant works.[14] It explores, for example, how the arbitrariness of tax officers was expressed, what were

[12] European Commission, *Tax Reforms in EU Member States – Tax Policy Challenges for Economic Growth and Fiscal Sustainability*, Institutional Paper 008, September 2015. http://ec.europa.eu/economy_finance/publications/eeip/pdf/ip008_en.pdf [accessed 14.10.2016], pp. 19–20.

[13] For example, Kazakos and Drakatos.

[14] See for example Tatsos, Glykou and Giouras.

the characteristics of the system that increased its complexity, where the frequent changes of tax legislation should be attributed to and whether and to what extent the state undertook measures to remedy the situation. The research presents not only the voices of entrepreneurs and taxpayers, but those of the members of the tax services too. It throws light on the difficulties that tax officers had to face when performing their duties in the context of a tax regime that offered them poor training and was confusing, constantly changing and disorganised. It also presents the perceptions of the Greek society about the issue. It shows that the poor functioning of the tax services was a systemic problem that affected all Greeks.

The monograph also throws light on some of the deeper causes of the big issue of tax evasion. The Greek citizens' 'innate resistance to taxation' has often been attributed to cultural forces.[15] Here, however, tax evasion is seen as an outcome of the problematic functioning of the tax system. The research employs a historical institutionalist methodology which examines the perceptions and beliefs of Greek entrepreneurs/taxpayers but also tax officers about the tax system. The analysis recognises the importance of the historical context within which such perceptions were shaped. It is argued that to a large extent, the tax system was perceived to be illegitimate and unfair and that this contributed to the level of tax evasion. By exploring tax evasion, this work also throws light on one of the causes of the great increase of the public deficit from the 1980s onwards.

Moreover, this research contributes to institutional analyses about the tax system. The Greek case offers a very good example of the vicious cycle connecting tax evasion and corruption. Specifically, it has been shown that, due to its inability to assess taxpayers' true taxable income, the Greek state resorted to arbitrary measures such as the 'presumptions of wealth' mentioned in the previous pages. Not all of the tax officers were corrupt. However, those who were corrupt, benefitted from an arbitrary system that gave them power to make their own decisions about taxpayers' income and therefore also to extort bribes. Such measures increased the illegitimacy of the tax system and therefore also taxpayers' willingness to evade taxes. The increase of tax evasion and the state's continuously

[15] Matthew Karnitschnig and Nektaria Stamouli, 'Greece Struggles to Get Citizens to Pay Their Taxes', *The Wall Street Journal*, 25.2.2015. http://www.wsj.com/articles/greece-struggles-to-get-citizens-to-pay-their-taxes-1424867495 [accessed 10.3.2016].

growing need for tax revenue led to even more arbitrary measures, again because of the inability of the tax mechanism to figure out taxpayers' income. This increased even more the illegitimacy of the tax system and therefore also the tendency to evade taxes.

Additionally, here the difficulties facing Greek entrepreneurship were not examined in terms of any ideas about Greeks' stance towards business, wealth accumulation, etc.[16] The lens used here is an institutional one, as this study focuses on the interaction between the system of taxation and Greek business. By doing so, the research done here contributes to the theory that explores the interaction between institutions and entrepreneurship.

Moreover, here the examination of the interaction between the Greek system of taxation and Greek business drew primarily on Baumol's perspective. His work indicated that tax rules affect the development of entrepreneurship and influence the forms of it that can emerge in different societal and economic contexts. However, Baumol's examination considered exclusively the level of taxes. The present study takes his perspective a step further, by suggesting that the explanatory power of his model can be enhanced by taking into consideration the importance of the tax regime as well, and examining how the way that the tax services function affects entrepreneurship. Research based on such an extended version of Baumol's model could provide useful insights, especially for the cases of countries in which tax administration seems to be a greater obstacle for entrepreneurial activity than tax rates.[17]

Bibliography

Web Resources

Dimitrelis, S., 'The 500 Tax Officers Who Are Ready for Greece', *Capital*, 7.2.2015. http://www.capital.gr/tax/2223675, in Greek.

Karnitschnig, M., and Stamouli, N., 'Greece Struggles to Get Citizens to Pay Their Taxes', *The Wall Street Journal*, 25.2.2015. http://www.wsj.com/articles/greece-struggles-to-get-citizens-to-pay-their-taxes-1424867495.

[16] Cf Sapelli, see pp. 18–19.

[17] See *Helping Firms Grow, European Competitiveness Report 2014.*

Official Publications

European Commission, *Helping Firms Grow, European Competitiveness Report 2014*, Commission Staff Working Document SWD (2014)277 final http://ec.europa.eu/growth/industry/competitiveness/reports/eu-competitiveness-report/index_en.htm.

European Commission, *Tax Reforms in EU Member States—Tax Policy Challenges for Economic Growth and Fiscal Sustainability*, Institutional Paper 008, September 2015 http://ec.europa.eu/economy_finance/publications/eeip/pdf/ip008_en.pdf.

Secondary Literature

Bucheli, M. and Wadhwani, R. D. (eds) *History, Theory* (Oxford: Oxford University Press, 2013).

Casson, M., *Entrepreneurship: Theory, Networks, History* (UK: Edward Elgar, 2010).

Drakatos, K., *The Big Cycle of the Greek Economy (1945–1995)* (Athens: Papazisis, 1997), in Greek.

Giouras, T., *Taxation and Politics, Political-Economic Problematic and Financial Thought* (Athens: Sakis Karagiorgas Foundation, 2000), in Greek.

Glykou, I., *State and Tax Policy, an Historical and Theoretical Approach and the Case of Greece* (Athens: Sakoullas, 2009), in Greek.

Hall, P. A. and Taylor, R. C. R., 'Political Science and the Three New Institutionalisms', *Political Studies*, XLIV (1996), pp. 936–957.

Kazakos, P., *Between State and Market* (Athens: Patakis, 2001), in Greek.

Sapelli, G., *Southern Europe since 1945, Tradition and Modernity in Portugal, Spain, Italy, Greece and Turkey* (London and New York: Longman, 1995).

Tatsos, N., *Shadow Economy and Tax Evasion in Greece* (Athens: Papazisi, 2001), in Greek.

Thelen, K., 'Historical Institutionalism in Comparative Politics', *Annual Review of Political Science*, 2 (1999), 369–404.

Bibliography

Unpublished Sources

a) Interviews
Ioannis Photopoulos 10.6.2014
Entrepreneur who requested anonymity no 1 28.7.2014
Ulysses Kyriakopoulos 31.7.2014
Entrepreneur who requested anonymity no 2 8.8.2014
Stelios Argyros 29.8.2014
Retired tax officer who requested anonymity 9.9.2014
Entrepreneur who requested anonymity no 3 11.9.2014
Charalampos Nikolakopoulos 22.7.2015
b) Unpublished theses
Florou, Christina, 'Comparative evaluation of the methods used to determine the aggregate net income of the Greek stock companies', (unpublished doctoral thesis, Aristotle University of Thessaloniki, 2009), in Greek.
Manesiotis, Vasilios, 'Tax structure change during economic development: the case of Greece', (unpublished doctoral thesis, Northwestern University, 1985).
Tsakas, Christos, 'Greek Business ahead of the European Challenge: State Strategy and Private Interests from the Association with the EEC to Democratic Transition' (unpublished doctoral thesis, University of Crete, 2015), in Greek.

Z. Pittaki, *Exploring the roots of systematic tax avoidance in Greece*, Palgrave Studies in Economic History,
https://doi.org/10.1007/978-3-030-71979-1

Primary Sources

CHROTEX Archive

'The Scopes of the Rearrangements', probably published in 1955 in *I Naftemporiki*

'Tax Courts', *I Naftemporiki*, 28.02.1957, p. 6.

'The Exports Problem', *O EconomicosTahidromos*, 15.04.1965, p. 1.

Board of Directors Meeting Minutes (1967–1977)

Historical Archives of the Piraeus Bank Group Cultural Foundation

Economic Development Financing Organisation Archive, *Report of Activities up to December 31, 1961*, p. 12.

Index of Parliamentary Discussions 1946–1967

Minutes from the Sitting of the Special Committee, 6/26.7.1955, pp. 56–62.

Professor Michalis Psalidopoulos Personal Archive

Bulletin of the Federation of Greek Industrialists (FGI) (1966–1988)

The Hellenic Literary and Historical Archive

The guild of hat making craft industries, 'Memorandum to the Ministries of Commerce and Industry', 16.03.1966.

IZOLA Files, Report of the Board of Governors for 1967 (no page number available).

IZOLA Files, Report of the Board of Governors for 1970, p. 6.

IZOLA Files, Report of the Board of Governors for 1976, p. 18.

The 'Konstantinos G. Karamanlis'Foundation, Ioannis Mpoutos Archive

File 6, 'Decadence', *I Avgi*, 09.01.1966, p. 1.

The 'Konstantinos G. Karamanlis'Foundation, Konstantinos G. Karamanlis Archive

Vol. 07, *A Period of Ordeal, 1963–1974* (Period B', 21.4.1967–24.7.1974), pp. 49–50.

Vol. 08, *The Restoration of Democracy, 1974–1977* (Period A', 24.7.1974–3.9.1975), p. 210.

Vol 09, *The Restoration of Democracy, 1974–1977* (Period B', 4.9.1975–21.10.1977), pp. 39–40.

The 'Konstantinos G. Karamanlis' Foundation, Konstantinos Papakonstantinou Archive

File 202A', Findings of the Economics Committee, 1959–1961, Notes on Tax Evasion, Measures against tax theft, p. 4.

File 202A', Findings of the Economics Committee, 1959–1961, Notes on Tax Evasion, Measures against tax theft, The Special Audit Team for the Implementation of the Tax Code, 'Note on the measures that should be assumed against tax evasion', p. 1.

File 12A, F01348, 'The Parliamentary Discussion on the Tax Bill', *I Naftemporiki*, 11.03.1960, p. 6.

File 12A, F01348, Spir. Lizardos, 'Tax Evasion', *I Naftemporiki*, 11.03.1960, p. 7.

Union of Corporations and Limited Liability Companies Archive

Board of Directors Meeting Minutes (1957–1989).

Vovolini Archive

File 30, Eftaxias Family, sub-file 1, Evidence no. 61, p. 2.

'Notes – Tax Evasion', *Viomichaniki Epitheorissis*, Vol. 20, September 1953, p. 302.

Viomichaniki Epitheorissis, Vol. 22, May 1955, p. 18.

Viomichaniki Epitheorissis, Vol. 26, 1959, Proceedings of the 2nd Congress of the Chambers of Commerce and Industry of Greece, 20–23.10.1957, pp. 53–54.

Viomichaniki Epitheorissis, Vol. 26, 1959, Proceedings of the 2nd Congress of the Chambers of Commerce and Industry of Greece, 20–23.10.1957, pp. 268–269.

Viomichaniki Epitheorissis, Vol. 32, 1965, Proceedings of the 5th Congress of the Chambers of Commerce and Industry of Greece—8th theme of the agenda, 14-17/6 1964, p. 318.

Viomichaniki Epitheorissis, Vol. 38, November 1971, 445, p. 11.

Newspapers, Magazines and Serial Publications

a) Newspapers

Dimokratia, Eleftheria, Empros, Imerisia (and new online), I Avgi, I Kathimerini, I Naftemporiki, O Economicos Tahydromos, Makedonia, Rizospastis, Ta Nea, To Vima, To Vima tis Kyriakis (in Greek).

A number of contemporary articles was also retrieved from the newspapers I Kathimerini, to Vima, Dimokratia, Capital and Imerisia (in Greek).

The Financial Times, The Guardian.

b) Magazines and Serial Publications

The Accountant, Tax Review, The Bulletin of Tax Legislation, Bulletin of the Chamber of Commerce and Industry of Athens.

Documentaries

'The Time Machine (I Mihani tou Chronou): The Dictatorship's fascism and spoils'. https://www.youtube.com/watch?v=x0lVB0-Cl8s [accessed 11.2.2014] (aired on NET, subsequently NERIT), in Greek.

'The trial of the junta' (aired on NERIT), in Greek.

Official Publications

Attica and Cyclades Union of Tax Officers, 'Mockery and Ridicule for the Technical Training Category', 31.3.2016.

Bank of Greece, *Bank of Greece Governor's Annual Report for 1967* (Athens: Bank of Greece, 1968).

Bank of Greece, *Bank of Greece Governor's Annual Report for 1968* (Athens: Bank of Greece, 1969).

Bank of Greece, *Bank of Greece Governor's Annual Report for 1969* (Athens: Bank of Greece, 1970).

Bank of Greece, *Bank of Greece Governor's Annual Report for 1971* (Athens: Bank of Greece, 1972).

Bank of Greece, *Bank of Greece Governor's Annual Report for 1980* (Athens: Bank of Greece, 1981).

Bank of Greece, *Long-term Statistical Series of the Greek Economy* (Athens: Bank of Greece, 1992), in Greek.

Bank of Greece, *Proposals of the Disincentives Committee* (Athens: Bank of Greece, 1979).

Bank of Greece, *Statement made by Governor Xenophon Zolotas at the Annual Meeting of the Bank of Greece, 20 April 1967* (Athens: The Bank of Greece, 1967).

European Commission, *Helping Firms Grow, European Competitiveness Report 2014*, Commission Staff Working Document SWD (2014)277 final. http://ec.europa.eu/growth/industry/competitiveness/reports/eu-competitiveness-report/index_en.htm [accessed 12.3.2016].

European Commission, *Tax Reforms in EU Member States—Tax policy Challenges for Economic Growth and Fiscal Sustainability*, Institutional Paper 008, September 2015. http://ec.europa.eu/economy_finance/publications/eeip/pdf/ip008_en.pdf [accessed 14.10.2016].

Federation of Greek Industrialists, *The FGI's Positions on Economy, Sustainable Development, Labour, the State and Institutions* (Athens: Federation of Greek Industrialists, 2017), in Greek.

Federation of Greek Industrialists, *The Suspended Step of the Stork* (Athens: Federation of Greek Industrialists, 2015), in Greek.

Federation of Greek Industrialists, *The Greek Industry in 1959* (Athens: Federation of Greek Industrialists, 1960), in Greek.

Foundation for Industrial and Economic Research, *The Taxation of Income in Greece* (Athens: Foundation for Industrial and Economic Research, 2018), in Greek.

Hellenic Statistical Authority, *Concise Statistical Yearbook of Greece*, issues 1962, 1982 and 1985–6.

Hellenic Statistical Authority, *Statistical Yearbook of Greece*, issues 1962, 2005 and 2009–10.

Hellenic Statistical Authority, *Statistical Yearbook of Public Finance*, 1966.

International Monetary Fund, *Annual Report 1959*. http://www.imf.org/external/pubs/ft/ar/archive/pdf/ar1959.pdf [accessed 14.12.2014].

International Monetary Fund, *Annual Report 1960*. https://www.imf.org/external/pubs/ft/ar/archive/pdf/ar1960.pdf [accessed 14.12.2014].

International Monetary Fund, *Greece, Selected Issues*, Country Report No.13/155, June 2013. https://www.imf.org/external/pubs/ft/scr/2013/cr13155.pdf [accessed 1.11.2015].

International Monetary Fund, *Corruption: Costs and Mitigating Strategies*, IMF Staff Discussion Note, May 2016. http://www.imf.org/external/pubs/ft/sdn/2016/sdn1605.pdf [accessed 8.10.2016].

Ministry of Coordination, *National Accounts of Greece 1948–1965* (Athens: State Printing Office, 1967), in Greek.

Ministry of Finance, *Annual Reports for the Execution of the Budget*, various issues (1955–1990), in Greek.

National Union of Tax Officers, 'Press Release-We Condemn the Aggravated Assault in DOY Acharnon Against Our Colleague' 13.2.2018.

The State Gazette, Tax Code, issue 1, no. 116, 5.5.1956.

Secondary Literature

Agapitos, G. I., *Income Taxation in Greece* (Athens: Centre of Planning and Economic Research, 1986), in Greek.

Argyriades, Demetrios, 'Greek Exit from the Crisis—A Pressing and Much-Needed Public Service Reform', *Social Sciences*, 2 (2013), 78–90.

Argyriades, Demetrios, 'Ethics and Governance from a Comprehensive Perspective: How Are We Going to Face the Multiple Challenges of Our Times', Panteion University of Political and Social Sciences, Centre of Governance and Sustainable Development. http://www.dee.gr/mediaupload/publications/20100618_ithiki_kai_diakibernisi.pdf [accessed 7.7.2015], pp. 1–26, in Greek.

Artavanis, Nikolaos, Adair Morse and Margarita Tsoutsoura, 'Measuring Income Tax Evasion Using Bank Credit: Evidence from Greece'. *Quarterly Journal of Economics*, 2016.

Baumol, William J., 'Entrepreneurship: Productive, Unproductive, and Destructive', *Journal of Political Economy*, Vol. 98, 5, 1 (Oct., 1990), pp. 893–921.

Baumol, William J., 'Formal Entrepreneurship Theory in Economics: Existence and Bounds', *Journal of Business Venturing*, 8 (1993), pp. 197–210.

Bitros, George K., 'Greece: How and Why Things Turned Upside Down', in *Essays in Applied Economics and Finance*, ed Giannis Katsoulakos (Athens: Athens University of Economics and Business, 2013), pp. 1–45, in Greek.

Bosworth, Barry and Trifon Kollintzas, 'Economic Growth in Greece: Past Performance and Future Prospects, in *Greece's Economic Performance and Prospects*, eds Ralph C. Bryan, Nikolaos C. Garganas and Georgios S. Tavlas (Athens: The Bank of Greece and The Brookings Institution, 2002), pp. 153–192.

Break, George F. and Ralph Turvey, *Studies in Greek Taxation* (Athens: Centre of Planning and Economic Research, 1964).

Casson, Mark, *Entrepreneurship: Theory, Networks, History* (UK: Edward Elgar, 2010).

Casson, Mark and Peter J. Buckley, 'Entrepreneurship and the Growth of the Firm: An Extension of Penrose's Theory' in *Entrepreneurship—Theory, Networks, History* (UK: Edward Elgar, 2010), pp. 88–111.

'Chronology' in *Greece in the 20th century, 1965–1970*, I Kathimerini – Epta Imeres (Athens: I Kathimerini, 12.12.1999), pp. 3–7, in Greek.

Clemens, Elisabeth S. and James M. Cook, 'Politics and Institutionalism: Explaining Durability and Change', *Annual Review of Sociology*, 25 (1999), 441–466.

Close, D. H., *Greece Since 1945* (Great Britain: Pearson Education Limited, 2002).

Demathas, Zacharias, 'Greek Economy and European Community', in *Greece in the 20th Century, 1980–1990*, I Kathimerini – Epta Imeres (Athens: *I Kathimerini*, 25–26.12.1999), pp. 22–23, in Greek.

Dertilis, G. V, *Ineffectual of Effective? Taxes and Power in the Neo-hellenic State* (Athens: Alexandria Publications, 1993), in Greek.

Dimitras, Panayote Elias, 'Changes in Public Attitudes', in *Political Change in Greece Before and After the Colonels*, eds Kevin Featherstone and Dimitrios K. Katsioudas (London: Croom Helm, 1987), pp. 64–84.

Douhan, Robin and Magnus Henrekson, 'The Political Economy of Entrepreneurship', *IFN Working Paper* No 716, Research Institute of Industrial Economics (2007). http://econfaculty.gmu.edu/pboettke/workshop/spring08/WP_PoliticalEconomy.pdf [accessed 10.11.2015], pp. 1–29.

'Drachma for 60 years', in *Four Interviews of Xenophon Zolotas in Economicos Tahidromos*, (Athens: Economicos Tahidromos,1988), pp. 3–18, in Greek.

Drakatos, Konstantinos, *The Big Cycle of the Greek Economy (1945–1995)* (Athens: Papazisis, 1997), in Greek.

Dritsas, Margarita, *The Colour of Success: The Greek Paint industry, 1830–1990* (Athens: Trohalia, 1995), in Greek.

Edmiston, Kelly D., 'Tax Uncertainty and Investment: A Cross-Country Empirical Examination', *Economic Inquiry*, 42, 3 (July 2004), 425–440.

Eliades, E. A, 'Stabilization of the Greek Economy and the 1953 Devaluation of the Drachma' Staff Papers, *International Monetary Fund*, 4, 1 (Sep., 1954), 22–72.

Estrin, Saul, Klaus E. Meyer and Maria Bytchkova, 'Entrepreneurship in Transition Economies', in *The Oxford Handbook of Entrepreneurship*, eds Mark Casson, Bernard Yeung, Anuradha Basu and Nigel Wadeson (Oxford: Oxford University Press, 2006), pp. 693–725.

Evans, Chris, 'The Operating Costs of Taxation: A Review of the Research', *Economic Affairs*, 21, 2 (2001), 5–9.

Evans, Chris, 'Studying the Studies: An Overview of Recent Research into Taxation Operating Costs', *eJournal of Tax Research* 1,1 (2003), 64–92.

Fear, Jeff, 'Mining the Past: Historicizing Organizational Learning and Change', in *Organizations in Time: History, Theory, Methods*, eds Marcelo Bucheli and R. Daniel Wadhwani (Oxford: Oxford University Press, 2013), pp. 169–192.

Freris, A. F., *The Greek Economy in the Twentieth Century* (London and Sydney: Croom Helm, 1986).

Galanos, George, 'The Greek Tourism Industry and the Challenge of the Economic Crisis', in *Greece's Horizons—Reflecting on the Country's Assets and Capabilities*, eds Pantelis Sklias and Nikolaos Tzifakis (Athens: Konstantinos Karamanlis Institute for Democracy, 2013), pp. 131–145.

Gallant, Thomas G., *Modern Greece* (London: Arnold, 2001).

Giannaris, N. V., *Greece and Yugoslavia, an Economic Comparison* (New York, Praeger, 1984).

Giouras, Thanasis, *Taxation and Politics, Political-Economic Problematic and Financial Thought* (Athens: Sakis Karagiorgas Foundation, 2000), in Greek.

Giouras, Thanasis and Michalis Psalidopoulos, *Occupation, Nazism and Greek Economy—Official Reports and Memoirs* (Athens: Metamesonikties Ekdoseis, 2015), in Greek.

Glykou, Ioanna, *State and Tax Policy, an Historical and Theoretical Approach and the Case of Greece* (Athens: Sakoullas, 2009), in Greek.

Goldscheid, Rudolf and Robert Lazarsfeld, 'Staatsozialismus oder Staatskapitalismus - Ein finanzsoziologischer Beitrag zur Lösung des Staatsschulden-Problems', *Archiv für Rechts- und Wirtschaftsphilosophie*, 11, 2 (1917/1918), 255–259.

Goldscheid, Rudolf, 'A Sociological Approach to Problems of Public Finance' in *Classics in the Theory of Public Finance*, eds R. A. Musgrave and A. T. Peacock (London: Macmillan&Co. Ltd., [1925], 1958), pp. 202–213.

Grigoropoulos, Gregory J., 'Shipping and Sustainable Economic Development: The Case of Greece', in *Greece's Horizons, Reflecting on the Country's Assets and Capabilities*, eds Pantelis Sklias and Nikolaos Tzifakis (Athens: Konstantinos Karamanlis Institute for Democracy, 2013), pp. 121–129.

Haig, Robert Murray, 'The Cost to Business Concerns of Compliance with Tax Laws', *Management Review*, 24, 11 (1935), 323–333.

Hall, Peter A. and Rosemary C. R. Taylor, 'Political Science and the Three New Institutionalisms', *Political Studies*, XLIV (1996), 936–957.

Harlaftis, Gelina, *A History of Greek-Owned Shipping—The Making of an International Tramp Fleet, 1830 to the Present Day* (London: Routledge, 1996).

Hassett, Kevin A. and Gilbert E. Metcalf 'Investment with Uncertain Tax Policy: Does Random Tax Policy Discourage Investment?', *The Economic Journal*, 109, 457 (July 1999), 372–393.

Hébert, Robert and Albert N. Link, *The Entrepreneur: Mainstream Views and Radical Critiques* (New York: Praeger, 1988).

Henrekson, Magnus, 'Entrepreneurship and Institutions', *IFN Working Paper* No 707, Research Institute of Industrial Economics (2007). http://www.ifn.se/Wfiles/wp/wp707.pdf [accessed 10.11.2015], pp. 1–30.

Hodgson, Geoffrey M., 'What Are institutions?', *Journal of Economic Issues*, XL, 1 (2006), 1–25.

Ioakimoglou, E. and J. Milios, 'Capital Accumulation and Over-Accumulation Crisis: The Case of Greece (1960–1989)', *Review of Radical Political Economics*, 25, 2 (June 1993), 81–107.

Ioakeimoglou, Ilias, 'The Greek Economy 1960–2007, Development, Productive Structure and Labour Market'. http://www.ine.otoe.gr/Upl/pdf/Greece_IneOtoe.pdf [accessed 15/2/2014], pp. 1–28, in Greek.

Johnson, Victoria, 'What Is Organizational Imprinting? Cultural Entrepreneurship in the Founding of the Paris Opera', *American Journal of Sociology*, 13, 1 (2007), 97–127.

Jones, Geoffrey and Rohit Daniel Wadhwani, 'Schumpeter's Plea: Rediscovering History and Relevance in the Study of Entrepreneurship', *Harvard Business School Working Paper*, No. 06-036 (2006). http://www.hbs.edu/faculty/Publication%20Files/06-036.pdf [accessed 10.10.2013], pp. 1–38.

Kalafatis, Thanasis, 'Construction Fever', in *Greece in the 20th Century, 1965–1970*, I Kathimerini – Epta Imeres (Athens: I Kathimerini, 12.12.1999), pp. 24–25, in Greek.

Kalyvianakis, K. et al., *Tax regime, Shadow Economy and Tax Evasion in Greece* (Athens: Papazisis, 1993), in Greek.

Karafillis, Athanasios, 'Certificates of Social Ideals: A Case of Social Justice or Injustice in the Selection of Candidate Students for the Pedagogical Academies'. http://eriande.elemedu.upatras.gr/?section=985&language=el&page706=1&itemid706=1113 [accessed 11.1.2016], in Greek.

Karakousis, Antonis, 'A Tumultuous Decade', in *Greece in the 20th Century, 1970–1980*, I Kathimerini – Epta Imeres (Athens: I Kathimerini, 19.12.1999), pp. 24–25, in Greek.

Karamitsopoulos, Vasilis, Antonis Koumpias, Orestis Pastellas and Mariela Tiliakou, 'Proposal for the Establishment and Functioning of a Special Economic Zone in Greece', in *Niches of Freedom and Development—Proposal for the Functioning of A Special Economic Zone in Greece* (Brussels: Friedrich Naumann Stiftung Für die Freiheit, 2016), pp. 6–20.

Kariotis, Theodore C., 'The Economy: Growth Without Equity', in *Greece in the Twentieth Century*, eds. Theodore A. Couloumbis, Theodore Kariotis and Fotini Bellou (Athens: Hellenic Foundation for European and Black Sea Studies, 2004), pp. 239–273.

Karnitschnig, Matthew and Nektaria Stamouli, 'Greece Struggles to Get Citizens to Pay Their Taxes', *The Wall Street Journal*, 25.2.2015. http://www.wsj.com/articles/greece-struggles-to-get-citizens-to-pay-their-taxes-1424867495 [accessed 10.3.2016].

Kazakos, Panos, *Between State and Market* (Athens: Patakis, 2001), in Greek.

Kirzner, Israel M., *Competition and Entrepreneurship* (Chicago: University of Chicago Press, 1973).

Korres, Georgios M. and Dionysios P. Chionis, *Greek Economy, Economic Policy and Analysis of the Basic Macroeconomic Magnitudes* (Athens, Stamoulis, 2003), in Greek.

Kostis, Kostas, *State and Enterprises in Greece, the history of 'Aluminium of Greece'* (Athens: Polis, 2013), in Greek.

Landström, Hans and Matts Benner, 'Entrepreneurship Research: A History of Scholarly Migration', in *Historical Foundations of Entrepreneurship Research*, eds Hans Landström and Franz Lohrke (UK: Edward Elgar, 2010), pp. 15–45.

Landström, Hans and Olle Persson, 'Entrepreneurship Research: Research Communities and Knowledge Platforms' in *Historical Foundations of Entrepreneurship Research*, eds Hans Landström and Franz Lohrke (UK: Edward Elgar, 2010), pp. 46–76.

Langrod, Georges, *Reorganisation of Public Administration in Greece—A Report* (Paris: OECD, 1965).

Legg, Keith R., *Politics in Modern Greece* (California: Stanford University Press, 1969).

Leibenstein, Harvey 'Entrepreneurship and Development', *The American Economic Review*, 58, 2 (1968), 72–83.

Lindbeck, Assar, 'Consequences of the Advanced Welfare State', *The World Economy*, 11, 1 (1988), 19–38.

Lipartito, Kenneth, 'Historical Sources and Data', in *Organizations in Time: History, Theory, Methods*, eds Marcelo Bucheli and R. Daniel Wadhwani (Oxford: Oxford University Press, 2013), pp. 284–305.

Louri, H., and I. Pepelasis- Minoglou, 'A Quantitative Exploration on the Determinants of (De-) Industrialisation: The Case of Greece', *International Review of Applied Economics*, 15, 4 (2001), 397–410.

Lyrintzis, Christos, 'Change and Demystification', in *Greece in the 20th Century, 1980–1990*, I Kathimerini – Epta Imeres (Athens: *I Kathimerini*, 25–26.12.1999), pp. 8–10, in Greek.

Makrydimitris, Antonis, *The Administration in Crisis, Texts on Administration and Society* (Athens: Nea Sinora-Livanis, 1996), in Greek.

Manesiotis, Vasillios G. and Robert D. Reischauer, 'Greek Fiscal and Budget Policy and EMU', in *Greece's Economic Performance and Prospects*, eds Ralph C. Bryant, Nikolaos H. Garganas and Georgios S. Tavlas (Bank of Greece and The Brookings Institution, 2002), pp. 103–149.

Markezinis, Vasilios, *Greece of Crises, a Personal Essay* (Athens: Livanis, 2011), in Greek.

Martin, Isaac William, Ajay K. Mehrotta and Monica Prasad, 'The Thunder of History: The Origins and Development of the New Fiscal Sociology', in *The New Fiscal Sociology, Taxation in Comparative and Historical Perspective*, eds Isaac William Martin, Ajay K. Mehrotta and Monica Prasad (Cambridge: Cambridge University Press, 2009).

Mayr, Thomas P. and Raymond H. McGrath, 'Tramp Shipping: The Role of Taxation in International Resource Allocation', *Maritime Policy & Management*, 24, 3 (1997), 261–283.

McDonald, Robert, *Pillar & Tinderbox: The Greek Press and the Dictatorship* (New York: Marion Boyars, 1983).

Meyer, John W. and Bryan Rowan, 'Institutionalized Organizations: Formal Structure as Myth and Ceremony', *American Journal of Sociology*, 83, 2 (1977), 340–363.

Meynaud, Jean, *Political Forces in Greece, vol. I*, trans. by P. Merlopoulos (Athens: Savvalas, 2002).

Michas, N. A., 'Economic Development, Social Mobilization and the Growth of Public Expenditures in Greece', *American Journal of Economics and Sociology*, 39, 1 (January 1980), 31–48.

Milios, Yiannis, 'The Greek Economy in the 20th Century'. http://users.ntua.gr/jmilios/Oikonomia_Eikostos1ab.pdf [accessed 20.12.2014], pp. 1–24, in Greek.

Mills, Lillian F., 'Corporate Tax Compliance and Financial Reporting', *National Tax Journal*, XLIX, 3 (1996), 421–433.

Mitchell, B. R., *International Historical Statistics: Europe 1750–2005* (New York: Palgrave Macmillan, 2007).

Moscholios, Nikolaos Mich., *Tax Incentives, Comparative Research, Greece-European Economic Community* (Athens, 1967), in Greek.

Moussis, Nicholas S., *Greek Industrialists and the Association of Greece with the Common Market* (Brussels, 1967).

Mouzelis, Nikos, *Modern Greece, Facets of Underdevelopment* (London: The Macmillan Press Ltd., 1978).

Mouzelis, Nikos, 'Capitalism and Dictatorship in Post-war Greece', *New Left Review*, I, (March–April 1996), 57–80.
Nikolakopoulos, Ilias, *The Cachectic Democracy-Political Parties and Elections: 1946–1967* (Athens: Patakis, 2001), in Greek.
North, Douglass C., 'Institutions', *Journal of Economic Perspectives*, 5, 1 (1991), 97–112.
North, Douglass C., *Understanding the Process of Economic Change* (Princeton: Princeton University Press, 2005).
Palaiologos, Yiannis , *The 13th Labour of Hercules* (Athens: Estia, 2014), in Greek.
Panselina, Georgia M. and Maria Mavroeidi, *The Federation of Greek Industrialists, 1907–2007—A Century in the Service of the Idea of Entrepreneurship* (Athens: Economia Publishing, 2007), in Greek.
Papakonstantinou, Petros, 'The Restoration of Democracy', in *Greece in the 20th Century, 1970–1980*, I Kathimerini – Epta Imeres (Athens: I Kathimerini, 19.12.1999), pp. 12–14, in Greek.
Penrose, Edith, 'Limits to the Growth and Size of Firms', *The American Economic Review*, 45, 2 (1955), 531–543.
Photopoulos, Ioannis, 'The Administration of the Greek Tax System', *Enterprise*, reprint, issue 63, 2010, pp. 893–907, in Greek.
Pougouras, Petros K. and Christos A. Kyttaris, *Tax Control of Commercial and Industrial Enterprises* (Athens, 1957), in Greek.
Provopoulos, G. A., *The Public Sector of the Greek Economy, Recent Trends and Economic Repercussions* (Athens: Foundation for Economic and Industrial Research, 1985), in Greek.
Psalidopoulos, Michalis, *Monetary Management and Economic Crisis—The Policy of the Bank of Greece, 1929–1941* (Athens: The Bank of Greece, 2011), in Greek.
Psalidopoulos, Michalis, *Desperate Supervisors, American Consultants in Greece, 1947–53—From Paul A. Porter to Edward A. Tenenbaum* (Athens: Metamesonikties Ekdoseis, 2013), in Greek.
Psalidopoulos, Michalis, *History of the Bank of Greece, 1928–2008* (Athens: The Bank of Greece, 2014), in Greek.
Rollings, Neil, *British Business in the Formative Years of European Integration, 1945–1973* (Cambridge: Cambridge University Press, 2007).
Rose-Ackerman, Susan and Bonnie J. Palifka, *Corruption and Government—Causes, Consequences, and Reform* (New York: Cambridge University Press, 2016).
Sandford, Cedric, *Hidden Costs of Taxation* (London: Institute for Fiscal Studies, 1973).
Sandford, Cedric, Michael Godwin and Peter Hardwick, *Administrative and Compliance Costs of Taxation* (Great Britain: Fiscal Publications, 1989).

Sapelli, Giulio, *Southern Europe since 1945, Tradition and Modernity in Portugal, Spain, Italy, Greece and Turkey* (London and New York: Longman, 1995).

Schumpeter, Joseph A, 'The Crisis of the Tax State', in *Joseph A. Schumpeter: The Economics and Sociology of Capitalism*, ed R. Swedberg (Princeton, NJ: Princeton University Press [1918], 1991), pp. 99–140.

Scott, W. Richard, *Institutions and Organizations—Ideas and Interests* (California: Sage Publications, 2008).

Schwab, Peter and George D. Frangos, *Greece Under the Junta* (New York: Facts on File, 1970).

Seferiades, Seraphim, 'Polarization and Nonproportionality: The Greek Party System in the Postwar Era', *Comparative Politics* 19, 1 (1986), 69–93.

Sellas, Stephanos Mich, *The Greek System of Taxation* (Athens: Papazisis, 1989), in Greek.

Shane, Scott, *A General Theory of Entrepreneurship* (UK: Edward Elgar, 2003).

Smith, Adam, *An Inquiry into the Nature and Causes of the Wealth of Nations*, Volume II (London: Methuen & Co., 1904).

Sotiropoulos, Dimitris A., *The Tip of the Clientelist State—Organisation, Staffing and Politicisation of the Higher Echelons of the Central Administration in Greece, 1974–2000* (Athens: Potamos, 2001), in Greek.

Stathopoulos, Georgios N., *Taxation of Indigenous and Foreign Companies* (Athens, Federation of Greek Industries, 1964), in Greek.

Stebilis, Dimitrios , '21 April 1967: The Ending of a Chronic Political Crisis and the Beginning of a Dark Period', *History—Theoretical Texts, Documents of the Revolutionary Movement*. http://istorika-ntokoumenta.blogspot.co.uk/2013/06/21-1967.html [accessed 20.12.2014], in Greek.

Steinmo, Sven, 'Historical Institutionalism', in *Approaches and Methodologies in the Social Sciences, a Pluralist Perspective*, eds Donatella Della Porta and Michael Keating (Cambridge: Cambridge University Press, 2008), pp. 118–138.

Suddaby, Roy, William M. Foster and Albert J. Mills, 'Historical Institutionalism', in *Organizations in Time: History, Theory, Methods*, eds Marcelo Bucheli and R. Daniel Wadhwani (Oxford: Oxford University Press, 2013), pp. 100–123.

Sutcliffe, A., *An Economic and Social History of Western Europe Since 1945* (London and New York, Longman, 1996).

Tatsos, Nikos, *Public Finance in Greece* (Athens: Sbilias, 1991), in Greek.

Tatsos, Nikos, *Shadow Economy and Tax Evasion in Greece* (Athens: Papazisi, 2001), in Greek.

Thelen, Kathleen, 'Historical Institutionalism in Comparative Politics', *Annual Review of Political Science*, 2 (1999), 369–404.

Tran-Nam, Binh and Chris Evans, 'The Impact of Cedric Sandford on the Discipline of Tax Compliance Costs', *Australian Tax Forum*, 17 (2002), 389–406.

Tsiouras, Athanasios, 'Return to Development with Direct Foreign Investment', in *Niches of Freedom and Development—Proposal for the Functioning of a Special Economic Zone in Greece* (Brussels: Friedrich Naumann Stiftung Für die Freiheit, 2016), pp. 2–5.

Tsoukalas, C., *The Greek Tragedy* (Harmondsworth, Penguin, 1969).

Tsoukalas, Konstantinos, *State, Society, Labour in Post-war Greece* (Athens: Themelio, 2005), in Greek.

Tsounakos, Othon, 'The Coup of 21 April 1967', in *Greece in the 20th Century, 1965–1970*, I Kathimerini – Epta Imeres (special issue) (Athens: I Kathimerini, 12.12.1999), pp. 12–14, in Greek.

Tsounakos, Othon, 'Resistance Movements', in *Greece in the 20th Century, 1965–1970*, I Kathimerini – Epta Imeres (Athens: I Kathimerini, 12.12.1999), pp. 19–21, in Greek.

Varoufakis, Yanis and Tasos Patokos, 'Business Taxation Amid the Crisis', Centre of Research—Athens Chamber of Commerce and Industry, in Greek.

Veremis, Thanos, 'Impromptu Ideologies', in *Greece in the 20th Century, 1965–1970*, I Kathimerini – Epta Imeres (Athens: I Kathimerini, 12.12.1999), pp. 15–16, in Greek.

Verheul, Ingrid, Sander Wennekers, David Audretsch and Roy Thurik, 'An Eclectic Theory of Entrepreneurship: Policies, Institutions and Culture', in *Entrepreneurship: Determinants and Policy in a European-US Comparison*, eds David Audretsch, Roy Thurik, Ingrid Verheul and Sander Wennekers (USA: Kluwer Academic Publishers, 2002), pp. 11–81.

Vetsopoulos, A., 'Efforts for the Development and Stabilization of the Economy During the Period of the Marshall Plan', *Journal of Modern Greek Studies*, 27, 2 (October 2009), 275–302.

Vlahopapadopoulos, G., *The Effectiveness of Tax Incentives in Greece and Suggestions for their Reform* (Athens: Centre of Planning and Economic Research, 1967), in Greek.

Wadhwani, R. Daniel, 'Historical Reasoning and the Development of Entrepreneurship Theory', in *Historical Foundations of Entrepreneurship Research*, eds Hans Landström and Franz Lohrke (UK: Edward Elgar, 2010), pp. 343–362.

Wadhwani, R. Daniel and Marcelo Bucheli, 'The Future of the Past in Management and Organization Studies', in *Organizations in Time: History, Theory, Methods*, eds Marcelo Bucheli and R. Daniel Wadhwani (Oxford: Oxford University Press, 2013), pp. 3–32.

Xanthakis, Manolis, *The Crisis of Greek Manufacturing and State Intervention* (Athens: Papazisis 1989), in Greek.

Xanthakis, Manolis D., *Tax Regime, Shadow Economy and Tax Evasion in Greece* (Athens: Papazisis, 1993), in Greek.

Yannopoulos, George, 'The State of the Opposition Forces Since the Military Coup', in *Greece Under Military Rule*, eds Richard Clogg and George Yannopoulos (London: Secker & Warburg, 1972), pp. 163–190.

Yannopoulos, G., 'Sensitivity of Industrial Sectors to Common Market Competition', in *The Mediterranean Challenge: IV, The Tenth Member—Economic Aspects* (Sussex: Sussex European Research Centre, 1980), pp. 77–121.

Yanoulopoulos, Yanis, 'Greece: Political and Constitutional Developments 1924–1974', in *Greece in Transition, Essays in the History of Modern Greece 1821–1974*, ed John T. A Koumoulides (London: Zeno, 1977), 64–91.

Zolotas, Xenophon, *Our Economic Problem—A TV Discussion* (Athens: The Bank of Greece – Surveys and Talks Archive, 1975), in Greek.

Web Resources

'At Least 350 Taxes in Favour of Third Parties Have Been Targeted by the Government and the Troika'. http://www.unitedreporters.gr/news/GR/Forologika_themata/forologika_themata/Sto_stohastro_kyvernisis_kai_troikas__toylahiston_350_foroi_yper_triton [accessed 5.2.2014], in Greek.

BBC, 'On This Day', *1974: Greek Military Rule Gives in to Democracy*. http://news.bbc.co.uk/onthisday/hi/dates/stories/july/23/newsid_2515000/2515819.stm [accessed 28.12.2014].

'Censorship During the Junta'. http://chatzelenisgeorge.blogspot.co.uk/2013/04/blog-post_21.html [accessed 13.7.2014], in Greek.

'CHROTEX', *The Company*. http://www.chrotex.gr/article_detail.asp?e_lang_id=0&e_cat_serial=001001&e_cat_id=2&e_article_id=417 [accessed 12.9.2015], in Greek.

'e-forologia', *Online Bank*, Legislative order 3843/1958. http://www.e-forologia.gr/lawbank/document.aspx?digest=48DBD85F893B6FC0.1D031AEA53&version=1958/09/3 [accessed 03.10.2014], in Greek.

'Europedia', *Author*. http://www.europedia.moussis.eu/author/?lang=en [accessed 11.11.2014].

'Federation of Greek Industrialists'. http://www.sev.org.gr/online/generic.aspx?id=12&mid=600&lang=gr [accessed 14.12.2014], in Greek.

'Greece: The Junta 5 Years After the Coup', *The Harvard Crimson*, 21.4.1972. http://www.thecrimson.com/article/1972/4/21/greece-the-junta-5-years-after [accessed 23.7.2015].

'Hellenic Parliament', *Constitutional History*. http://www.hellenicparliament.gr/Vouli-ton-Ellinon/To-Politevma/Syntagmatiki-Istoria/ [accessed 20.11.2015], in Greek.

'Hellenic Parliament', *The Institution*. http://www.hellenicparliament.gr/Vouli-ton-Ellinon/O-Thesmos/ [accessed 1.12.2015], in Greek.

http://mba.aegean.gr/attachments/article/87/ArgyrosSteliosCV.pdf [accessed 7/12/2015].

'Iospress', *The Forgotten Scandals of the 'Nation-Saving' Revolution*. http://www.iospress.gr/ios2010/ios20100725.htm [accessed 2.12.2015], in Greek.

Ministry of Foreign Affairs of Greece, 'The Country's Course in the European Union'. http://www.mfa.gr/exoteriki-politiki/i-ellada-stin-ee/i-poreia-tis-elladas-stin-europaiki-enosi.html [accessed 05.10.2014], in Greek.

'National Centre for Public Administration and Local Government', *Mission*. http://www.ekdd.gr/ekdda/index.php/en/2012-06-29-09-59-33 [accessed 2.11.2014], in Greek.

Revenue Statistics, OECD.stat. https://stats.oecd.org/Index.aspx?DataSetCode=REV [accessed 13/12/2015].

Spiros Dimitrelis, 'The 500 Tax Officers Who Are Ready for Greece', *Capital*, 7.2.2015. http://www.capital.gr/tax/2223675 [accessed 20.2.2016], in Greek.

'Stockwatch' *Stelios Argyros*. http://www.stockwatch.com.cy/nqcontent.cfm?a_name=bod_view&bodn_id=5747&lang=en [accessed 7/12/2015].

'The Course of the Union of Corporations and Limited Liability Companies', *Union of Corporations and Limited Liability Companies*. http://sae-epe.gr/istoriko [accessed 8.11.2015], in Greek.

'The General Secretariat of the Government', *Alexandros Papagos Government*. http://www.ggk.gov.gr/?p=1194 [accessed 15.10.2014], in Greek.

'The General Secretariat of the Government', *Georgios Papadopoulos Government*. http://www.ggk.gov.gr/?p=1261 [accessed 9.12.2015], in Greek.

'The General Secretariat of the Government', *Georgios Papandreou Government*. http://www.ggk.gov.gr/?p=1239 [accessed 10.11.2014], in Greek.

'The General Secretariat of the Government', *Governments from 1909 to Date*. www.ggk.gov.gr/?page_id=776&sort=time [accessed 10.01.2015], in Greek.

'The General Secretariat of the Government', *Konstantinos G. Karamanlis Government*. http://www.ggk.gov.gr/?p=1206 [accessed 15.10.2014], in Greek.

'The General Secretariat of the Government', *Tzanis Tzanetakis Government*. http://www.ggk.gov.gr/?p=1294 [accessed 4.2.2015], in Greek.

'The Hellenic Centre for European Studies', *Stathis Efstathiades*. http://www.ekem.gr/index.php?option=com_content&view=article&id=77&Itemid=61 [accessed 20.12.2014], in Greek.

The 'Konstantinos G. Karamanlis' Foundation, 'Historical Archive', *Konstantinos Papakonstantinou*. http://www.ikk.gr/Default.aspx?tabid=236 [accessed 26.10.2014], in Greek.

The Republic of Cyprus, 'Press and Information Office', *The 1974 Turkish Invasion and Its Consequences*. http://www.moi.gov.cy/moi/pio/pio.nsf/All/6F5DD418DD053ED1C2256D6D001E7571?OpenDocument [accessed 28.12.2014].

'The Right of Voting in Greece', *Kyros-Education*, 18.2.2002. https://kyros.wordpress.com/2012/02/18/δικαίωμα-ψήφου-στην-ελλάδα/ [accessed 26.2.2016], in Greek.

'TVXS', *Attila II: The Last Chapter of the Cyprus Tragedy*, 14.8.2010. tvxs.gr/news/κόσμος/αττίλας-ιι-το-τελευταίο-κεφάλαιο-της-κυπριακής-τραγωδίας [accessed 30.3.2014], in Greek.

'What Is Bribery and Corruption?', *Tackling Bribery and Corruption*. http://www.anticorruption.ie/en/acjs/pages/fq08000018 [accessed 8.10.2016].

Index

Z. Pittaki, *Exploring the roots of systematic tax avoidance in Greece*, Palgrave Studies in Economic History,
https://doi.org/10.1007/978-3-030-71979-1

The manufacturer's authorised representative in the EU is Springer Nature Customer Service Centre GmbH, Europaplatz 3, 69115 Heidelberg, Germany. If you have any concerns regarding our products, please contact ProductSafety@springernature.com

ed and bound by CPI Group (UK) Ltd, Croydon, CR0 4YY

23/09/2026

02221520-0010